THE
MOUNTAINS
OF
EUROPE

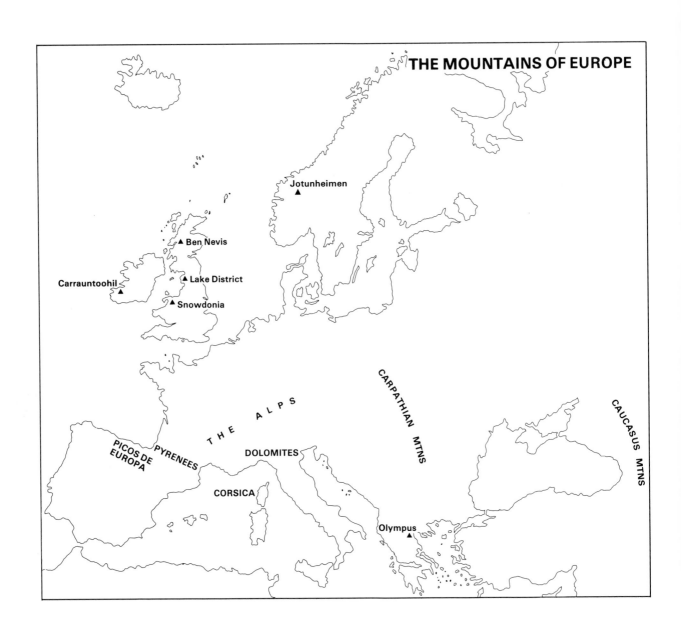

THE MOUNTAINS OF EUROPE

Jotunheimen ▲

▲ Ben Nevis

Carrauntoohil ▲

▲ Lake District

▲ Snowdonia

THE ALPS

CARPATHIAN MTNS

CAUCASUS MTNS

PICOS DE EUROPA

PYRENEES

DOLOMITES

CORSICA

Olympus ▲

THE
MOUNTAINS
OF
EUROPE

Edited by Kev Reynolds

The Oxford Illustrated Press

The Oxford Illustrated Press

© 1990, Kev Reynolds

ISBN 0 946609 84 5

Published by:
The Oxford Illustrated Press Limited, Haynes
Publishing Group, Sparkford, Nr Yeovil, Somerset
BA22 7JJ, England.

Haynes Publications Inc, 861 Lawrence Drive,
Newbury Park, California 91320, USA.

Printed in England by:
J. H. Haynes & Co Limited, Sparkford, Nr Yeovil,
Somerset.

British Library Cataloguing in Publication Data:
The Mountains of Europe.
  1. Europe. Mountains – Visitors' guides
  I. Reynolds, Kev
  914'.04558
  ISBN 0-946609-84-5

Library of Congress Catalog Card Number:
  89-85713

Contents

This book is dedicated to the memory of Dudley Stevens
whose love of mountains shone clear.

Introduction

An interest in mountains and mountain activity has never been more popular than it is today. The far-flung ranges of Asia, Africa and the Americas are becoming as familiar to armchair adventurers from Europe as were the Alps to the pioneers of mountaineering a century and more ago. Yet mystery and romance still remain within our own continent, and no matter how often one walks or climbs in a particular range there is always something new to learn, some new facet to be revealed that will bring additional pleasure to one's days among the hills. Long after every possible 'Last Great Problem' has been settled, the mountains will continue to work their magic upon the mind of man.

The idea for this book was conceived many years ago when my own passion for walking and climbing in new mountain regions was matched only by a desire to learn as much about them as I could. That process of learning meant delving into specialist libraries, poring through musty volumes, drooling over maps, studying photographs, devouring magazines and journals and, it must be admitted, thoroughly enjoying every moment of it. But it was a time-consuming process, and then only partly-satisfying since most of the books and magazine articles consulted were either written for the non-active layman, or for the committed climber—one sought to share an enthusiasm in general terms, the other tended to make assumptions about the reader's involvement and concentrated on technical detail. What I longed for was a volume that would have a wider scope, that would both enthuse and inform, would make the reader eager to visit the area under review and at the same time give practical advice to aid the planning of that visit. A book that would offer advice on where to climb and walk, would make mention on occasion of other things besides the mountains; the lakes, flowers, villages, birds and animals whose presence adds something special to the climber's—and walker's—experience.

In 1969 *The World Atlas of Mountaineering* appeared, edited by Wilfred Noyce and Ian McMorrin. A splendid book, it has given countless hours of inspiration and dream-fodder over the years. Ten years later John Cleare wrote and illustrated *Collins Guide to Mountains and Mountaineering*, another volume full of dreams and inspiration, but also offering worthwhile practical information. Both books are recommended to all who love mountains, for they were written by experts who possessed not only knowledge born of personal experience, but an infectious enthusiasm too.

Where this book differs from those that have gone before is in its concentration on the mountains of just one continent—Europe. And what a magnificent variety of mountains there are here! From the low crags of Snowdonia to the lofty ice-caked giants of Russia's remote Caucasus, from the granite spine of Mediterranean Corsica to the arctic tundra of Norway, from rain-lashed Ireland to sun-baked Greece, from the well-documented Alps to the lesser-known Picos de Europa, the range and extent of Europe's mountains are nothing if not multi-dimensional and truly fascinating.

To take on the mountains of Europe single-handed would be too much for any one person; the subject is too large and complex. In recognising this from the start I invited other writers to join me in the project. Each district, then, is treated to a separate chapter contributed by a specialist writer–mountaineer with an intimate knowledge and enthusiasm for that particular region gained from his own climbing experience. It's a talented team of writers, many of whom are of international repute and well-respected figures in mountaineering circles, and I should like to acknowledge a deep gratitude to them for their involvement in this book. They are: Steve Ashton, Louis Baume, John Brailsford, Cecil Davies, Dave Durkan, Jerzy Gajewski, Joss Lynam, Cameron McNeish, C Douglas Milner, Tim Salmon, Victor Saunders, Dudley Stevens and Walt Unsworth. I am immensely grateful to each one for their willingness to share their knowledge and experience, and for their advice and encouragement which I value highly.

In addition I am grateful to the following for information, suggestions and/or the loan of photographic material: George Band, John Barry, Hamish Brown, Serge Coupé, Mick Fowler, Adrian Garlick, Tony Howard, Hamish MacInnes, Guy Martin, Ernst Sondheimer, H Stevens, the Irish and Northern Ireland Tourist Boards, the Swiss National Tourist Office and West Col Productions.

Jane Marshall and Anna Wynn at Oxford Illustrated Press have given welcome encouragement at every stage and as always have been most supportive. They are warmly thanked too for allowing this book to grow beyond its originally contracted size. But even so, any attempt to encompass the mountains of Europe will necessarily face limitations and I have been forced to be selective in the regions for study. I apologise to any reader who seeks information about one of the continent's more obscure ranges and finds it not represented in this book. In spite of considerable freedom it has been impossible to include every single mountain district, while it must be admitted that the amount of space allocated to the mountains of Great Britain and Ireland is, quite clearly, disproportionate to their size. Yet among them mountaineering has a tremendous historic significance and by virtue of the numbers of activists drawn to them, I am convinced that a chapter devoted to each area is well justified. Read Cameron McNeish on Scotland, Walt Unsworth on the Lakes, Steve Ashton on North Wales and Joss Lynam on Ireland and you'll agree. Even the most ardent of Britain's committed hill-men will surely find something new and entertaining here.

All who have fallen under the spell of mountains are incurable dreamers, be they climber or walker or armchair adventurer. This book, I hope, will add inspiration to dreams. It sets out to reveal some of the mysteries of Europe's wild places and to entice with their romance. It is neither Atlas nor Gazetteer but a collection of essays designed to entertain, enthuse and enlighten. I hope it will be used also as a work of reference, as an aid to planning a visit to one of our many diverse ranges. It was designed with that in mind; at once a weaver of dreams and a spur to action.

Kev Reynolds
Kent 1989

CAMERON McNEISH
Scotland

Bothies and ballads, bealachs and burns; peat fires and folklore, *fasaig* sound and hoar frost; Caledonian pine, red gnarled and twisted; ancient rocks, wind-scoured and rough; high lochans, still and black, kelpie haunted and remote.

Sgurrs and Carns, Monadhs and Mullachs and Mealls, Ciste's and Creags, Stobs and Stucs, Bidean and, of course, Bens and Beinns.

Is it possible, I ask, to take the hills of Scotland and disassociate them from the quintessential element that is as natural here as the earth and the air, the fire and the water? I don't know the name of it; 'heritage' is too weak, too misused. It could be spiritual, an indwelling Holy Ghost born of Celtic ancestry which binds us to a land that is uncompromising in its hold. A land that brings tears to nostalgic eyes, and at the same time music to the lips.

Sadly the nostalgia and the music have been misinterpreted by many.

What makes a land? Is it the people, or the landscape itself? Or is it a combination of both, the intertwining of culture and history, life and death, with the very natural features that have shaped them? If so, what happens when you take the people from that land?

Let me tell you. You are left with a natural wilderness with whiffs and taints of days gone by. You can never shrug aside the ghosts of yesterday. You can't ignore the ancient sheilings and the dry stane dykes, the run rigs and the gable wall still standing. There's a familiarity there that belies explanation. It's in the soul. And sometimes it causes you to weep, and at other times it makes you rejoice in all its splendour and glory and pride.

The people have largely gone but the rocks remain.

Aye, the rocks have seen the passage of history from maybe twenty or thirty million years gone by. The rocks were higher then and extended westwards beyond what are now the worn and blunted teeth of St Kilda, but the constant scouring of water, then ice, carved this great tableland into shapes; hundreds of them.

The great plain that linked Scotland with Norway vanished below the North Sea and westwards the hills sank in a similar fashion, leaving only the tops as islands. Vast seas continued to scourge and carve, eating their way into the land mass, creating long fjords from the westward running glens.

Natural subsidence continued and faults appeared, separating the bottom part of the country from the mountainous north, or the high lands. Individual mountain

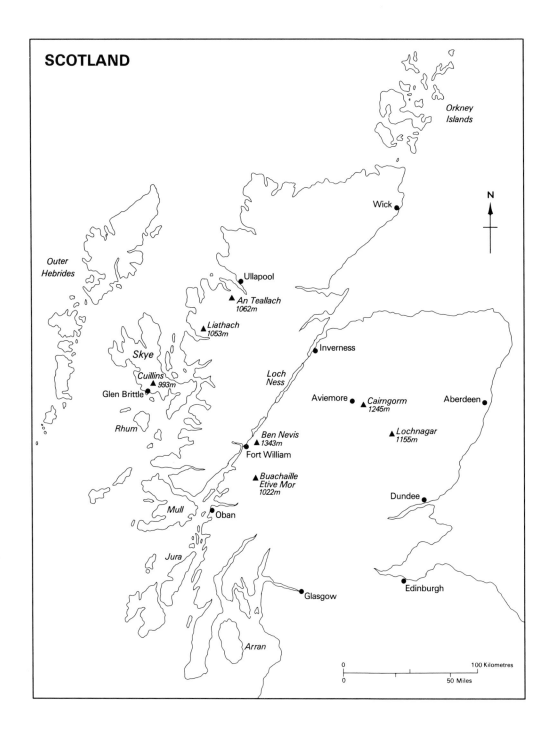

SCOTLAND

Orkney
Islands

N

Wick

Outer
Hebrides

Ullapool

▲ An Teallach
1062m

▲ Liathach
1053m

Skye

Inverness

Loch
Ness

Cuillins
▲ 993m

Glen Brittle

Aviemore ● ▲ Cairngorm
1245m

Aberdeen

Rhum

▲ Lochnagar
1155m

Ben Nevis
▲ 1343m

Fort William

▲ Buachaille
Etive Mor
1022m

Dundee

Mull

Oban

Jura

Edinburgh

Glasgow

Arran

0   100 Kilometres

0   50 Miles

masses were created, great ranges with dominant features, and elsewhere, smaller individual peaks which rose in solitary fashion from the flatness of the surrounding terrain. Old grain lines and transverse valleys filled in with water and the lochs were created, the lochs which so often reflect the grandeur of the hills, the lochs which change colour with lighting to reflect sombre moody skies, or the sparkle of a summer sun. In reflecting the mountains and the open sky they reflect their own glory, a characteristic element of the Scottish environment, along with the biting sea lochs, the raging rivers, the ancient forests and, of course, the mountains.

People have been walking and climbing the hills of Scotland since history began. The roads are recent, laid down less than two hundred years ago, and before that people used tracks, or just took to the heather.

This history of pedestrianism in Scotland is therefore an old one, and it still persists today. Its parallel tradition of free access to the hills and moors is still jealously guarded and this is why the mountaineering ethos in Scotland fails to understand the compulsion that drives folk to negotiate long-distance footpaths. Likewise the signposts and cairned tracks that are becoming so commonplace are foreign to a tradition which instils self-reliance. Scotland is well mapped and the Ordnance Survey maps are among the best in the world. So why do we need signposts and cairned tracks? If you can't read a map and follow it with the help of a compass you just shouldn't be there. And that's not élitism, just common sense.

In 1889 the Aberdeen based Cairngorm Club and the Glasgow based Scottish Mountaineering Club were officially constituted. The great age of discovery had begun. One SMC member, Sir Hugh Munro of Lindertis, published his *Tables of Heights Over 3,000 Feet,* listing almost 300 mountains. The list appeared in the second edition of the SMC Journal and it has been available and argued about in some form or other ever since.

Sir Hugh Munro gave his name to the hills he listed, and the 277 three thousand footers (914m) have ever since been known as 'Munros'. The first mountaineer to climb all the Munros was the Rev. A E Robertson in 1901. Nowadays, well over 500 people have climbed them and some have completed them in a single expedition, even in winter conditions.

Munro-bagging can be anything from a lifetime's incidental pastime to a fierce passion. And there are dangers—not all objective ones. The danger of addiction is very real. When Munro's *Tables* becomes your Bible and takes permanent residence at your bedside to lull you to sleep with dreams of numbers and ticks; when your weekend trips are planned with the number of Munros as the prime objective; and when you would rather visit an area which offers five dull Munros than one which offers two good hills; when you judge the success of a trip not solely by the aesthetic enjoyment of being in the hills but by the number of Munros you've climbed . . . then you must take stock of the situation.

By that time though, you will have probably reached the incurable stage. You can only hope and pray that by the time you've climbed up Number 277 you will have

13

purged the offending disease from your blood. Sadly, this is not usually the case. Round Number Two often becomes the next target, or another one, an incomprehensible desire to start on the Corbetts, the list of hills over 2500 feet (762m).

But if the advantages of the Munros are manifold, so too are the disadvantages. Lists are surely something we try to flee from on a Friday night. Numbers and lists shouldn't have a place in the hills. The great joy of a long walk by the coast is diminished if your heart tells you that you should really be knocking off tops. And probably worst of all, some of the superb hills which offer everything other than the desired elevation above the level of the sea are so easily ignored. I wouldn't swop the lowly Cobbler, or Stac Pollaidh, or Cul Beag, for a dozen Munros. Who would prefer the relative dullness of the Monadhliath, or the Geal Charns, or Wyvis to the splendour of Arkle, or Quineag, or Ben Loyal, or Rum's Askival? How can you begin to compare an island Munro like Ben More on Mull with the exciting granite ridges of Goat Fell, Beinn Tarsuinn, Cir Mhor and Caisteal Abhail on the Isle of Arran?

To judge a hill solely on its height is insane. Or is it? The Munro fever rages still, and probably always will.

For a long time the Ayrshire coast was a popular area with Glaswegian holidaymakers. One of the great attractions was the rugged shape of the Isle of Arran, close at hand over the waters of the Firth of Clyde. Its outline became familiar to generations of holidaymakers, the 'sleeping warrior' shape created by the outline of Goat Fell, Cir Mhor and the other Arran ridges.

Arran is usually reached by car ferry from Ardrossan and amongst Scottish islands it is unique. There is none of the starkness of the Hebrides here; it's a living landscape of whitewashed cottages with bright cornfields which run to the shore line. The glens are well wooded and the farmlands are rich. And behind rise the peaks, tops that form the culmination points of high and airy ridges.

Sixteen peaks are linked by these high granite ridges, the principal and most enjoyable day being the long ridge walk from Ben Nuis to Suidhe Fhearghas over the tops of Beinn Tarsuinn, the superb A'Chir Ridge, Cir Mhor, Caisteal Abhail and down from Suidhe Fhearghas to Sannox Bay.

Arran also boasts a multitude of rock climbing crags, the best routes being on the north-east face of Cir Mhor and the south face from the Fionn Choire. Arran granite is second only to Cuillin gabbro for roughness, being coarsely crystalline, and the great feature of Arran climbing is in the 'cyclopean wall' formation of its crags. This is caused by the cracking of the rock during cooling and the subsequent weathering by wind and frost over the years has shaped it into great blocks. They tend to look like a huge pile of boiler plates, all lumped on top of each other by some immense supernatural force.

Ben Lomond, at 973 metres, is a popular and, in many ways, a gentle hill. It tends not to dominate the surrounding countryside, possibly because it itself is dominated by Loch Lomond, Britain's largest sheet of inland water.

But while Ben Lomond perhaps lacks the grandeur of a Buachaille Etive Mor or a Ben Nevis, it is nevertheless a proud looking hill, raising its bluff head above broad purple shoulders to lift it above all other hills in the nearby vicinity. The usual route to the summit is via the footpath from Rowardennan, on the east shores of Loch Lomond a few miles north of Balmaha.

To the north-east of Ben Lomond lies the craggy land of the Trossachs. This area of hill and loch lies on the very edge of the Highland Fault, the geological boundary between the Highlands and Lowlands. As such, it was very much a frontier land in days gone by, when civilisation was thought to stop at the village of Aberfoyle. Beyond was a land infested by the clans, cattle reivers and murderers, through which no gentlemen should travel alone. The infamous Rob Roy McGregor roamed and ruled this area.

The highest hill in the Trossachs is Ben Ledi, at 876 metres. Other worthwhile expeditions include Ben Venue, and the imposing little crag of Ben A'an which overlooks Loch Achray.

North-west of Ben Lomond the unmistakable outline of the Cobbler dominates all higher peaks of the Arrochar Alps. At only 881 metres above sea level the Cobbler, or Ben Arthur, has a character and attractiveness worthy of a hundred higher Munros. Its three tops are formed by mica schist crags which offer some of the best rock climbing in the Southern Highlands, and indeed one has to scramble with hands and feet to reach the centre peak which is the summit. Many a humble walker has cried tears of frustration after walking up to the summit ridge from Loch Long-side to discover that he or she doesn't have the necessary head for heights to stand on the summit block.

First of all you have to scramble through a narrow eye in the rock, usually on hands and knees. This carries you onto a narrow sloping ledge which has to be traversed along the side of the summit block. A couple of lengthy reaches and pulls and you're on the top, lording it over the long and sinuous Loch Long and the other hills of the Arrochar Alps: Beinn Narnain, Beinn Ime, Ben Vane and Ben Vorlich.

From the head of Loch Lomond the long high pass of Glen Falloch carries you below some fine hills to Crianlarich, dominated by the sweeping slopes of Ben More. Crianlarich lies at the junction of Strathfillan and Glen Dochart, where the Perth and Stirling road comes in from the east. Follow that road west, towards Tyndrum, and you'll catch a glimpse of one of the finest mountains in this area, Ben Lui.

Beinn Laoigh, to give it its proper name, is 1130 metres in height and is best approached from Glen Cononish, close by the Crianlarich-Tyndrum road. From the long walk to it the hill's major feature, its east face, is seen to best advantage, soaring upwards to its double-topped summit. Two craggy spurs enclose a bowl-shaped corrie which holds snow well into the spring, and the finest feature of this corrie, and indeed of the mountain, is a long gash of a central gully which offers a magnificent snow climb of easy grade in winter. This is a classic climb, but beware. A great cornice often overhangs the top of the corrie, bringing a sting in the tail to an otherwise straightforward ascent.

Northwards from Tyndrum the A9 road pushes on valiantly over the great mattress of the Rannoch Moor. This immense area of rough boggy moorland is large enough to take the entire Lake District. There is nowhere else in Britain quite like it.

There's a surrealist quality to this road over the moor. The skies are wide and in all points of the compass there are brooding hills. Stark lochs reflect the clouds or grey mists and the road, for large parts, is as straight as a die. There's a rise in the gradient, you slowly swing round on a left-hand bend and there before you unfolds a scene that thrills the heart of anyone interested in climbing mountains.

Rising almost sheer from the flat moor is the grey bulk of the Buachaille Etive Mor, the Great Shepherd of Glen Etive. As you drive closer its shape becomes more and more impressive. An archetypal mountain shape, it rises in buttressed flanks throwing up red cliffs to its sharp summit. Here and there great gashes and grooves reveal the inky depths of the classic gullies and the long curving ridges cap some of the mountain's classic cliffs.

One route in particular takes a spectacular journey to the top. Curved Ridge is a Moderate rock climb but it offers an easy staircase of red rhyolite, rough and secure. Climbing upwards from an obvious waterslab, it offers a gallery viewpoint of the Rannoch Wall, a steep uncompromising cliff which holds some of the best climbs on the mountain.

Beyond the Buachaille the jaws of Glen Coe gape widely. A great toothed ridge defends the northern aspect of the Glen from the north: the Aonach Eagach ridge, believed by many to be the finest ridge traverse on the Scottish mainland.

Across the glen the Bidean nam Bian massif throws out three outliers, the Three Sisters of Glen Coe: Beinn Fhada, Gearr Aonach and Aonach Dubh. The whole massif is steep sided and rocky and offers some splendid rock climbing on the great Diamond and Churchdoor buttresses, and winter climbing on the cliffs of Aonach Dubh and Stob Coire nan Lochan.

Further north, beyond the 14 kilometre long ridge of the Mamores, lies the highest mountain in Britain, Ben Nevis (1343m/4406ft). From the Corpach road towards Mallaig it looks like a great crouched giant, huge in bulk but lacking the intrinsic features which would make it a classic mountain. But the Ben keeps its secrets for those willing to exert a bit of effort. From the long glen of the Allt a'Mhuillin, it slowly unfolds those awesome secrets: 3 kilometres of magnificent rock architecture. Buttresses, great ridges, pinnacles and towers form the ramparts of this bastion which offers a tremendous variety of rock, snow and ice climbs.

Among the easier classics are the long and superb North-East Buttress route, and Tower Ridge, the winter ascent of which was described by Dr Norman Collie as being similar to the Italian Ridge of the Matterhorn. Modern classics include Orion Face, Pointfive and Zero Gullies in winter, and Sassenach, Centurian and the Bat in summer.

Ben Nevis is usually climbed by the tourist path from Achintree Farm on the right bank of the Nevis Water. It's a long trail to the top and is not the most exciting mountain walk in the country. But despite that, it affords a route to thousands of

Rock climbing in Glen Coe. The pass of Glen Coe behind. (Photo: Cameron McNeish.)

visitors each summer, eager to tramp the highest mountain top in the country.

The view from the summit is extensive in all directions. It ranges from Ireland to Torridon in the north, and from the Outer Hebrides in the west to the blue outline of the Cairngorms in the east. South across Glen Nevis the whole ridge of the mighty Mamores can easily be traced, and beyond it the flat featureless plain of the Rannoch Moor.

At the south-east shoulder of the mountain an airy ridge curves its way towards the north to join with Carn Mor Dearg. Eastwards Aonach Mor and Aonach Beag abut onto the westwards extension of the Grey Corries ridge, a long switchback sweep of hills capped by grey quartzite. The traverse of the Aonachs and the Grey Corries offers an expedition every bit as exciting as that of the Mamores to the south and a complete circumference of the Ben, the Aonachs, the Grey Corries and the Mamores, in one continuous expedition, offers a trip without equal for sustained high-level walking in the country. Unbelievably the whole route has been walked within 24 hours.

Perhaps the finest area in the West Highlands is Knoydart. This is the wild and remote peninsula which lies in its rough limbo between the Loch of Heaven, Loch Nevis, and the Loch of Hell, Loch Hourn. These two sea lochs offer Knoydart a character rare in other areas of Scotland. No roads penetrate the fastness of this quarter and mere tracks line the 58 kilometre coastline. Access by foot involves long overland journeys through difficult country although a ferry does run from Mallaig to Inverie, the major settlement on the peninsula.

The main mountain of the district is Ladhar Beinn, at 1019 metres the most westerly of all the mainland Munros. Its north-east face is its most spectacular, seen to advantage from Barrisdale Bay on Loch Hourn. Other principal tops are Luinne Bheinn and Meall Buidhe.

Loch Hourn is linked to the Great Glen, the great geological fault that runs from Fort William to Inverness, by Glen Garry. North of here lies Glen Sheil, part of an 80 kilometre trough which lies across the Highland watershed. This is a spectacular glen, with its south side lined by a long ridge connecting no less than nine Munros, culminating in two superb tops, Sgurr na Sgine (944m) and The Saddle (1010m). The latter is the finest mountain in the area, with an interesting ridge, the Forcan ridge, offering the most challenging route to the summit.

Across Glen Sheil the Five Sisters of Kintail are easily recognisable, especially from the low ground to the west near the start of the Mam Ratagan pass which crosses to Glenelg. Beyond them the hills of Glen Affric, Glen Cannich and Strath Farrar stretch eastwards and northwards, reached from the east, for these glens are all roadless in their western extremities.

The major tops include Carn Eige, Mam Sodhail and Sgurr nan Ceathreamhnan, all around the 1160 metre mark. All are big hills in isolated positions, linked by ancient rights of way connecting the east coast village of Beauly with Kintail in the west.

Skye is the largest of the Inner Hebrides, a great indented island where no part of the land is any more than eight kilometres from the sea. The coastlines are populated by crofting communities, while the hinterlands are composed mainly of peaty moorland and low hills. In the north, in the peninsula of Trotternish, a long basalt spine offers a superb high-level ridge walk from the ancient volcanic slip of the Quiraig southwards to the town of Portree, the main town of the island.

But the real mountains of Skye, indeed some would say the finest in all Scotland, lie in the south of the island. The Cuillin Hills rise to a height of 993 metres; twenty tops exceed 914 metres (3000ft), of which twelve are Munros, although one of these, Blaven, lies east of the main Cuillin ridge, separated by the wide gulf of Glen Sligachan.

The main ridge swings north and north-east, curving around Loch Coruisk to reach its high point on Sgurr Alasdair. Much of the ridge is narrow and steep-sided, the peaks are sharp and well-defined and completion of the ridge requires more than the usual hill walker's skills. Here and there it becomes necessary to rock climb up to a V. Diff. standard. The complete traverse of the main ridge gives over 3000 metres of climbing and is the finest mountaineering expedition to be enjoyed in the country.

The coarse gabbro of the Cuillin is well suited to rock climbing, although after a day on the crags your hands know all about it. The best centre for rock climbing on Skye is Glen Brittle.

From the Skye Cuillin, a large island to the south dominates the seaward views. The Isle of Rum is owned by the Nature Conservancy Council and is second only to Skye in terms of scenery and mountaineering potential. The Cuillin of Rum offers a superb day's rock scrambling, a zig-zag ridge with seven summits. The highest and shapeliest of the peaks is Askival, which also boasts a lot of good climbing on its flanking buttresses.

The main peaks of the Torridon area offer a triptych of contrasting mountains, each in its own persona a real gem that would be outstanding in any mountain area.

First there's Beinn Eighe (1008m), with its incredible Coire Mhic Fearchair, whose Triple Buttresses offer sport to the finest of rock and snow and ice climbers. There can be few more breathtaking corries in all the country. Then Liathac (1053m) whose pinnacled ridge tops steep slopes and in recent years has seen an explosion in standards. And Beinn Alligin (985m), the jewel of Torridon with her great natural 'cleft' and amazing 'horns'.

North, across the beautiful Loch Maree stands Slioch (981m), a magnificent prospect with a commanding presence. Beyond lies the Great Wilderness, a vast area of wild unspoilt land which boasts some of the most inaccessible Munros in the country: A'Mhaighdean (967m), Ruad Stac Mhor (919m), Beinn Tarsuinn (936m), Mullach Coire Mhic Fearchair (1014m), Sgurr Ban (974m), Beinn a'Chlaidheimh (914m) and An Teallach. This latter hill is one of the most popular in Scotland on account of its high airy ridge, taking in the high eyries of Lord Berkeley's Seat and the Corrag Bhuidhe Buttresses. But the most incredible feature of An Teallach is her 518 metre deep corrie, Toll an Lochan, which compares with Coire Mhic Fearchair of Beinn Eighe and the Garbh Coire of Braeriach in the Cairngorms as Scotland's finest corrie. An Teallach is 1062 metres in height.

Northwards beyond Ullapool lie four Munros: Ben More Assynt and Conival, Ben Klibreck and the most northerly Munro, Ben Hope (927m/3042ft). But the stark and sterile landscape of Sutherland offers more than Munros. Up here, in the far north, lie a clutch of Scottish hills which are grander than the vast majority of Munros and all lie under the 3000 feet plimsoll line. Ben More Coigach, Stac Pollaidh, Cul Mor and Cul Beag, Suilven, Canisp, Quineag, Arkle and Foinavon. Each is a gem and all are worthy of a visit.

There is no mountain area in Scotland under more threat than the Cairngorms. Recognised by international organisations as being very important in world environment terms, the Cairngorms are seen by local authorities as a place where downhill skiing should be developed. A chairlift to the principal summit of the range carries thousands of visitors each year, offering quick and easy access to a 1200 metre (4000ft) Arctic environment which is extremely fragile. The tramp of boots is slowly destroying it.

But for all that the Cairngorms offer an experience that is unique in Scotland. With the biggest land areas over 600 (2000ft), 900 (3000ft) and 1200 metres (4000ft) in Britain, the climate on the tops and on the high level plateaux is Arctic, with an associated bird and plant life. Up here you can see and hear ptarmigan all the time. The dotterel has been breeding successfully on the high bare gravelly slopes for many years, and the song of the cock snow bunting early on a spring morning is one of the real joys of the hills. Reintroduced reindeer roam these hills, while the eagle and the peregrine falcon reign supreme amongst the high crags.

Seen from a distance the Cairngorms don't particularly impress, but these great hills offer the best views to those who are prepared to sweat a bit and climb the summits. It's then, when you look down into the vast corries, the steep-sided trenches and the glacier-scoured fissures, that you begin to realise their true worth. Four lie above 1200 metres (4000ft): Cairngorm, Beinn Macdui (the second highest mountain in Britain), Braeriach and Cairn Toul. A round of these four tops offers a hard and exhilarating mountain day, while an even longer challenge would be to include two other summits, Ben Avon and Beinn a'Bhuird—a long way for a day trip but feasible in two days with an overnight at the Fords of Avon Bothy.

The Shelter Stone Crag beside Loch Avon, below the northern slopes of Cairngorm itself, offers some of the best rock climbing in the area. Other good crags include the cliffs of Coire an Lochan, and further south, the impressively gaunt Creag an Dubh Loch beyond Lochnagar. In winter most of the crags freeze up to offer superb climbing and even if there is little snow about, Cairngorm mountaineers often enjoy their sport on frozen turf, torquing their ice axes into tiny cracks in the rocks and using them as handholds. They breed 'em tough in the Cairngorms!

WALT UNSWORTH

The Lake District

The English Lake District is an area of ancient tradition where many words left behind by the Norsemen are still in common use; thus a mountain becomes a *fell,* and what is called hill walking or mountain walking in other areas is here known as fell walking. The fact that the name has spread beyond the region is indicative of the influence the Lake District has always had on the British love of mountains.

The region sprang into national prominence during the Romantic movement which began in the mid-eighteenth century. Travellers, who had formerly thought of landscape only in terms of usefulness, now began to have a sense of excitement at the mountain scene. 'Beauty, Horror and Immensity united', was how one described it, and though the horror and immensity was soon lost, the beauty remained. A visit to the Lake District became almost *de rigueur* for young men who wished to be considered 'travelled'.

Wordsworth and the Lake Poets simply added impetus to a tourist industry which was already considerable. When the railways reached the area and the day-trip became possible from the mill towns of Lancashire and Yorkshire, a new working-class public came to appreciate the district. Once when Canon Rawnsley was appealing for funds for the newly-formed National Trust, he received a letter containing two shillings (10p): 'I am a working man,' it said, 'and cannot afford more than two shillings, but I once saw Derwentwater and can never forget it.'

It wasn't long before some of the Romantics were exploring the fells and that in turn led to rock climbing. Was the sport invented here? Possibly, but in any case the first ascent of Napes Needle by Haskett Smith in 1886 is as good a symbolic start as any. Wasdale Head was the centre for the new sport because only Dow, of the major crags, could not be reached from Wasdale, whereas the great triumvirate of Scafell, Pillar and the Napes were only a short walk from the little inn there.

Early in the nineteenth century Wordsworth had described the valleys of the Lake District as being like the spokes of a wheel whose hub was Esk Hause and though the analogy breaks down when considering the eastern fells, it serves well enough. The high ridges run between and also meet centrally, and it is this configuration which not only makes the area so suitable for walking tours, but which has prevented it from being overrun by motor roads. From central Lakeland only one motorable pass breaks out to the east, Kirkstone, between Ambleside and Patterdale, and only three to the west: Whinlatter, between Keswick and Cockermouth; Honister between Borrowdale and Buttermere, and the Wrynose-Hardknott combination which leads from Langdale

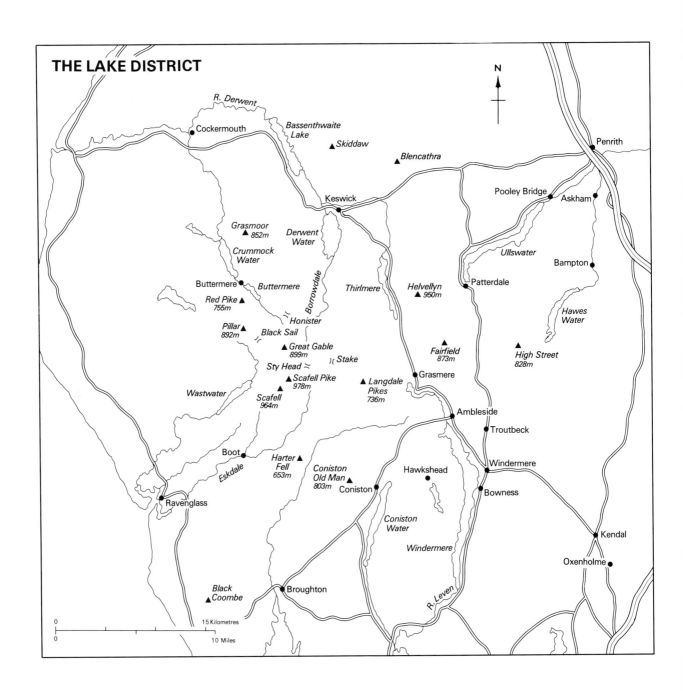

THE LAKE DISTRICT

N

R. Derwent

Cockermouth

Bassenthwaite Lake

▲ Skiddaw

▲ Blencathra

Penrith

Keswick

Pooley Bridge

Askham

Grasmoor ▲ 852m

Derwent Water

Ullswater

Bampton

Crummock Water

Buttermere ● Buttermere

Thirlmere

Helvellyn ▲ 950m

Patterdale

Hawes Water

Red Pike ▲ 755m

Borrowdale

Pillar ▲ 892m

Honister

Black Sail

▲ Great Gable 899m

Fairfield ▲ 873m

High Street ▲ 828m

Sty Head ≈

)(Stake

Grasmere

▲ Scafell Pike 978m

▲ Langdale Pikes 736m

Wastwater

Scafell 964m

Ambleside

Troutbeck

Windermere

Boot

Harter ▲ Fell 653m

Coniston Old Man ▲ 803m

Hawkshead ●

Bowness

Eskdale

Coniston

Ravenglass

Kendal

Coniston Water

Oxenholme ●

Windermere

Black ▲ Coombe

Broughton

R. Leven

0   15 Kilometres

0   10 Miles

to Duddon and then Eskdale. In addition there are some moorland roads here and there but they are all narrow and not for nervous drivers.

To compensate for this there is an extensive footpath network partly based on the old pack-horse tracks, though some are very much older than that. High Street, which crosses the mountain of that name, is certainly Roman and probably earlier.

The M6 motorway which bounds the Lake District on the east provides rapid access from other parts of the country, but the main road through the district runs north-south from Keswick to Ambleside over the easy Dunmail Raise pass, then on via Windermere to Kendal. Fortunately heavy lorries have been banned for some years.

Access by rail is surprisingly good. The main London-Glasgow line passes through Kendal (actually on the outskirts at a place called Oxenholme) and Penrith. From Oxenholme a branch line serves Windermere. Less well-known, however, is the Cumbrian coast line which travels from Lancaster to Barrow round Morecambe Bay, then up the west coast and along the Solway to Carlisle. Anyone contemplating a walking holiday using rail travel should seriously consider this west coast line as offering a splendid means of access away from the busy Windermere honeypot.

One of the stopping places on this line is Ravenglass where it is possible to transfer to the narrow gauge Ravenglass and Eskdale Railway, which travels up Eskdale to a hamlet called Boot—surely a place for walkers! The railway is affectionately known as 'La'al Ratty' and I always find it ironical to think that one of the remotest valleys in England is accessible by rail from London, when so many more important places are not!

Accommodation of all sorts—hotels, youth hostels, camp and caravan sites—is plentiful, but on high days and holidays it might well be full. The fame of the area ensures that there are many other visitors besides walkers and climbers—this is one of the world's most popular tourist areas. Lonely it ain't!

As in the Alps of old, a Lakeland fell walker can either choose to be a centrist or an ex-centrist. That is to say, he or she can either stay in one centre, such as Ambleside, and go off in different directions each day, or start somewhere like Windermere and do a circular tour of the district, moving on from valley to valley as time and inclination allow.

The latter is an infinitely better way of getting to know the place—I was introduced to the Lakes this way as a spotty schoolboy during the war and never forgot the wonder and magic of that first tour. Each day was a new horizon beyond which were fresh discoveries to be made—the grandeur that is Wasdale, the sublime beauty of Eskdale, the prettiness of Borrowdale. However, it does mean you have to carry all your gear with you over the fells and to press on regardless of weather if you have booked accommodation ahead. But it is worth every ounce of effort, every degree of frustration.

With climbing it is different. I have actually done a walk round the Lakes, climbing on different crags as I went along, but these days there is so much gear (often carried on climbs where it isn't necessary) that it is more practical to stay in one place—a campsite or club hut, of which there are many.

What follows is a circular tour of the Lake District which would give anyone a good introduction to this delightful area, and from time to time I will introduce some of the crags and climbs.

So let's assume that we have arrived fresh-eyed and fit as a ferret at Windermere railway station, ready for our first tour of the Lake District. Which way to go? Well, the old advice to 'go west, young man' seems appropriate, setting us off on a clockwise tour. Down to the lake and across the ancient ferry, then by Claife Heights to Hawkshead and from there by Tarn Hows to Coniston. This walk embraces Lakeland at its most intimate: all woods and rocky knolls. Up on Claife Heights you'll probably meet nobody; at Tarn Hows you'll probably meet everybody.

A day could be spent in Coniston doing the classic round of the Coniston Fells, Wetherlam, Swirl How and the Old Man, coming down past lonely Goat's Water and the towering Dow Crag; one of the district's finest climbing crags. There is no more compact group of high fells in Lakeland and none where the art of fell walking can be so readily appreciated.

Climbing on Dow Crag's buttresses—A,B,C and D—rising from steep screes above a lonely tarn, is that of the grand gesture, often surprisingly strenuous. There are some superb routes: Giant's Crawl, for example, is excellent for beginners, while Hopkinson's Crack, Great Central Route, Murray's Route, Eliminate A and Sidewalk (graded E2) are all classic climbs.

West from Coniston over the old Walna Scar road, where packhorses once picked their way, to Seathwaite in Dunnerdale and then over the stepping stones of the Duddon and across the moor to Eskdale, taking in Harter Fell en route. This is a gorgeous little mountain of craggy outcrops which can be scrambled up or avoided as you wish, and seen from Eskdale many walkers regard it as the loveliest peak in the Lakes.

Eskdale itself has a quiet beauty all its own. The pools of the Esk are delectable on a hot summer's day and the central part of the valley does lend itself to riverside walks, with a diversion to one of the district's finest waterfalls, Stanley Force. The head and tail of the valley are different. The head gives the very tough Eskdale Ring, a mountain circuit which includes the highest peaks in England and encloses the lonely wastes of the upper Esk. Crinkle Crags, Bowfell, Scafell Pike and Scafell are included in a very strenuous day. On the other hand, the walk down the valley to Ravenglass over the little known Muncaster Fell is sheer delight.

West again, across Burnmoor with its lonely, lovely tarn and steeply down into Wasdale Head, the dale that was said to have 'the deepest lake and the biggest liar in England'. The lake is still there, but the liar was the nineteenth-century owner of the inn, Will Ritson, who presided over the birth of rock climbing at his little hostelry, though he could never comprehend the sport. 'Aren't fells heigh enuff?' he would demand. Certainly some of the highest fells are accessible from Wasdale Head—the Scafells and Gable, for example—though perhaps the best expedition is the Mosedale Horseshoe which starts with Yewbarrow (a tough little fell), then travels over Red Pike, Steeple, Pillar and Kirk Fell to end back in Wasdale Head. Less strenuous walks include the High Level route by Robinson's Cairn to Pillar Rock and the Climbers' Traverse of Great Gable. The latter is unusual in that it brings the walker into the heart of the climbers' world below the Napes Ridges, including the famous Napes Needle, an 18-metre free-standing pinnacle.

This was the earliest climbing area in Britain, known far and wide for The Needle. Needle Ridge is good for novices while Eagle's Nest Ridge is much more difficult and exposed, as is Tophet Wall, both graded Severe. On a little crag nearby lie two old classics: Innominate Crack and Kern Knotts Crack (both VS), whilst on the Ennerdale side of Gable is Gable Crag with the delectable Engineer's Slabs of the same grade.

The great crag of Scafell rising so majestically above the corrie known as Hollow Stones to the south of Napes Needle, is really only part of a complex of rock faces hereabouts. Chief among others is the East Buttress (over the col called Mickledore) and Pike's Crag, facing Scafell Crag across the corrie. There are only easy climbs on Pike's Crag, but few easy ones on Scafell Crag and none at all on the East Buttress. Almost every route has merit. Among the easier one might mention Jones's Direct and Moss Ghyll, whilst among the harder it is almost impossible to choose but one must mention Central Buttress (HVS), done in 1914 and for many years the hardest climb in Britain.

Our onward journey now starts to turn north as we leave Wasdale by the deep, dark Mosedale and cross first the Black Sail Pass into upper Ennerdale and then the Scarth Gap Pass into Buttermere. On the Ennerdale flanks of Pillar Fell rises monolith-like one of the most famous rock features in Britain—Pillar Rock. Among the many fine climbs to be made here are the New West and North Climb, both hard for their grade (D), and Walker's Gully (HS) and North West Climb (VS).

The contrast between Buttermere and the sombre valleys of Wasdale and Ennerdale could hardly be more marked. Buttermere hamlet rests on a flat strip of land between the lake of the same name and Crummock Water, and is perhaps everybody's vision of the Lake District. The finest walk here is the Red Pike to High Crag ridge over High Stile, returning through the Burtness Woods along the shores of the lake. It is a very good introductory walk for anyone not used to fell walking, providing the weather is fine. It can be extended over Haystacks and Fleetwith Pike and even continued over Dale Head, Hindscarth and Robinson back to Buttermere, but the full circuit is a long and fairly hard day.

Buttermere also has a number of crags with good climbs, including Buckstone How near Honister Pass where Cleopatra and Honister Wall are two established classics. Eagle Crag in Burtness Combe has Eagle Front (VS), and the adjacent Grey Crag has a number of easy climbs which would give a novice a good day's outing.

From Buttermere the natural route leads to Keswick, which is the principal town of the northern Lakes. There are several ways of doing this walk, all of them interesting, but perhaps the best is to take the high level route from Robinson to Dale Head, then follow the ridge north over Maiden Moor to Cat Bells, with extensive views over Derwent Water to Skiddaw. The going is easy after the initial climb and you come down off the fell only three or four kilometres from the town.

Keswick is a good place to take a break, but it can also be used as a centre from which to climb Skiddaw and Blencathra—two great lumpy slate mountains north of the town. Blencathra is very fine if traversed by Hall's Fell Ridge and Sharp Edge—this latter is probably the trickiest walker's ridge in the Lakes, though the difficulties are short and easily overcome with care and commonsense. To the west of the town there is a longer and more traditional walk called the Coledale Horseshoe which starts and ends at Braithwaite, taking in all the fells around Coledale Hause including the shapely Causey Pike and the great bulky plateau of Grasmoor.

Keswick can also be used to explore Borrowdale, one of the loveliest of all the Lakeland dales. At its head there is a splendid traverse of Glaramara with a return along Langstrath Beck, where on a hot day there are deep pools for dipping. It is usual to do Scafell Pike from here too, and Gable, for though the distances are greater than from Wasdale accommodation is less restricted.

But Borrowdale is not really about high fells. It is about exploring the woods and rocks of the valley. It is about Watendlath; that gorgeous little hamlet hung in the sky that Walpole made the home of his sexy heroine, Judith Paris. It is about the Bowder Stone, and Castle Crag and poking about in nooks and crannies. It has what I consider to be one of the finest low-level walks in the area, along the western shores of Derwent Water by paths that, just beyond Grange, join the Old Toll Road, a stony highway that leads to Seatoller. The walking is easy and the views magnificent.

For some time now Borrowdale has been the most popular Lakeland valley for climbers; the crags are usually only a few minutes from the road and there's a lot of them, offering climbs of every type and grade. In the upper valley and its side valleys, there are some bold mountain crags such as Raven's Crag on Glaramara and Gillercombe Buttress on Grey Knotts. Langstrath also has its big bold crags including Sergeant Crag, Heron Crag and Eagle Crag.

Lower down the dale things are different. The crags are often hidden in the woods and routes tend to be shorter. Most famous of these is Shepherd's Crag, a series of rocky bays with numerous popular climbs including Brown Crag Wall and Ardus, Eve, and Little Chamonix.

The walker's route along the shores of Derwent Water and Borrowdale can be used to escape from Keswick on our circular tour, which is now heading east. By following the Toll Road as far as Rosthwaite and then going up the Stonethwaite Beck to Greenup Edge, a way can be made down Far Easedale to Grasmere and then by Loughrigg Terrace to Ambleside. This is a long day, especially carrying a pack, but since there is a bus service at either end it is always possible to cheat!

Ambleside is to the central Lakes what Keswick is to the north. A good bus service runs the length of Langdale from the town and enables the walker to tackle the fells at the head of the valley, such as Bowfell, Crinkle Crags and, of course, the Langdale Pikes. These latter dominate the valley, not so much by their height, but by their shape and grouping. There is hardly a more distinctive group of hills in Britain, but they are all show, I regret to say—climbing them is easy.

The walk up Milk Gill to that curiously named fell, Pavey Ark, is the most popular in Langdale. At the head of the gill the great crags brood over Stickle Tarn, and running across it from bottom right to top left is a curious sort of ledge known locally as a 'rake'. This one is by far the finest of all, known as Jack's Rake, and it can be followed in its entirety across the cliff. Needless to say this is not something to be embarked upon with small children and dogs—though both have done it. Despite appearances to the contrary, much of Jack's Rake is not at all exposed because of a natural rock wall, almost like a bannister, which protects the walker on the outside edge. Higher up, however, there's a stretch where nothing comes between you and a drop of several hundred feet.

Langdale's crags, along with those of Borrowdale, are amongst the most popular in the district, not only because they are easy of access but also because they offer a wide spectrum of climbing from the easiest to the hardest. Relatively small crags, like Raven Crag and Middlefell, assume significance out of all proportion to their size because of these two factors.

Old Dungeon Ghyll Hotel and Middlefell Buttress, Langdale. (Photo: Walt Unsworth.)

Of the bigger crags the best known are Bowfell Buttress, Pavey Ark, White Gill and Gimmer Crag. The original route on Bowfell is a bold but fairly easy V. Diff., a classic of its kind. So too are Crescent Slabs and Stoat's Crack on Pavey. White Gill has its Chimney and Slip Not (MVS). On Gimmer one is spoilt for choice: B Route, with its brutal Amen Corner (S), Asterisk (HS) and The Crack. Harder routes of quality abound: Gimmer String (E1) and Kipling Groove on Gimmer; Do Not (E1), Laugh Not (HVS) and Haste Not (VS) on White Gill; Astra (E1), Arcturus (HVS) and Rake End Wall (VS) on Pavey.

But the smaller, handier rocks should not be neglected for despite their popularity they are still very good—routes like Centipede, Revelation and Original on Raven, graded either Mild Severe or Severe, not to mention beginners' routes like Route 1, Scout Crag and Middlefell Buttress, both Diffs.

Tucked away in the adjacent valley of Easedale is Deer Bield with three great classics: Deer Bield Chimney, Deer Bield Crack and Deer Bield Buttress, going from Severe to E1 in grade and each reckoned the hardest thing of its kind in 1908, 1930 and 1951 respectively!

Loughrigg Fell is a short excursion from Ambleside with good views of the Langdale Pikes, especially from Loughrigg Terrace across Grasmere. The terrace is a broad belvedere of a path overlooking the lake and is very popular. The finest of Ambleside's walks, however, is the Fairfield Horseshoe, which takes in the peak of that name as the crux of the 'horseshoe' whose arms are two long ridges reaching down towards the town.

The best way to continue the journey west is to cross Grisedal Hause from Grasmere to Patterdale. This is a wild and lonely crossing; a melancholy place on a winter's day and yet it leads to one of the pleasantest and cheeriest of lakes, Ullswater. The mobs go to Windermere but the nobs go to Ullswater, if only to see Aira Force, one of the best waterfalls in the district.

Patterdale, the valley at the head of the lake, is a good centre for walks, two of which need special mention. The first is the low level walk along the lake shore below Place Fell, from Sandwick to Patterdale. You can climb Place Fell first and return to the shore walk or be completely lazy and reach the start by means of a lake steamer. In either case it is a superb excursion.

Striding Edge is quite different and is not only the most popular walk from Patterdale but one of the most popular in the Lake District. The ancient terrors which once clung to the rocky ridge have disappeared completely and sometimes the narrow crest seems like Blackpool Promenade. People still get killed there. In winter it is matched only by the Blencathra traverse described earlier—and winter is when it should be done, provided you are competent enough and have the right gear. The traditional circuit is to return by the adjacent ridge called Swirrel Edge and this is still the best plan.

Scattered throughout the Eastern Fells are crags which have had a mixed fortune over the years. Hardly known at all before the war they gained prominence in the 1960s and then, except for two or three, lapsed back into relative obscurity. Amongst the best known are Raven Crag Thirlmere, Castle Rock of Triermain and Dove Crag. The routes tend to be hard and there is practically nothing worthwhile for the beginner. Classic lines in the VS grade are Communist Convert, Raven Crag; Hangover, Dove Crag; and Jim Birkett's famous Overhanging Bastion on Castle Rock. Harder routes include the Medlar (E3) and Totalitarian (E2) on Raven; North Crag Eliminate (E1) and Agony (HVS) on Castle Rock; Extol and Hiraeth (both E2) and Dovedale Groove (E1) on Dove Crag.

But now the circle is closing and the way lies south to Windermere, where we started our perambulation. It can be ended on a high note by following the Roman way across High Street to Troutbeck and finally the great lake itself. From Patterdale the path not only passes one of the prettiest mountain tarns, Angle Tarn, but with a little management you can actually pick up nine 600 metre (2000ft) tops in one little walk. That really is ending on a high note!

There isn't a single mountain in the Lake District that cannot be walked up, so mountain climbing isn't relevant. There are three important activities which lie beyond the scope of mere fell walking, however, and they are scrambling, winter climbing and rock climbing.

Scrambling has become immensely popular in recent years, especially since Brian Evans published his classic guide, *Scrambles in the Lake District*. It consists of routes which require the use of hands as well as feet but which are too broken or discontinuous to be regarded as proper climbs. There are two types in the main, the ridge scramble and the gill or gully scramble, and both are to be found throughout the district. Typical of the ridge scramble is the celebrated Pinnacle Ridge on St Sunday Crag above Patterdale. Broken rocks lead to a fine saw-tooth ridge of pinnacles which are very airy and certainly not for the faint-hearted.

More enclosed but also more serious, is Sandbed Gill, a deep fissure on the eastern side of St John's Vale. Slippery rock predominates and the climb becomes a relentless struggle with numerous cascades, but the rock scenery is most impressive.

Not all the gills are as difficult as Sandbed Gill, but nobody should attempt scrambling in the mistaken belief that it is an easy option. It may be technically easier than rock climbing but it is inherently more dangerous, with slimy gills and fragile rock—a scrambler would do well to have some rock climbing experience behind him. If in any doubt about the sort of difficulty that scrambling entails, a good yardstick is to remember that Jack's Rake on Pavey Ark, mentioned earlier, counts as the *easiest* sort of scramble.

In a sense scrambling leads on to winter climbing, for what might be mere scrambles in summer can make very fine ice climbs. The Lake District seldom has the sort of winters which seem guaranteed in Scotland, but there are usually two or three weekends in which conditions are right.

Easily the most famous winter playground is formed by the gullies of Great End in the Scafell massif. They vary from grade I to grade III, so they are not beyond the ability of most winter climbers and if for this reason alone (and the fact that they are the most likely to be in condition) they tend to be crowded, especially the ever-popular Central Gully (200m, grade II). Actually, the great snow funnel at the top of Central Gully needs careful watching—it has been known to avalanche.

Another area often in condition is the eastern side of the Helvellyn range. Here again there are plenty of easy to middle grade routes above Red Tarn and in the imposing corries at the head of Grisedale Beck.

If we leave out summer rock climbs done under winter conditions there are still routes of great quality to be found when the conditions are right. One such is Raven Crag Gully in Combe Ghyll, Borrowdale (150m, grade III) or Dove Crag Gully in Buttermere (90m, grade IV). But condition is everything and the Lakeland winter climber travels more in hope than expectation.

Until a few years ago rock climbing in the Lake District meant exclusively the large crags which dominate the core of the area; igneous rock of the so-called Borrowdale Volcanics, big and bold and sound as a bell. Recently however, some of the rocks which lie on the fringes of Lakeland have come into their own, such as the Eden valley sandstone and the limestone of Chapel Head Scar and the Warton area. This adds variety, especially to the upper grades, as does the quarry climbing on slate at Hodge Close in Little Langdale.

It is the great crags of the principal valleys which command most attention, however, even in these days of esoteric tastes. There may be a slight air of faded glory about Dow or Pillar and distinctly so about the Napes, but Scafell maintains its place as one of the great crags of Britain, with many of the climbs there being true classics.

STEVE ASHTON
North Wales

North Wales is not a wilderness. Rather it is a sprawling range of little mountains dotted with villages and chopped into day-sized bits by a network of roads; old, worn mountains that on fine summer weekends are over-subscribed several times over—an adventure playground for grown-ups. But never mind the weary image of eroded paths and polished rock pedalled by its detractors, because those coming fresh to North Wales will see it with inquisitive eyes and be delighted. Regulars naturally cling to memories of the good old days, but the tangible changes wrought by a century of mountaineering are small. The despair of cynics is misplaced; remote crags and hidden cwms await with new adventures.

Geological upheaval and subsequent glacial erosion sketched the outlines of the present landscape many thousands of years ago. Rock-walled cirques, drumlins, truncated spurs and U-shaped valleys remain as irrefutable evidence of the ice age, but in recent history the fine adjustments of natural erosion have been dwarfed by the crude daubs and slashes of industry. Of these, the most influential in texturing the character of today's landscape is sheep grazing. A few stunted hawthorns are all that remain of the once wooded slopes, and the stone walls and fences that stake out summer grazing are encountered even on some of the highest summits. A few patches of natural woodland survive in some valleys to remind us of the deciduous forests that once flourished there, but these are rare exceptions to the unvarying blocks of conifers which now cling to the lower mountain slopes. Some hills have been gnawed away for slate or burrowed into for copper. Few mines and quarries are worked today although the spoil heaps and ruined buildings remain to remind us of the harsh lives lived in the mountains before we came along with our, perhaps misplaced, aesthetic sensibilities.

Not all North Wales mountains are gentle, sheep-grazed domes. In the rocky summits, knife-edged ridges and squat buttresses we see the bones of an ancient landscape—and the wherewithal to rediscover primitive instincts of climbing and survival. We share these rugged peaks with ravens, buzzards and falcons—and on fine weekdays with RAF jets and helicopters on training exercises. We might also glimpse a feral goat, showing off his magnificent curved horns on some sunlit rock promontory before returning to the shadows of the cliff.

A damp and generally unpredictable climate makes it difficult to plan expeditions in advance. The only certainty is that an overcast sky on the coast means that it will be raining in the mountains. Under the influence of north-westerlies, bands of showers drench the hills between interludes of dazzling sunshine—exhilarating for the walker

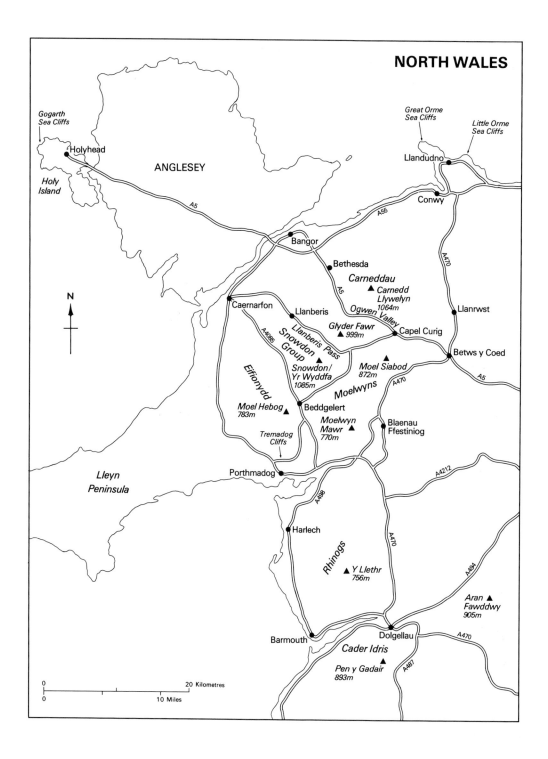

NORTH WALES

Gogarth Sea Cliffs

Holyhead

ANGLESEY

Holy Island

A5

Great Orme Sea Cliffs

Little Orme Sea Cliffs

Llandudno

Conwy

A55

A470

Bangor

Bethesda

A5

Carneddau

▲ *Carnedd Llywelyn 1064m*

Llanrwst

Caernarfon

Llanberis

Ogwen Valley

Llanberis Pass

Glyder Fawr ▲ *999m*

Capel Curig

A4086

Snowdon Group

Moel Siabod ▲ *872m*

Betws y Coed

A5

A470

Eifionydd

Snowdon/ *Yr Wyddfa* ▲ *1085m*

Moelwyns

Moel Hebog 783m ▲

Beddgelert

Moelwyn Mawr ▲ *770m*

Blaenau Ffestiniog

Tremadog Cliffs

Porthmadog

A498

A4212

A470

Harlech

Lleyn Peninsula

Rhinogs

▲ *Y Llethr 756m*

A494

Aran ▲ *Fawddwy 905m*

Barmouth

Dolgellau

A470

Cader Idris

A487

Pen y Gadair 893m ▲

N

0   20 Kilometres

0   10 Miles

but frustrating for the climber. More rarely, and most often in late autumn or early spring, an unexpected calm descends on the mountains as high pressure brings a week of clear days and frosty nights. While temperature inversions fill the valleys with mist, crocodile backs of ridges bask in the sunshine above. Snow collects in gullies of the highest cwms from November to May, but complete cover exists only for a few weeks of the year. Typically it will fall during one or two days, drift from high ground to hollows over a couple more, linger for a week, and finally shrink to a few paltry strips during the inevitable period of mild south-westerlies. But whatever its state, this ever-changing landscape revitalises jaded appetites and presents endless challenges to the winter mountaineer.

Each mountain group has its own characteristic shape and terrain. You can choose to stroll among gentle hills one day and scramble over rugged peaks the next. Most walks are 15 to 25 kilometres in length although the geography is such that several may be linked by those who have the time and stamina. The best known of these is the Fourteen Peaks walk which links all summits in excess of 3000 feet (914m)—of which, curiously, there are fifteen. This demanding two-day—or crippling one-day—expedition takes you from a bivouac on Snowdon's summit, across the rocky ups and downs of the Glyders, and onto the delicious undulating ridges of the Carneddau. An annual fell race follows the less satisfactory metric equivalent over the 1000 metre peaks. Those with a taste for solitude and less frenetic challenge will find both in the Arans, Rhinogs and Moelwyns on the fringes of the National Park.

Barren, rounded summits characterise the Carneddau, northernmost of Snowdonia's mountain groups. Here is the best ridge walking in North Wales and each flank of the group can boast a grand horseshoe traverse which has Carnedd Llewelyn, at 1064 metres the highest mountain of the group, at its apex. The southern horseshoe linking Pen Yr Ole Wen, Carnedd Dafydd, Carnedd Llewelyn and Pen yr Helgi Du is generally thought to be the finest.

The Glyders form the spiritual home of North Wales hill walking. Curious rock piles littering the summit plateaux of the two highest peaks—Glyder Fach (994m) and Glyder Fawr (999m)—have inspired mountain walkers ever since the late eighteenth century, when Thomas Pennant illustrated his exploits with pen drawings of strange obelisks. Both peaks can be ascended by uncomplicated walks, but in fair weather the most satisfying route begins by scrambling over Tryfan (917m) before gaining the Glyder plateau by the exciting Bristly Ridge.

Snowdon (Yr Wyddfa) is just one of nine peaks in the Snowdon group, but its commanding height (1085m/3560ft) and central location ensure its dominance over all others. A walk that failed to incorporate Snowdon summit would feel only half complete. The summit itself is cluttered with erections and debris associated with the rack railway on which stubby little engines puff and pant throughout the tourist season, toiling up the north-west ridge from Llanberis. Nine paths, all maintained to some degree and all extremely popular, converge on the summit cone from beginnings among featureless southern slopes or rocky northern cwms. In summer the Sherpa bus service links their starting points to facilitate different combinations of ascent and descent. However, the most famous is a circular combination of the Crib Goch and Lliwedd approaches. This route, the Snowdon Horseshoe, is arguably the finest of Britain's ridge scrambles outside Scotland.

Snowdon and the Glyders absorb most of the heavy traffic, so days spent on the grassy tops of the Moelwyns will be relatively tranquil. Paths here are fewer, narrower, and less well documented. Detritus from abandoned slate mines and quarries presses in on villages tucked close beneath and offends or intrigues according to temperament.

South of Snowdon a dog-leg ridge of high ground surrounds Cwm Pennant. Part of this circuit integrates simple rock scrambles with slender grass ridges for the delightful Nantlle Ridge. The Lleyn Peninsula extending south-west from here places its small hills in picturesque juxtaposition with a coastline spared the usual commercial ravages. Here stands the enigmatic triptych of The Rivals, on whose heathery slopes are found remnants of Iron-Age settlements.

South of Eifionydd an attractive ridge parallels the coastline in a series of dips and peaks. Intractable terrain at its northern end deters many, but those who persevere with its heather and boulders will be rewarded by the Carneddau-like turf of the southern limb.

With its deep cwms, rocky headwalls, and radiating ridges, Cader Idris has more in common with Snowdon or the Glyders than its gentle neighbours in this southern extremity of Snowdonia. An uncomplicated, if uninspiring, ascent from the north wins widespread popularity for the summit of Pen y Gadair itself (893m), although discerning walkers will begin from the south and approach via the encircling ridge of Cwm Cau.

Until recently Aran was plagued by access difficulties which soured relations between visitors and local farmers. Now a series of courtesy paths have been negotiated which, while limiting the freedom to roam, at least provide a good introduction to this quiet corner of Snowdonia. The best of these traverses the main ridge from north to south and over the two highest summits, Aran Benllyn (884m) and Aran Fawddwy (907m). A more convenient circular route from Cwm Cywarch in the south incorporates the higher of the two.

North Wales ridges and snow gullies were climbed during the Golden Age of alpinism as winter practice. But these alpine miniatures soon began to charm their pioneers and by the turn of the century the 'practice' tag had been dropped. Some of the more difficult routes of this period were completed during Easter visits, when snow banks and icy chockstones blurred the distinction between summer and winter climbing. Several among these tax climbers today. Apart from Archer Thomson's aberration in the Devil's Kitchen, major icefalls awaited the equipment revolution of the late Sixties and Seventies.

Winter mountaineering in North Wales can be categorised as follows:

1) Ordinary hill walks under snow cover. Most walks are unaffected by light snow cover, but conditions are notoriously difficult to predict and you might encounter

anything from frosted grass to knee-deep powder. Ridges stripped of loose snow by cross winds can give effortless walking in magnificent surroundings, while intervening cwms choked by drifts are all but impassable. The optimum surface of crisp snow is infrequent and short-lived.

2) Wintery ridge scrambles. Conditions on these routes are even more variable. Erstwhile simple scrambles like Crib Goch and Bristly Ridge are extremely precarious under verglas or deep powder and are then best avoided. Ideal conditions arrive when a sudden freeze halts a gradual thaw, but unfortunately by then most ridge crests have already been stripped bare. At their best these routes give superb outings of Alpine character.

3) Gullies. This category includes everything from simple snow couloirs to vertical fissures. They are the most long-lived of winter routes and in a good year the popular snow couloirs like Parsley Fern and Central Trinity are climbable on at least a couple of days each week from December to April. Couloirs accumulate snow to a depth of several metres, surviving thaws and consolidating to a perfect consistency for late-season ascents. The more difficult gullies require a build-up of ice and so attain climbable condition less often. All gullies are best avoided during times of thaw or heavy snowfall as avalanches are not uncommon.

4) Icefalls. These are generally found at mid altitudes because to form they require an uninterrupted source of water. The big icefalls on cliffs take ten days of continuous sub-zero temperatures to form properly, although some routes are climbable after just four or five. Timing is critical. Most icefalls appear at least once each winter but they may be climbable on only one or two weekends in the entire season. Huge low-level waterfalls like Aber Falls and Maesglasau may freeze fully only once in a decade, so be ready!

On the Carneddau few of the ridge walks are entirely free of short scrambling sections, but difficulties are rarely prolonged or excessive. They are at their best after winds have stripped their crests of loose snow. Much of the best climbing will be found in the gullies of Craig yr Ysfa and Black Ladders. Under firm snow conditions the 250 metre Great Gully (III/IV) on Craig yr Ysfa is the finest of its type in Wales while the infamous Western Gully (IV) on Black Ladders provides a more difficult and sustained outing of a similar length. Both cliffs also contain several less demanding gullies which nevertheless share the evocative atmosphere of their more difficult neighbours.

Except under light snow cover the Glyders range is not ideal winter walking terrain. Snow-covered boulders make it hard going and few approaches on the more interesting northern side are without complications. At a more ambitious level, Tryfan's North Ridge, Bristly Ridge and the Gribin can be linked in a magnificent, if arduous, circuit. The Tryfan gullies are good but take little drainage and consequently accumulate ice slowly. Those on Glyder Fach, especially Central Gully, are better, while those on Glyder Fawr's Upper Cliffs are unaccountably ignored. Without doubt the most reliable winter route is Clogwyn Du Gully in the Nameless Cwm. Its left-hand branch includes a superb grade IV ice pitch which forms readily. Snow in grade I couloirs at the head of the Nameless Cwm remains long after that in the remainder of the Glyders has melted away. Low-grade couloirs within the arms of Y Garn are also good survivors. At a lower level, the normally repulsive Devil's Kitchen cliffs develop a dozen icefalls after a prolonged freeze. The stream course to the left of the crag freezes sooner than any other in North Wales and gives excellent pre-season practice. On the cliff proper, South Gully (IV) is the finest of the traditional routes. The Kitchen Cleft itself was the scene of an astonishing feat of endurance by Archer Thomson who, over a period of seven hours during the big freeze of 1895, hacked his way up the frozen waterfall with the aid of a coal hatchet purloined from Ogwen Cottage. To the right of the Cleft forms the most famous ice climb in Wales, and one of the most sought-after in Britain—the 125 metre Devil's Appendix (V). This awesome cascade of ice forms most years, but rebuffed all attempts until 1978, since when it has been climbed frequently.

Along with Cwm Idwal the south side of the Llanberis Pass contains the best icefall climbing in Wales. Those on the 100 metre open face of Craig y Rhaeadr are all grade IV or V and intimidating. Climbing of a more conventional nature awaits in upper Cwm Glas. Parsley Fern Gully (grade I or II according to line followed) is the most durable winter climb in Wales, which is just as well because it is also the most popular.

Winter walking on Snowdon is never straightforward, even allowing for a 'settling down' period after heavy snow. For instance, the featureless upper part of the Watkin can become a treacherous ice sheet through sun action, while the Zig-Zags on the Pig Track often drift over and a substantial cornice may develop at their exit. Crib Goch is crossed often despite the seriousness of the undertaking (technicalities rarely exceed grade I but the route is inescapable). Under ideal conditions the traverse is magnificent. The 150 metre altitude advantage enjoyed by Clogwyn y Garnedd over other winter crags in Wales ensures its continuing popularity—despite a two-hour approach. Large accumulations of water ice are rare here, so it is worth waiting for deep, consolidated snow. The shallow Trinity Gullies (grades I to III) are the favourites, although the nearby Ladies Gully and Cave Gully (both grade III in good conditions) are more interesting. The 300 metre cliffs of Lliwedd promise superb winter climbing of Alpine character. Unfortunately, minimal drainage prevents a build-up of ice on the faces and snow usually melts away before it has a chance to consolidate. The gullies also suffer from a lack of drainage although snow sometimes holds long enough to give difficult and serious climbs at grade IV. Winter climbing on Clogwyn Du'r Arddu is restricted for the same reasons although in good winters the perpetually oozing Black Cleft develops into a huge boss of ice which can be climbed at grade V with an extremely difficult mixed finish. Originally ascended over two days during the freeze of 1963, this was the forerunner of modern icefall climbing. That is, if you don't count Archer Thomson's Devil's Kitchen escapade of 1895.

Nowhere in Britain is there such a varied collection of rock climbs as in North Wales. From 300 metre mountain crags on the flanks of Snowdon to 30 metre limestone sea cliffs, there is something here to suit every taste and ability.

Exposed scrambling on the Braich-tu-du Face of Pen yr Ole Wen above the Ogwen valley.

Most routes are 60 to 120 metres in length and situated on crags less than an hour's walk from the road, so it is not unusual to climb three or four in one day. Comparisons with the Lake District are inevitable. Essentially there is little difference in length, outlook and intrinsic merit of mountain rock climbs, although approach walks are shorter. Rock on the easier classics is likely to be more polished and on the harder routes, less reliable. And yet most climbers would agree that North Wales has the edge. Why? Because North Wales also contains several south-facing coastal cliffs that make climbing possible throughout the year when the high crags are cloaked in mist or covered in snow.

Rock climbing began in North Wales about a hundred years ago. At that time the main attractions were gully and ridge routes on the big mountain crags. By the turn of the century, attempts to justify rock climbing in terms of pseudo-alpinism were abandoned and some notable outcrop climbs resulted—principally those pioneered by Archer Thomson. Otherwise attention remained focused on Lliwedd and Ogwen, where rambling cliffs seamed by ledges suited the rope techniques of the day. Most of the Diff. and V. Diff. favourites of today belong to this period. Not surprisingly the holds on many of these routes have since become polished to a slippery sheen by decades of eager boots.

The Great War dispersed the ranks of early pioneers and few of those who returned to North Wales in peacetime did so with effect. It took a new generation of climbers in the late Twenties and early Thirties to establish the Very Severe grade, and thus solve the problem of Clogwyn Du'r Arddu (or 'Cloggy', as it became known) and to realise the true possibilities of the Llanberis Pass. The main thrust came from Colin Kirkus and Menlove Edwards, though others of equal ability produced important individual climbs. Most of today's classic VSs owe their origin to this period of bold climbing.

Momentum was lost again during the Second World War. Harding and Moulam began a post-war revival, which in the Fifties was taken up by members of the Rock and Ice Club—and by Joe Brown and Don Whillans in particular. These were the years of the great Extremes in the Llanberis Pass and on Cloggy: Cenotaph Corner, Cemetary Gates, The Grooves, Vember, White Slab, Shrike. Today these E1 and E2 climbs are the core and the inspiration of all Extreme climbing in North Wales.

Throughout the Sixties the Extreme ethos was applied by Brown, Crew, Ingle, Boysen and others to previously neglected low-level crags at Tremadog and awesome sea cliffs at Gogarth. As the number of Extremes grew from dozens to hundreds, then likewise the hundreds capable of climbing them grew to thousands. Despite this, the 6a technical barrier remained intact.

Pete Livesey's ascent of Right Wall (E5, 6a) on Dinas Cromlech in 1974 showed what was possible with the proper application of training and preparation, though it was several years before new climbs of this grade became the norm. The late Seventies were noted for blitzes on the Pass and Gogarth as remaining lines at the new grade were picked off.

Throughout the Eighties the search for the ultimate test-piece continued. Fawcett,

Moffat, Redhead, Pollitt and Dawes each left masterpieces that in the future will be seen as the historical milestones of our time. These were the years of the limestone sea-cliffs, of the great Llanberis slate quarries and of audacious routes on Cloggy's Great Wall. And so it will continue. Meanwhile, climbers of the next generation will be discovering the delights of rock climbing on the old classics, sharing stances and enthusiasm with those of ten, twenty or thirty years' experience for whom history is incidental, not pivotal, to their own passionate enjoyment of the North Wales mountains.

Ogwen is the traditional base for novices and mountaineers. The Milestone Buttress and Idwal Slabs remain popular among the low-level crags despite polished holds and, on the Slabs, scant protection. Of the higher mountain crags, Tryfan's friendly East Face remains a favourite, while the summit cliffs of Glyder Fach and Glyder Fawr present more serious challenges on equally good rock. The full spectrum of difficulty is represented on the remote crags of the Carneddau—Craig yr Ysfa and Llech Ddu.

Short approaches to famous routes on south-facing cliffs endear the Llanberis Pass to crag climbers. In fact many of the routes on the Three Cliffs on the north side (there are four main crags and several minor ones, but who's counting?) are loose, undistinguished and polished. By far the best crag on the north side is Dinas Cromlech, where exhilarating wall and corner climbs survive all criticism. Perpetual weekend queues below Left Wall, Cenotaph Corner and Cemetary Gates are evidence of its status in British climbing. In Cwm Glas, on the opposite side of the valley, the shadowy form of Dinas Mot counters with greater variety. Some say it is the best crag in the Pass. Poorly protected slab climbing on the Nose contrasts with gymnastics on the Wings and Plexus Buttress. Higher up in Cwm Glas, Cyrn Las surprises with climbs comparable in quality and difficulty to those on Cloggy.

Cloggy is something special and all who climb here are brought under its spell. Its northerly aspect and high standard of routes (VS or harder) restrict climbing to the few dry weekends in the period from May to September. Steep slab climbing on the West Buttress (Great, Bow, Sheaf, West Buttress Eliminate, White, Longland's) complements the fierce walls and cracks on the East Buttress and Pinnacle (The Corner, Troach, Curving Crack, Vember, Great Wall, Llithrig, Pinnacle Arête, Octo, Shrike). On the opposite side of Snowdon, low-grade but serious mountaineering routes of up to 300 metres on Lliwedd provide the historical echo.

Neglected peripheral crags add to the charm of North Wales climbing. Delightful slabs of rough rock in the Moelwyns are ideal for first climbs, as are those on the Great Slab in Cwm Silyn (where grooves and arêtes on the adjacent Ogof Nose await later expertise). Big mountain crags on the flanks of Cader Idris and Aran are looser, but even quieter. All outlying crags lie within daily travelling distance of central regions.

South-facing coastal cliffs among the trees at Tremadog are a tremendous asset to North Wales climbing. Quality of rock and climbing on these mostly two-pitch routes bear comparison with any in the country. Inevitably most of the best routes are VS or harder but there are Severes here (Creagh Dhu Wall, Poor Man's Peuterey, Christmas Curry, Merlin) as good as any in Wales. In the harder grades, walls and overhangs on Vector Buttress (Vector, Weaver, Void) complement the slabs, corners and arêtes of Peuterey Buttress (Pincushion, Silly Arête, Barbarian, Scratch Arête).

As for sea cliffs, the weather on the western tip of Anglesey is even better than at Tremadog and routes on the Gogarth sea cliffs even more numerous. However, the climbing is more serious because of tidal approaches and poorer rock. The seaside atmosphere of some sea cliffs is entirely absent and most people climb here in a state of unrelieved trepidation. Route lengths are typically 45 to 120 metres. Worthwhile routes are HVS or harder, whether on the crumbling ramps, chimneys and overhangs of South Stack or on the smoother, less ephemeral faces of the Main Cliff and Wen Zawn. Sea cliffs on the Great Orme near Llandudno are comparable in length, difficulty and quality to inland limestone crags in the Peak District (that is, short and sweet), while those on the Little Orme are reminiscent of the more unfriendly Gogarth zawns (big and ugly).

JOSS LYNAM

Ireland

Ireland cannot boast of any high mountains—only two break the thousand metre contour, but most of them rise from the coast, so that every metre of height must be climbed. The mountains are very varied. You can take your choice amongst the quartzite cones of Connemara, the sandstone summits and coums of the south-east, Cork and Kerry and Mayo, the varied granites of Donegal, Mourne and Wicklow. Apart from Wicklow and Mourne, all ranges have one thing in common; climbers and walkers are rare, and paths even rarer. To my mind this is the great joy of the Irish hills; you need to use your map, your compass and your head to find your way, and when you do meet someone on the hill, you are glad to stop for a greeting and a chat.

Ireland has a dire reputation for bad weather. Faced with statistics it would be impossible to deny that rain falls on more than two hundred days per year on most Irish mountains. What the statistics don't tell you is that there is rarely a day when for at least a few minutes the wind will not blow the mist away and the sun gleam through the clouds to pick out the greens and russets of the hillsides, and reflect off the wet rock. The proximity of the Gulf Stream ensures that there is little snow on the hills in winter.

There are efficient Mountain Rescue teams in the more popular areas, but the only helicopter base is near Dublin, so reaction may be slow. Add to this the changeable weather, the lack of paths and lack of people, and you have a situation where any group on the Irish hills should be self-sufficient. As long as you come to Ireland expecting to look after yourself, I'll guarantee you an enjoyable mountain holiday.

South of Dublin rises the big whaleback of the Wicklow Hills. It is a granite batholith heaved up in the Caledonian Mountain Building and now, stripped of most of its mantle of metamorphic schist, it displays a series of rounded summits with gentle heathery slopes, boggy cols and plateaux. The highest mountain is Lugnaquillia (926m/3039ft), one of the two Irish 'Munros' outside of Kerry.

At first sight it is not a very interesting area for the hill walker. However, Wicklow is redeemed by its valleys. The glaciers of the Ice Age worked hard here to gouge out fine corries, many of them now lake-filled and very beautiful. My personal favourite is the Lough Dan–Lough Tay valley, dominated by the big Luggala crag, but Glendalough, site of an early Christian complex, is a close second. It, too, has an excellent climbing crag.

The sheer size of the area is also impressive. Admiring Lough Tay from White Hill to its east with a French journalist recently, she exclaimed at the wildness of the hills

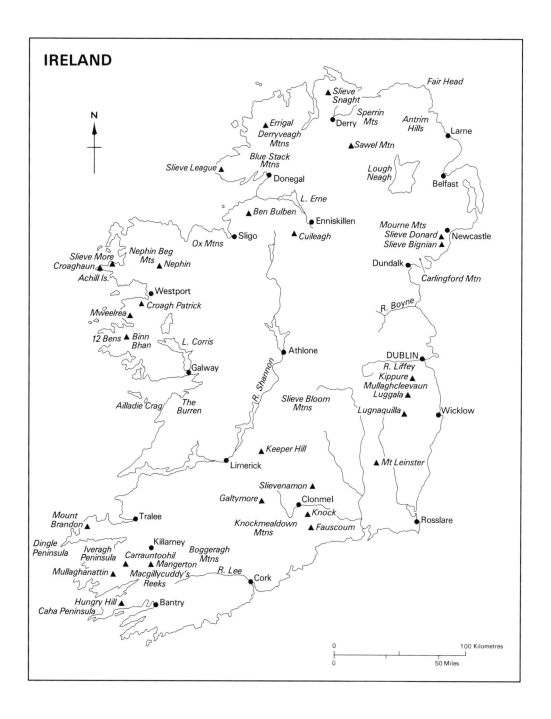

IRELAND

N

▲ *Slieve Snaght*

Fair Head

▲ *Errigal*
Derryveagh Mtns

Sperrin Mts
● Derry

Antrim Hills

● Larne

▲ *Sawel Mtn*

Blue Stack Mtns

Slieve League ▲

● Donegal

Lough Neagh

● Belfast

L. Erne

▲ *Ben Bulben*

● Enniskillen

Mourne Mts
Slieve Donard ▲
Slieve Bignian ▲

● Newcastle

Ox Mtns
● Sligo

▲ *Cuileagh*

Slieve More
Croaghaun
Achill Is.

Nephin Beg Mts
▲ *Nephin*

● Dundalk

Carlingford Mtn

● Westport

▲ *Croagh Patrick*

R. Boyne

Mweelrea ▲

12 Bens ▲ *Binn Bhan*

L. Corris

DUBLIN ●
R. Liffey
Kippure ▲
Mullaghcleevaun
Luggala ▲

● Athlone

● Galway

Ailladie Crag
The Burren

Slieve Bloom Mtns

Lugnaquilla ▲

● Wicklow

▲ *Keeper Hill*

● Limerick

Slievenamon ▲

Galtymore ▲

Mt Leinster ▲

● Clonmel
▲ *Knock*

Mount Brandon
● Tralee

Knockmealdown Mtns

▲ *Fauscoum*

● Rosslare

Dingle Peninsula

● Killarney

Boggeragh Mtns

Iveragh Peninsula
Carrauntoohil ▲
▲ *Mangerton*

R. Lee

● Cork

Mullaghanattin ▲
Macgillycuddy's Reeks

Hungry Hill ▲
Caha Peninsula

● Bantry

0   100 Kilometres

0   50 Miles

and moors and when I thought about it, there was not a dwelling (bar the big house nestling under Luggala) between us and Lackan 17 kilometres away as the crow flies. And that is the *breadth* of the range. The *length* is nearly 60 kilometres! Yet civilisation is never far away; from the same viewpoint the television mast on Kippure is clearly visible, and almost invisible but cutting north-south right through the wilderness, is the Military Road, built by the British after the 1798 Rebellion to root out the guerillas who had retired to these hills.

Because of their proximity to Dublin, the relatively good bus services and the network of youth hostels, the Wicklows are the most popular of our mountains, and you are bound to meet company if you walk them at a weekend. The finest walk is also the longest; from the outskirts of Dublin to the top of Lugnaquillia, some 53 kilometres and 2300 metres of ascent, following the main north-south ridge and taking in most of the main summits of the range, including Kippure (754m), Mullaghcleevaun (847m) and Tonelagee (819m). If you doubt your ability to finish the walk, you can arrange to be picked up at Sally Gap or the Wicklow Gap, where roads cross the ridge.

This is a large area and there are dozens of good walks I have not space to mention. I will single out the Sugarloaf, a mere 501 metres high but a fine scramble up a gleaming quartzite cone. Situated well to the east of the main range it is quite isolated and with views all round, from the big mountains on the west to the Irish Sea and (on a clear day) the Welsh hills beyond.

Product, like the Cork-Kerry Mountains, of the Hercynian Mountain Building, the sandstone mountains of the south-east are aligned east-west—unlike their northern neighbour Mount Leinster (796m), the southernmost outlier of the north-south alignment of Wicklow granite.

These are varied hills. The Comeragh Mountains have a huge summit plateau of dissected bogland, supported by dark vegetated walls of rock which enclose lake filled coums; one of which, Coumshingaun on the east, can claim to be the finest in Ireland. The disc-shaped plateau has an appendage running out to the north, like the tail of a tadpole, which forms the ridge of Knockanaffrin (753m). Dry underfoot and falling steeply to the east, this makes a very pleasant walk. The best way to taste the Comeraghs without too much bog-trotting is to climb the ridge on the south side of Coumshingaun (some scrambling involved here), which will lead you quite quickly to the highest point of the range, Fauscoum (789m). If the prospect daunts you, then you can skirt the top of Coumshingaun and return down the ridge which bounds it on the north. But it is worthwhile to brave the peat hags and cross the plateau to gaze down on Coumalocha and the Spilloge Loughs before returning to the north ridge of Coumshingaun.

West of the Comeraghs the Knockmealdowns, rounded heathery summits, march westward along the Tipperary-Waterford border. This ridge makes pleasant walking. It is dry underfoot, not too heathery, and if the cloud is down the county boundary ditch will keep you walking in the right direction. The best walk is the eastern half, starting from the Clonmel-Youghal road. This takes you over half-a-dozen

well-defined summits, including the highest, Knockmealdown (793m). You finish at
The Vee, a spectacular gash across the range, through which snakes the Cahir to
Lismore road.

*View west from
Galtymore. (Photo:
Hamish Brown.)*

North across the fertile Mitchelstown vale are the Galty Mountains, another string
of sandstone summits. Boasting a Munro, Galtymore (919m/3018ft), this ridge makes a
great walk. The Galtys are mostly grassy underfoot, the summits are well-defined,
there are fine corrie lakes below the scarp to the north and great views south to the
Knockmealdowns and north over the rich farmland of the Glen of Aherlow. It also
boasts the most beautifully-situated youth hostel in Ireland, Mountain Lodge, nestling
in the woods on the southern flanks of the range.

There are plenty of other hills in the south and east—isolated Slievenamon (719m),
the Slievefelims, the Silvermines Mountains and Keeper Hill (694m). But we must
push on towards the biggest and highest concentration of mountains in Ireland, in
Cork and Kerry.

The east-west Hercynian Mountain Building which created the mountains of the
south-east, formed in Cork and Kerry a series of parallel folds which have weathered
into the finest concentration of mountains in Ireland. The sea has flooded the troughs
of the folds, leaving four gnarled and knobbly fingers projecting into the Atlantic.

The Cork and Kerry mountains are all sandstone and because of the temperate
climate due to the proximity of the Gulf Stream they carry much vegetation. The

44

typical mountain here is quite steep with outcrops of rough purple rock appearing amidst dark green-brown vegetation. Gloomy corries with dark, wet crags are common. The ridges vary; sometimes, as on the Reeks, they are true arêtes. More often, as on Brandon, they have one steep and one gentle slope or, as in the Beara Peninsula, the ridges are broad and level, but cliff-edged.

The most northerly finger is the long, narrow Dingle Peninsula, culminating in Mount Brandon (950m), named for St Brendan who, tradition says, sailed to America and back. His oratory is on the summit and is reached by a long plod up gentle slopes from the west. The exciting side of Brandon is the east, a line of cliffs stretching 3 kilometres above a series of lakelets strung together like beads on a rosary. The walker follows the ridge running up from Faha above Cloghane, then, to avoid a high rock step, diagonals off down to the highest lakelet directly below the summit. I have been there in snow and it looks impossible to get to the summit without serious climbing, but the path—yes, there is a path—zig-zags back to the ridge without any real difficulty.

The slightly lower mountains east of Brandon suffer by their proximity to its overwhelming presence, but the ridges and coums of Slieveanea, Stradbally Mountain and Beenoskee—the highest at 824 metres—are well worth a visit, as are the equally high Slieve Mish, overlooking Tralee.

The second finger, the Inveragh Peninsula, has at its base the Macgillycuddy's Reeks, containing all but three of Ireland's Munros and culminating in Carrauntoohil (1038m/3414ft), Ireland's highest mountain. These peaks—justifiably called peaks—are not only the highest but can claim to be the steepest mountains in Ireland. Certainly the 'Reeks Walk', 18 kilometres and 1800 metres of ascent, from the Gap of Dunloe in the east along the narrow ridges of the Eastern Reeks and up the stony slopes of Carrauntoohil, would be a classic anywhere. The walk descends over Caher but the best route of all is to follow the jagged arête across to Beenkeragh (1010m), with slopes falling precipitously 300 metres or so to Coumloughra on the west and the crag-girt Devil's Looking Glass on the east. The walker can avoid any rock climbing by keeping below the jagged section of crest on the west and when he reaches it again he is rewarded with a view of the rocky north face of Carrauntoohil falling 600 metres to the Hag's Glen.

The rest of the Peninsula might be an anti-climax, but it isn't. Overlooking Dingle Bay is the Coumasaharn Horseshoe—highest point 772 metres. Easy ridge-walking but with fabulous views into a series of huge coums, each with a lake. In a rare triumph for conservation two of these coums have just been rescued from the threat of a hydro-electric scheme.

Separated from the Reeks by the narrow gash of the Ballaghabeama Pass is a whole range of fine rocky peaks, including Mullaghanattin (771m) and Knocknagantee (677m). This has to be the wildest and most remote mountain area in Ireland. There is a kind of central dish, ringed with summits and drained by a stream which falls 200 metres nearly vertically over the plateau rim. I have been up there at night and there is not a light to be seen except as you pass one narrow gap disclosing the lights of Sneem far away. There are big expanses of bare, beautiful, rough, light purple-brown rock, and getting up to, and more importantly, down from, the plateau can be a problem. It is hard to find a walker's route through the crags, but it is well worth the effort.

The third finger is the Beara Peninsula. The Caha Mountains, backbone of the peninsula, are unfrequented and not very high; Hungry Hill (685m), which makes a good short walk from Glanmore Lake, is the highest. There is much dissected bogland on the other summits which makes for boring walking, but here too are fine lake-filled coums and to walk the whole 45 kilometres length of this range is a fine excursion for those who like to be solitary on the hills.

The fourth finger has no mountains, but before we leave Kerry I must mention the mountains east of The Reeks. Killarney town, the Gap of Dunloe and the Killarney Lakes are tourist traps to be avoided, but Mangerton (837m), whether climbed from the Devil's Punch Bowl or the Horse's Glen, is a worthwhile summit, both for itself and for the views over the Killarney lakeland and the Ridge of the Reeks.

On our way north to Connemara we pass The Burren. Since the highest point, Slieve Elva, is only 343 metres, we can hardly claim this to be a mountain region. Nevertheless there are 380 square kilometres of bare limestone hills, most attractive to the rambler, especially in May when the flowers are at their best. The area is full of interesting caves and has a fine sea-cliff for rock climbing at Ailladie. Further south the Cliffs of Moher are magnificent—for looking at!

The road from Galway to Oughterard, apart from a rare glimpse of Lough Corrib, meanders dully between hedges. Then it climbs out of a wooded dell just beyond Oughterard into a different world. The foreground is a flat plain, a jigsaw pattern of land and lake; the backdrop is a long line of rocky summits, their quartzite slabs gleaming white in the sunlight, or looming darkly out of the clouds. They are not high, these mountains—the highest is 703 metres—but they start almost from sea level and are the steepest and rockiest mountains in Ireland.

There are two groups, separated by the wide, level, boggy Glen Inagh. To the east is the ridge of the Maum Turks, named for the pass (*Mám*) of the Boar (*Tuirc*) which crosses it. The walk along the ridge, starting from near Maum village, crossing a dozen summits and finishing 25 kilometres and 2500 metres of climbing later at Leenaum, is to my mind the finest mountain walk in Ireland. It has been run in 4½ hours but normal humans should allow 9-11 hours. It is not, of course, necessary to do the whole ridge. The central section from Mám Éan over the highest summit, Binn Idir an Da Log (703m), to Mám Ochóige, can be comfortably done as a circular walk from Maum. The views of the east-facing coums are particularly fine.

To the west are the Twelve Bens (you can argue forever as to which of the fifteen or sixteen summits are the real twelve). It is as if you had taken the long string of Maum Turks and tied it up in a knot. Deep valleys run into the very centre of the range, separated by rocky ridges and conical summits. In general the Bens are steeper and rockier than the Turks. The best walk (again, one of the finest in Ireland), is the circuit of Gleann Chóchan, which will net you six Bens. This walk can be conveniently done from Ballynahinsh (stay at the youth hostel or the hotel, depending on the depth of your pocket), and will take you into the very heart of the group at the three-way pass Mám Eidhneach, and to the very wildest part of it, the high plateau of bare rock between Binn Dubh and Binn Choirr. And when you have done all that, there is still the white rock and scree cone of the highest, Binn Bhán (730m), waiting for you. The rock climber will also find, on the north side of Binn Choirr, the biggest climbing crag in Ireland, with 300 metre classics like Carrot Ridge and Seventh Heaven.

Killary Harbour and the Maum valley are the boundary between Counties Galway and Mayo, but more importantly for us, the boundary between quartzite and sandstone. The bare rocky slopes of the Bens are replaced with dark, rocky, vegetated coums. Once again we have the amalgam of hills and the sea; the long, deep Killary fjord (deep enough to house the British fleet, pre-World War One), and its continuation, the Erriff valley, split this group of mountains down the middle and offer superb dawn and sunset views.

The finest of the sandstone mountains of South Mayo is undoubtedly Mweelrea, the highest in the Province of Connacht, which rises in one unbroken slope to 819 metres above Killary Harbour. Probably the best way to climb Mweelrea is from the east, from Delphi, named by a nineteenth century landowner for its alleged resemblance to the Greek original. (One dissimilarity is there—it is the wettest place in Ireland!) However, on a dry day the Delphi horseshoe over Ben Lugmore and Ben Bury, high above the dark Coum Dubh (Black Corrie) to Mweelrea and back over Killary, is a great walk. Or if you want a more intimate acquaintance with Coum Dubh, its bounding ridges make a great scramble from the road west of Doo Lough. (Do these walks soon, as the area is under threat of being torn up for open-cast gold mining.)

I have no space to tell of Mweelrea's neighbours, the Sheeffrys and Ben Gorm, or the high, bleak, peaty plateau of Maum Trasna. But I must mention the quartzite cone of Croagh Patrick (762m) overlooking Clew Bay which allegedly contains one island for each day of the year. Croagh Patrick is the only really well-trodden mountain in Ireland. On the last Sunday in July 20,000 pilgrims climb (some in bare feet) to St Patrick's shrine on the summit!

Under a heading of North Mayo and Sligo we have a *mixum gatherum* of mountains, with no clear common factor except that they fit geographically between the Connemara-South Mayo group and the Donegal mountains.

North of Clew Bay, and well-seen from Croagh Patrick, is a group of rolling sandstone hills, the Nephin Beg range. Nephin itself (806m) is a solitary quartzite dome overlooking Lough Conn. You can penetrate into the middle of them by following the road alongside Lough Fee up to Srahmore Lodge, hidden amongst the forestry plantations. From this road you can pick out a route to climb any of the summits to the west—Corranabinnia (711m) and Glennamong are the most interesting, with a real arête between them overlooking two west-facing coums. But *the* walk of the range is to start from Mullaranny and follow the ridge north for 32 long kilometres of heather and bog, with never a building in sight, over the eponymous Nephin Beg and the highest summit of the range, Slieve Cor (717m), to the main road at Bangor Erris.

Projecting into the Atlantic like an arrowhead is Achill Island, with two fine isolated peaks, Slievemore (671m) and Croaghaun (665m). Croaghaun especially is worth a visit. The summit is right at the edge of an almost sheer drop into the Atlantic, with nothing between you and America except the narrow snaking arête leading to Achill Head on your left.

In total contrast are the limestone mountains of Sligo, spilling over into neighbouring Leitrim. Here we find typical vertical scarps and that rarity in Ireland, dry-going underfoot. The big prow of Ben Bulben (525m), celebrated in W B Yeats' poetry, thrusts itself upon our attention as we take the road north from Sligo town, but the prow itself is certainly not for the hill walker and the rock is so loose that rock climbers don't like it either. For a good walk go round to the north into Gleniff and climb up the east side of Ben Whiskin; once on the plateau you can go as far as you like, to King's Mountain, or even Ben Bulben. On your return you can descend an old road at the head of the valley.

West of Sligo is another limestone hill, Knocknarea (329m), overlooking the Atlantic. This gets a mention for two reasons. It is crowned by a burial cairn of the legendary Queen Maeve and . . . it was the first mountain I ever climbed, at the age of six!

The Donegal Mountains, half quartzite and half granite, are the oldest hills in Ireland. Going north the first group we come to are the Blue Stacks, worn-down granite only partly rejuvenated by the ice and therefore a little dull. However Lough Eske, and Lough Belshade above it, are not far from Donegal town and should be visited. Belshade is notable for the amount of bare granite to be seen and the fine climbing crag above it. There is a new small hydro-electric scheme here and it remains to be seen what damage it does.

At the west-most tip of the county, on either side of Glencolumbkille, are tremendous quartzite sea cliffs which we must class as mountains since they rise almost sheer to 601 metres at the summit of Slieve League. The walk (which includes some rough scrambling) from Teelin west along the Slieve League cliff crest to Glencolumbkille and then (preferably after a night's rest there!) back north-east over Slieve Tooey to Maghera, is one of the best in the land, with magnificent views down the high cliffs to rocky stacks pounded by the big Atlantic swell.

Further north is the quartzite cone of Errigal (752m), with the only slightly lower summits of the Aghlas and Muckish in line behind it; a fine rough ridge walk with plenty of ascent and descent, especially at the beautiful Altan Lough, confined on two sides by the steep flanks of Errigal and Aghla More. From the top of Errigal you have a full-circle view; north and west is the bare Atlantic coast, south-east you look down to Dunlewy with its lake and stark roof-less church backed by the crag-rimmed ridges which encircle the Poisoned Glen. The flat bottom of this valley (named for the

Euphorbia Hyberna which used to grow there) runs deep into the Derryveagh Mountains; granite hills with much glistening white bare rock, culminating in Slieve Snaght (683m). The flanks of this range offer fine long climbs on superbly rough granite, a little out of favour these days because some routes are rather vegetated. The Glenveagh National Park (a deer sanctuary), in a lake-filled valley at the north-east corner of this area, is worth a visit.

Not to be confused with its Derryveagh namesake is Slieve Snaght in Inishowen (615m), the northern-most mountain in Ireland.

Moving into Northern Ireland we come to the Sperrins. Straddling the county boundary between Londonderry and Tyrone, these schistose mountains form an extensive area of boggy upland, part grass and part heather, with hardly a rock to be seen except below the top of Dart (622m), western neighbour to the highest summit, Sawel (678m). A quick run up these two from one of the road passes which cross the range is perhaps all that is really worthwhile, but the ardent bog-trotter will find the Sperrin Skyway, which embraces the whole 32 kilometre length of the range, to be a fine walk. The lazy may prefer to admire the beautiful Glenelly valley south of the main ridge.

I would like to explore with you the glens and hills of Antrim (including Fairhead, whose sea cliffs provide the best rock climbs in Ireland), but space is short and we must hurry on to the Mournes. These are a compact group of granite hills of Tertiary age and consequently much less worn down than the Wicklows. There are rounded ridges, but there are also conical summits, often crowned with rocky tors, so that from the south-west one of them, Slieve Bignian (747m), looks just like a Stegosaurus ready to leap into the Irish Sea.

Belfast gets its water supply from the Mournes, with some marked effects. Firstly there are three reservoirs, which in an otherwise lakeless area add to, rather than detract from, the scenery. Secondly, in these sad days there tend to be quite a few of the military checking to make sure you are not trying to blow up the said water supply; thirdly there is a stone wall right around the catchment area, which makes navigation easy and used to provide the route for the annual Mourne Wall Walk, now abandoned because it was causing ecological damage. (No reason why individuals should not follow it, the finest walk in the Mournes—but avoid the spring growing season.)

Like so many Irish mountain areas the Mournes are close to the sea and the best base for a walk up Slieve Donard (850m), the highest point of the province of Ulster, is the seaside resort of Newcastle. From the little tower at the summit there are good views over the trident ridges to the south, the rocky tors on Slieve Bignian and Slieve Bearnagh (739m), and 'The Castles of Commedagh'.

Across Carlingford Lough from the Mournes are the mountains of the Cooley Peninsula. Rough volcanic hills, they were the scene for The Cattle Raid of Cooley, the best-known epic of Irish mythology, when Queen Maeve of Connacht was foiled by the Ulster hero, Cuchulainn, when she tried to steal the Great Bull of Cooley. Carlingford town at the foot of Slieve Foye (589m) has fine medieval ruins.

DAVE DURKAN
Norway

Norway was created from Ginnungagap, a concept of inner reality concealed by an outward appearance of great emptiness. Yet in this abyss existed potential life.

The fiery realm of Muspell in the far, far South kissed the frozen wastes of North. From fusion came Chaos and the birth of Ymir, father of the Frost Giants and ancestor to all. Three gods slew Ymir, turning his bones to mountains and his flesh to soil, while his blood flowed to form Sea. Four dwarfs raised his skull above World, his brains became the clouds which in turn brought rain, thus allowing his hair to grow as vegetation. The gods caused time to exist for man, giving life, senses and understanding.

There is another, and less probable, genesis; that 5–600 million years ago, after the planet had cooled, sedimentation due to erosion lay in a deep sea basin. Under heat and pressure the metamorphosis of mud was rock. Some 300 million years later pressure caused the Caledonian earth-crust fold; rocks were to be quartz, felspar, mica and granite. Seemingly aeons passed before ice covered and sculptured the land. It receded and today the mountains of Norway rise virtually from sea level.

Some believe that agents such as wind, rain and ice completed the mountain make-up with vegetation adding the final cosmetic, whilst you and I know it was the Troll-people who formed and twisted the rocks to reflect their own needs and nature. Man's entry is but a momentary digression, yet he has placed upon the valleys, the lakes and the peaks that particular stamp of his presence. He has given the mountains a living history.

Norway is known as the Home of the Trolls; Land of the Midnight Sun—titles that conjure images of supernatural peoples, Vikings, valley farms and home-bound fishing boats.

At first glance Norway gives the appearance of a curving jagged backbone with little in the way of substance. This is deceptive, for although never really wide, it is interesting to note that the distance from Oslo to North Norway is approximately the same as from Oslo to Rome; and of this over 70 per cent is mountainous.

Of the southern ranges the Rogaland-Setesdal Highlands are a blend of low mountain, wooded valley, lake and river landscape. Some sections are naked, rocky plateaux and whilst some big crags have been opened of late, it is predominantly a walker's area. There are a number of six to nine-day hut-to-hut walks in the region.

To the west is Folgefonna, a glacier covering 259 square kilometres and remote to the point that most groups visiting it must be pretty self-sufficient and experienced. Its

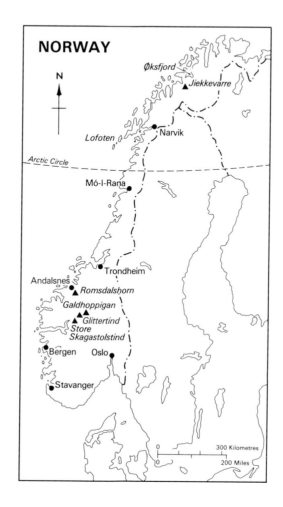

northern end is a fantastic place which lies so close to the sea that you can approach it from the west with the whole Atlantic as your backcloth. On reaching the top it is only a matter of crossing a few hundred metres before you can look down into the Hardanger Fjord.

Its big neighbour is the Hardangervidda mountain plateau where variety is the norm. High mountain moorland and glacier terrain in the north gives us Hardangerjøkulen. Finse is the starting point, reached by train on the Oslo-Bergen line. The highest point is 1860 metres and there are glacier guide services for those wishing for a day on the ice. Moving onto the plateau the walker will be well-rewarded with small, and not so small, peaks sneaking up here and there. Hårteigen, at 1690 metres, is the highest of them all and a worthy grail.

The *vidda* covers an area exceeding 15,000 square kilometres at an altitude of between 1060 and 1300 metres and is crossed by more than 1600 kilometres of marked tracks. These usually take in some place of interest, such as reindeer pits from prehistoric times, impressive waterfalls or ribbons of small lakes. Fishing is allowed but permits are necessary. There are herds of wild reindeer and the lucky walker may find whole antlers that are shed yearly, plus a rich flora with over 400 plant types.

The hut situation is excellent and run by the Norwegian Touring Association (DNT). A membership organisation with over 110,000 members, DNT has a national coverage, and both members and non-members may use the facilities. There are both staffed and un-staffed huts, the latter being self-catering only, whilst manned huts offer varying degrees of service. Additionally, some unstaffed huts have provisions that may be used, and paid for. Others do not, so it is worth checking on facilities provided—and opening dates, which may vary—before setting out. Members receive priority for beds, with substantial reductions in fees, yet no-one is ever turned away and the cost of membership is recouped after just a couple of nights' stay. Membership is therefore highly recommended.

The Finse-Fillefjell Ranges are popular with well-marked paths and comfortable huts. Again, Finse is the main starting point leading to the famous 'British Route'. This consists of five days of walking on a wondrous path along a series of small lakes connected by a river, leading to a series of impressive waterfalls; all good hiking.

One should not forget winter travel, for Norway is the birthplace of cross-country skiing. These regions are ideal for touring and for proficient, and not so proficient, skiers I would recommend for a first visit joining one of DNT's organised touring groups. There are special groups to meet all requirements, but general to all is that they use the huts and have proficient leaders.

The Rondane Mountains are situated in a National Park and are popular with geologists and mountain walkers alike. The numerous cirques are appealing, which with 'spooky' peaks create images of long-forgotten Troll strongholds rising in grand solitude amidst peaceful surroundings. Vegetation and animal life is sparse although what there is attracts naturalists. The main disadvantage is the area's popularity, which effectively reduces the possibilities of solitude during the main season.

W.C. Slingsby was the acknowledged 'Father' of Norwegian mountaineering and his book, *The Northern Playground*, is compelling reading and a true classic, much of it relating to ascents in the Jotunheimen. A word of warning though; do not try to emulate his times as he obviously had very little excess fat to carry.

The Jotunheimen, known as Norway's Alps, ranks as one of the country's finest mountain regions. It boasts some 250 peaks over 1800 metres, some rising above 2400 metres, and with more than sixty glaciers. The range consists of a number of independent groups, all of which are connected by paths, normally with no more than six hours' walking between huts. A number of these paths cross high passes and glaciers, so good route planning is necessary.

In reality the area demands a book to itself but because of limitations of space I simply note the areas of Falketind, Smørstabbtind, Bygdin-Gjende ranges, Leirvassbu and Raudalen as being worthy of attention and having their own devotees. At the heart is Norway's highest peak: Galdhøpiggen (2469m), the true 'Home of the Giants'. Glittertind, the country's number two, challenges its position, for although its rock summit is only 2452 metres, it has a snow summit reaching 2470 metres. So which is the highest? This is a long-term debate, but my daughter's school books say Galdhøpiggen.

To reach Galdhøpiggen's main peak, an energetic ascent from Spiterstulen is popular and well recommended. It can be completed in a 5-9 hour round trip. My preference is for the easy snow gully on the south side; four hours to the summit, and the standard descent. Or, a solitary traverse from the unnamed peak on the west ridge; a ten-hour day as taxing as it is enjoyable. Guide services are available for both novice and expert at the hotel, but another centre for starting for the summit is Juvasshytta. Here large economic parties are roped together looking rather like Chinese New Year dragon parades. Don't knock it though, as many a famous mountaineer started his career after receiving his first taste through a package glacier crossing.

Climbers in this region might turn their attention to the South West Wall of Veslepiggen (2369m), a seven-pitch route with reasonable rock, sustained climbing but somewhat complex route-finding. At grade VI it should be courted only by strong VS to HVS parties. Easier, but nicely exposed, is the South-East Ridge of Skardstind (2373m), grade IV+, again comprised of seven pitches and a mountaineering character.

Of all the groups my choice is the Hurrungane, a massif of nearly twenty peaks affording well-situated ridges and reasonably stable glaciers. An ideal area for attaining and practising basic alpine skills, it also boasts some big wall climbs. From the hotel at Turtagrø one to three-day routes of all standards may be enjoyed. The hut at Bandet is an ideal advance base camp and opens up days of sport. The gem is Store Skagastølstind (2405m), the country's third highest and most coveted peak. The first ascent was by Slingsby when he soloed the top section, which is impressive, to say the least. The easiest route is grade III+, which involves a demanding approach and boasts some very exposed climbing near the summit, and a spectacular abseil situated 650 metres above the Slingsby Glacier. As a guide I climbed this peak by the standard routes nearly thirty times and never grew tired of it.

Those wishing for something more demanding might turn their attentions to the West Face for sustained grade V and VI climbing on solid rock, varied and in spectacular positions. It is also worth considering the sadly neglected South Face, for although not a great line, it takes you through some impressive lunar scenery and has a sting in its tail. A long day, at grade III to IV, it is ideal for competent Severe parties, though the exit rocks can be tough-going after a fresh fall of snow, or if iced.

The surrounding peaks, namely Støre Midt Maradalstind (2057m), Søndre Dyrhaugstind (2074m) and Støre Ridngstind (2124m), all provide splendid days for the all-round mountaineer. Add swirling mist to this backcloth and you have an atmosphere to compete with both the Alps and Tolkien.

It is worth considering Norway as a winter venue, not just for skiing, but for climbing. The objectives are there in their thousands, from ridge traverses of the classics, to first winter ascents. Of late, waterfall climbing has come of age; a veritable Mecca. Here the whole size of the country comes into play; logistics are more complex and whilst summer days are long, remember that winter days are short—certainly as you move farther north. The best time is usually from the end of January to the end of March or early April. Equipment and experience should then be on a par with those required for venturing in the Alps during the same season.

The Jostedal Glacier may be reached on foot in four days, though the sane will use a car. This is Ranulph Fiennes country. He parachuted in, and the account in his excellent autobiography, *Living Dangerously*, leaves one feeling exhausted. Yet one should not be put off, for there is scope for us mere mortals too.

Rising above the surrounding peaks it resembles the ice caps of Greenland, at a height reaching nearly 2000 metres. It lies between the Jotunheimen and the North Sea, covers 475 square kilometres and is the largest icefield on the continent of Europe. A complete north to south (or south-north) journey for experienced skiers in good conditions takes about twenty skiing hours. However, ascents and descents must be taken into consideration; also that the area experiences the joys of both coastal and high mountain weather patterns! Most parties will be content to utilise the well-situated huts on both sides, so making a variety of glacier crossings, west to east and east-west. As in other areas DNT hold glacier courses here and guide services are available.

Travelling farther north you come to the Sunnmøre Alps. The towns of Øre or Ørsta are good starting points, with a traverse of the never-ending ridge system of Skartind (1500m) being good value. The Kolastind Pinnacles (1432m) or Råna (1586m) are also worthy of attention. Slogan, at 1564 metres, is impressive, but the ascent is not too taxing. The Patchell Hut makes an ideal base. There is a feeling of isolation here and some peaks demand the use of a boat to reach them, so homework is necessary. This, however, is not so in Romsdal, for there the big walls overlook a main highway.

Romsdal is the most famous climbing area in Norway, mainly because of its multi-day big wall climbs. Åndalsnes is the main centre and a taxi can deposit you under the mighty Trolltind (1795m) only ten minutes' from the heart of the town. The Troll Wall is said to be Europe's only vertical mile, and whilst not quite factual, it is a masterpiece of mountain architecture. The famous Troll Pillar is an overrated two-day climb. Its value lies in its position in Norwegian mountaineering history, being the longest and most difficult route in northern Europe at the time of its first ascent, by Arne Randers Heen and Ralph Hoibakk, in 1958. The route offers over 600 metres of very mixed climbing, which ranges from vertical to near-overhanging grass and mixed gunge, to about ten difficult pitches that would tax most HVS leaders, all combined with more than usually complex route-finding. Few parties manage it in one day, with one to three bivis being recorded. Worth doing if only as an eye-opener to The Wall itself, and to get over the rigours of travel.

The Wall itself is greatly foreshortened from below and once you have completed the approach up the giant scree slope you realise why so many have held it in awe. It's a

Romsdal—The Troll Wall, famed as Europe's only vertical mile. (Photo: Hamish Brown.)

giant, so big that El Capitan could nestle under its protective shadow.

The Rimmon, or English Route, has become the trade route, yet it should not be underestimated. Out of twenty-four pitches, half of them are sustained HVS (E2), and even the easy pitches demand respect. The climbing is varied and some pitches, such as the two up the Great Wall, are classic XS (E1) if done free. A slightly more than vertical finger crack, some jugs and good protection, then a 'thank God' belay. Hand and foot jams past a roof, up and up to a belay with uncertainty above; an exposed escape, and there is more still to come. Flake Crack, Narrow Slab and the overhanging Exit Chimney were names many of us grew up reading about, and Tony Howard and his party became household names after their 1965 ascent. Although the route has now been climbed free, it is usual to use some aid, and most parties take two to three days.

The Swedish Route is of the modern idiom, offering far more sustained and difficult climbing than the above. The positions are also in a class of their own. We aimed and reached a bivi under the Grey Wall after an early start and a long day's climbing. Day Two produced mind- and body-jarring excitement leading to the Hilton Ledge. This juts out over what felt like sitting on a prow of an ocean-going liner above a vertical mile. Tired after two days' hard and very sustained climbing I started to hallucinate; the smell of the sea, the sound of gulls, women on the sand, ice cream cones etc. My mentor, Greg Hall, could probably have dragged me up the remaining three pitches but deemed we take advantage of this magnificently situated ledge. We feasted and drank mugs of hot chocolate, told tales and settled down for the night with our respective dreams but awoke to mist and heavy rain, a drop in temperature resulting in slush. But what a bivouac, what dreams; not to be missed! Only competent parties need apply.

Not everyone wants to play gladiator and the Romsdal region has enough for all tastes. As such it is ideal for larger parties with mixed aspirations, with Store Vengetind (1852m) or Romsdalshorn (1550m) offering splendid days. Biskopstind tempts with a good route by the South-East Pillar where competent Severe parties should find the solid rock and interesting climbing just reward. Do not be put off, it looks harder than it is. Neither should you be shy about taking bivi equipment on some of the peaks, as a little map reading can lead to all sorts of exploratory adventures, at varying standards.

Dovre is a national preserve offering excellent walks, with Snohetta (2286m) being a popular objective. This peak was once thought to be the highest mountain in Norway, as well as in Europe! The small herds of wild reindeer, imported musk ox from Greenland, and the rich and rare plant and bird life, all add to its appeal. Crossing it by the Old King's Road, visiting historic travellers' inns, is a novel way to see the mountains.

Farther on is Trollheimen, where a spider's web of paths covers the 'Home of the Trolls'; an intoxicating area which in turn can lead to Nordmore. Nordmore is popular with novice and expert alike and is a walker's paradise. Innerdal Hut is the centre for climbing courses and is renowned for its hospitality. It has excellent crag climbing in fine mountain surroundings. Information can be gleaned locally and often a climbing partner found. There is a yearly Ladies' Climbing Meet held here, which has a strong following of both genders. Innerdalstårnet (1450m) is a long outing with reasonable grade III climbing to the summit. There are great views and the long slog up passes surprisingly quickly in reverse. The serious walker and scrambler would be well advised to venture deeper into this area.

A word on transport. Public transport brings the ranges within reach in one or two days—except for the far north. The main rail routes meet up with local bus routes but check carefully or an enforced bivouac in a desolate station may result. Personal transport is recommended as it opens up other areas en route, serves as a useful base, allows for alternatives when Thor (God of Thunder) is angry, and with food costs being high allows for stocking up at home.

Language is no barrier, with English being a useful social introduction. Many a climber has met a beautiful blonde on the dance floor and, claiming ignorance of language and steps, has been taken in hand. The basic steps, moves and throws are soon mastered to the tune of accordion and fiddle. Don't be shy. They are often dry affairs (the dances), so many locals sport hip flasks of the infamous *Hjemmebrent* which, under the eye of the local vicar, finds its way into pint pots of Coke. A warning though, do not mix drinking with driving in this land (nor any other), as the strong arm of the law puts you inside for 21 days.

The summer season extends from June to September and one should allow for wet, windy and cold days, although weeks of sunshine are by no means uncommon. Basically, the walker should be decked out with Scottish summer gear and the climber with Alpine summer or Scottish winter gear. Technical equipment should allow for double ropes and, as many descents are by abseil, some extra slings should be added.

Earlier generalisations pale as we journey towards the Arctic Circle. The concept becomes one of involvement as paths disappear, cairns are few and far between, huts are few and spartan, and approaches terminate below vast unclimbed walls.

The Okstind Glacier lies to the north of Mosjoen, a wild glacier area surrounded by alpine peaks. Further north, from the town of Mo i Rana, Svartisen (Black Ice Glacier) dominates, offering fine hikes and glacier crossings with the western sector harbouring interesting ascents. Again, this is DNT course country. There are also a number of cave systems with a lot of activity from both local and British cavers.

The Sulitjelma region is of interest to those seeking isolation and who wish to explore, with glacier crossings into the lower Swedish mountains.

Bodo is an ideal starting point for the Folda region, where climbers and walkers need to be self-sufficient when exploring new routes and reaching the last of the lost valleys.

An increasingly popular area is Tysfjord. Stetinden (1381m) is a magnificent and natural obelisk where the most popular route demands good technique (or brawn for the hand traverse), and it sports two modern masters that should grace any edition of Super Extreme Big Wall Climbing. Slingsby described it as 'nature's giant anvil', a true masterpiece of natural sculpture.

At this point it seems appropriate to quote from the late Ove Skjervan: 'Mountains are the basic resource of climbers; we should take good care of them and keep them clean.' Ove did not just mean litter; he was propagating a deeper ethic. Perhaps we should agree that the importance placed on the conquest of a mountain is an outlived premise, forming an emphasis now on basic discovery, be we walker or climber. This, instead of reducing the experience to 'how many hours' or how many and how difficult the technical points are on a given route.

We do need developed and documented areas with their guidebooks acting as yardsticks to the development of our sport, and to ourselves as individuals. To share information is healthy. We need our first ascents to enrich our history. We need tales of bravado to balm our egos and to humour us. Yet could we perhaps be satisfied for certain areas to have no route descriptions at all? That when we climb a new route we do not claim it, nor document it, nor publicise it?

In some areas of Norway this ethic is practised, an ethic that might be viewed as worthwhile, one to encourage and to safeguard. Add to this the Professor Arne Naess line of thought, 'It is not important to reach the top, but it is important *how* you reach the top,' and you're airing views put forward over sixty years ago. Yes, in the north you are entering undeveloped regions; have you the strength of character, of spirit, to leave them so for future generations?

The Lofotens consist of over eighty islands; a region in semi-limbo. Some descriptions do exist. A favourite of my own penmanship was: 'Climb the wall behind the village, 16 hours, great views.'

Moskenesoy is a gem sporting numerous spires that grace complex ridges. Climbs here can be quite alpine and are worthwhile. Hinnoy Isl is notable, and the island of Austvagoy was designed with climbers in mind. I steal from Per Prag: 'Strip the Dent Blanche of its ice, double the number of its arêtes, making them more jagged, cut off all but the upper 1000 metres, plant it by the seashore, and a fair idea will be had of Vegekallen.' Not bad for a peak that only reaches a height of 942 metres. Add the peaks in Kabelvag, Svolvoer, Rulten, Troll Fjord and you have unprecedented sport.

One famous 'tourist' outing is the ascent of Svolvaegeita (The Goat), 569m, the summit being two 4.5 metre high pinnacles known as 'De to Elskende'—the Two Lovers—which are separated like Adam and Eve on Tryfan by a narrow gap. However, owing to the difference in height, a 1.5 metre leap is necessitated. All this, 300 metres above the local cemetery.

Langoy Island sports a spectacular peak, Reka (609m). When remembering that everything starts at sea level, this is a reasonable ascent and the ridge is reminiscent of Crib Goch.

Every area has its local Matterhorn. In the Narvik region it is Rombakstotta (1243m). There is plenty of scope in the surrounding area, with the island of Andoy being ideal for congenial parties who have no pressing ambitions. Here, like Lofoten, one can combine local living—by renting an old fisherman's cottage—with mountaineering. Further north we reach Tromsø, which has its devotees and an active climbing club.

The Lyngen Peninsula is one of the least spoilt mountain areas in Europe, covering over 1398 square kilometres. Here a number of ascents have been made and recorded, but very little information exists. The Tromsø Climbing Club is working on a guidebook, but that is for the future. A traverse of Lakselvtinder (1617m) is a joy for those proficient in our craft. Jægervasstindan (1540m) is a most alluring peak first climbed by the British mountaineer, Elizabeth Main, in 1898. The more proficient alpinist may turn towards Jiekkevarri (1833m), a huge rock massif dotted with small icefields and flanked by several glaciers. Its South Face resembles the Brenva Face on

Mont Blanc and there have been British ascents of its East and South-East Faces. With information scarce, other parties may be able to experience the joy of exploration, the pioneer spirit being needed for this great beast of the north.

Our Odyssey continues to reach the north of Lyngen, the Skjervoy region. The main islands are Arnoy, with peaks rising to over 1000 metres and offering some climbing, and Vannoy which is in the main unexplored. Access and weather conditions have deterred most parties in the planning stage.

The Oksfjord region is an isolated part of Finmark with low mountains offering pleasant expedition conditions. Climbing here is reminiscent of Skye and while most peaks may be reached by gentle slopes, the opposite sides afford pleasant routes of passage on good gabbro.

Mountaineering may be defined as being the art of moving safely in potentially dangerous places. Norway's mountain ranges are many, diverse, splendid and worthy of attention. But it is a vast country with limited rescue facilities and when these are mobilised the time, energy and costs can be staggering. So take the scale into consideration and respect the weather gods, as there is no instant rescue.

One chapter alone cannot hope to do justice to Norway and her mountains. The aim here has been to promote questions, general discourse, and to open a window on the wilderness. To lean once more on Ove Skjerven:

'Sometimes we must protect them from large-scale commercial tourism, sometimes abstain from writing about them (leaving them as a gift to future generations). . .But don't take any of this to mean that you should not come to Norway and climb our mountains. As long as you share some of these attitudes. . .when the cold rain stops pouring down, you can make new ascents that have been made before.'

INTRODUCTION BY KEV REYNOLDS
The Alps

The Alps are both the birthplace of mountaineering and the best-known of any mountain range in the world. They stretch in a great arc for more than 1000 kilometres from the Mediterranean coast near Nice in south-east France, through Switzerland, Liechtenstein, northern Italy, parts of Germany and Yugoslavia and terminate near Vienna in eastern Austria.

Formed during the Tertiary period when the African tectonic plate collided with that of Europe, the range contains more than eighty summits in excess of 4000 metres (according to definition) and reaches its highest point on the snow dome of Mont Blanc (4807m). There are some 1200 glaciers, the largest being that of the Grosser Aletschgletscher which flows for 25 kilometres south of the main crest of the Bernese Alps in Switzerland, but even where glaciers have long departed many great U-shaped valleys still bear witness to the work of icefields of the past. The permanent snowline varies between 2500 and 2900 metres, adding a certain stature and an indefinable beauty to the range.

Snowfields and glaciers, and the summits themselves, held no appeal or interest to the native population until visitors began to arrive in search of knowledge and adventure in the late eighteenth century. Indeed, the word 'alp' was that given by peasant farmers to the upper pasturelands and it was only through a misunderstanding that the whole mountain range became so named. For centuries many summits were considered to be the home of demons and the pioneers of mountaineering had not only to battle with the difficulties of a sport using only rudimentary equipment, but also with the superstitions of local people. Nowadays, of course, tourism in the shape of mountain activity is a major industry, both winter and summer, and there are few secrets or superstitions left.

Beginning in the south-west the craggy peaks of the Maritime Alps rise north of Nice and reach their highest point on Punta del' Argentera (3297m), first climbed by W A B Coolidge in 1879. These give way on the Col de Larche to the Cottian Alps, named after King Cottius. In 218 BC Hannibal is thought to have crossed somewhere in this chain of mostly snow-free mountains, whose crown is Monte Viso (3851m). William Mathews (1828-1901), one of the founder-members of the Alpine Club, made the first ascent in 1861.

The mountains of Dauphiné continue the line beyond the Cottian Alps and are treated to a separate chapter. Then come the Graians; West, Central and Eastern, forming part of the frontier between France and Italy. The Western Graians include the delightful Vanoise National Park, contain 107 summits over 3000 metres in height, and the second largest snowfield in the Alps. The Central Graians run from Col du Mont Cenis to Col de la Seigne and share the boundaries of both the Vanoise National Park and part of that of the Gran Paradiso Park. The Eastern Graians are topped by the peak of Gran Paradiso (4061m), climbed first in 1860 by J J Cowell and W Dundas, with the guides J Tairraz and M Payot.

Then come the Mont Blanc and Pennine ranges, and the Bernese Alps standing apart and divided from the Pennines by the deep trench of the Rhône valley. To the south and east of the Bernese Alps the Lepontine and Adula Alps send their ridges down towards Italy. The Rhaetian Alps include the Albula and Bernina ranges, the latter containing the easternmost 4000 metre summit in the Alps (Piz Bernina), beyond which the Ortler is the first of the groups in northern Italy. These lead directly into the Dolomites.

North and north-east of the Rhaetian Alps stretch the many lovely groups that make up the Austrian and Germanic Alps, while the Dolomites of northern Italy give way to the Julian Alps of Yugoslavia.

JOHN BRAILSFORD
Dauphiné

In the sixteenth and seventeenth centuries the administrative region of Dauphiné stretched from close to Lyon in the north-east, to Montélimar in the south-east, Le Pont de Beauvoisin in Savoie and Briançon, Queyras and Gap in the south-west.

The modern *départements* of Isère, Drôme and Hautes Alpes equate to the region as it was in the seventeenth century. A large region, it is full of contrasting landscapes, geology, culture and origins which tend to give it a richness and depth to delight the visitor whatever his or her interests in life.

The climate is kinder than almost anywhere in the Alps. The influence of the Mediterranean is considerable and prolonged fine weather is a feature of the southern half of Dauphiné in particular, where it is unusual to suffer more than three days of storm before the sun returns. This warmer climate does result, however, in a variation of high mountain conditions from year to year and a heavy spring snowfall can alter approaches and climbs out of all recognition to guidebook descriptions.

The year 1492 saw not only Columbus's discovery of the Americas, but the ascent of Mont Aiguille (2086m), a bold, monolithic outlier in the Vercors (Isère) region of Dauphiné. This ascent by Antoine de Ville de Dompjulien, who was chamberlain to Charles VIII, was a real expedition and as such is seen by many as the beginning of true rock climbing.

To approach the Vercors from the west via Pont en Royans offers the traveller some of Europe's most spectacular roads, with the impressive limestone cliffs of Presles above Choranche where one enters the Gorges de la Bourne. The narrow, tortuous, overhung road climbs steadily upwards to level out at about 5 kilometres from Villard de Lans and although the descent to the city of Grenoble is less impressive, it is still craggy and evocative.

The Chartreuse massif lies north-east of Grenoble and is similar in character to Vercors. Rock climbing has been of a high order in these two limestone regions for more than a generation and the original guidebook by Serge Coupé is still available in Grenoble. Apart from Presles and Mont Aiguille, a continuous wall of vertical rock runs north to south parallel to the river Isère, with notable isolated buttresses such as Gerbier, Pleynet, Deux Soeurs, and Rochers du Parquet. These offer climbs of up to 300 metres in all grades. Chartreuse climbing has not proved so popular with British climbers, but it is equally well documented, although the actual climbs tend to be shorter in length.

Due east of Grenoble lies the true Alpine massif of Belledonne, culminating in the

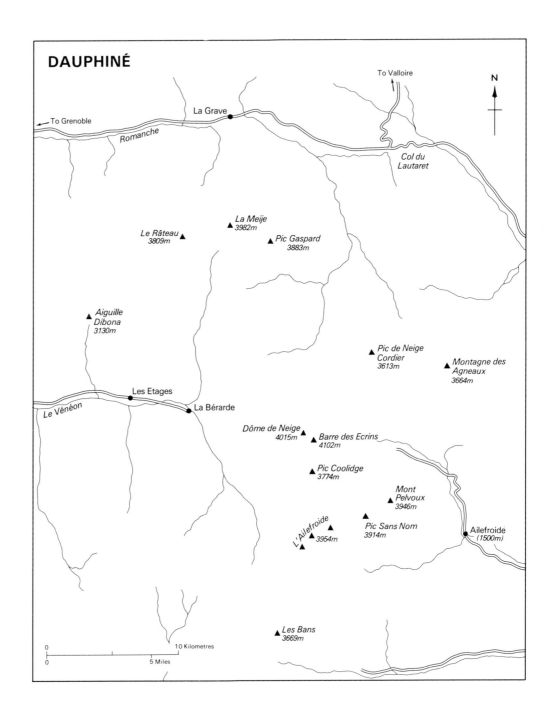

DAUPHINÉ

To Valloire

N

To Grenoble

La Grave

Romanche

Col du Lautaret

La Meije
3982m

Le Râteau
3809m

Pic Gaspard
3883m

Aiguille Dibona
3130m

Pic de Neige Cordier
3613m

Montagne des Agneaux
3664m

Les Etages

La Bérarde

Le Vénéon

Dôme de Neige
4015m

Barre des Ecrins
4102m

Pic Coolidge
3774m

Mont Pelvoux
3946m

L'Ailefroide
3954m

Pic Sans Nom
3914m

Ailefroide
(1500m)

Les Bans
3669m

0   10 Kilometres
0   5 Miles

Grand Pic de Belledonne at 2926 metres. It is a region of sharp rocky peaks, small glaciers and *névés* and a veritable jewel box of sparkling lakes, rising trout and running streams. Waterfalls cascade at almost every turn and when approached in the early morning, with mist swirling around the crags, they appear awesome.

Belledonne is really a walker's paradise. The Grande Randonnée, or long distance footpath, No 549—along with other, numerous waymarked routes—provides a network of Alpine travel in a mid-altitude situation, safe for families and young people.

The huts, as elsewhere today, need advance booking if one is to be sure of a meal and a bed. Sleep is less sure in the high summer months of July and August as the pressure is so great. Alpine starts, before 7.00 am, need to be arranged between your party and the guardian, who may leave your breakfast drink in a flask rather than get out of bed before the walking fraternity, who also tend to be late going to bed.

The classic climb is that pioneered by the late Gaston Rébuffat on the North Face

Mont Aiguille, first climbed in 1492, the year Columbus discovered America. (Photo: John Brailsford.)

of the Grande Pic de Belledonne and graded TD. The traverse of the Grand Pic to La Croix de Belledonne is also well worthwhile and the 300 metre glissade to the valley is as safe as it is exciting. Belledonne is easily approached from Grenoble via Uriage and Chamrousse. From Le Recoin a cable car rises to La Croix-de-Chamrousse from which point a descent of twenty minutes leads to Lac Robert.

The sites of winter ski pistes are soon left behind and true Alpine ambience takes over the place. Obviously winter ski activity is intense, but the spring skiing is good too, with open, guarded huts being available.

To the south-east of the Massif de Belledonne lies the Maurienne. Both these groups border Savoie and Italy respectively and access may be gained from either aspect.

Mont Thabor and the Aiguilles d'Arves are the principal peaks, while the GR5 links with the GR5B to offer a traverse between Forneaux, close to the railway at Modane, and the Névache/Clarée valley close to Briançon in the south. Other well-marked paths thread throughout the massif, and alpine huts are frequent. Some are supported by the Club Alpine Français (CAF), others are privately owned. *Gîtes d'étape* also serve valley bases and offer cheap, clean accommodation where, again, advance booking is wise. Also in this slice of the eastern part of Dauphiné one finds the GR54 and GR549 to the east of Alpe d'Huez and the Massif du Cerces, which stretches from the RN91 at the Col de Lautaret to the Vallée Etroite close to Bardonecchia in Italy.

The mountain hub of this wheel of our old administration is known to the French as l'Oisans, or the Massif des Ecrins. During the 'Golden Age' of the middle and late 1800s, first ascents were made by English-speaking alpinists, with Whymper, Tuckett and Coolidge prominent among them. Coolidge, with maps by Duhamel, provided the first guidebook to Dauphiné in 1892. Hautes Alpes thus became the third large massif to be exploited after Mont Blanc and the Bernese Oberland/Valais districts.

Departing Grenoble on the RN91 one soon leaves the industrial ugliness of chemical works of the lower Romanche valley, to arrive at the junction with the road which descends from the Maurienne via Col du Glandon, some eight kilometres before Bourg d'Oisans. The town itself is tourist-orientated but it retains a pleasant atmosphere in a fine setting. Roads leading to Alpe d'Huez, La Mure and La Bérarde as well as the N91 to Briançon, start from, or just outside, the town. The N91 rises sharply via the sombre barrage of Lac du Chambon, then less steeply to La Grave, one of the main points of access to the eastern flank of the *Parc National des Ecrins*.

The North Face of La Meije dominates the valley. Gravelotte was the first to make a route up this 750 metre wall in 1898, a climb which is still graded *Difficile* today. The narrow ice gully leads to the Brèche Zsigmondy, which is shown on the map between the Grand Pic (3982m) and the Dent Zsigmondy. Zsigmondy himself fell to his death on the south flank of the mountain. The rocks of the brèche collapsed into the Etançons valley in 1964. (The profile change is evident from pictures I took in 1960 and 1964.)

The North Face direct route was first climbed in 1962 by Ginel and Renaud, two guides from the *Ecole National de Ski et Alpinisme* in Chamonix. It is a serious, if well-protected climb with the descent either to the Promontoire Hut (the normal route), or the classic 'traverse of the arêtes' to the Aigle refuge. This aptly named tiny wooden hut hides itself for security behind a rock pinnacle at 3450 metres on the true right bank of the Tabuchet Glacier. The route to and from the Aigle Hut is long (5-6 hours) and demands mountaineering skill. The Promontoire refuge serves climbs on the south flank of La Meije and also the higher summits of the Etançons valley such as the Pavé-Gaspard normal route or traverse, the Rateau by its easy approach and the ancient passage via the Brèche de la Meije between La Bérarde and the Val Vénéon and La Grave. The passage of the Enfetchores Buttress on the north flank is relatively easy in good weather, but great care is needed in adverse conditions.

The traverse of La Meije is still a much-valued classic expedition of AD standard and must be high on the list of club mountaineers. Routes on the south and south-west flanks are in the higher grades of TD and ED, their popularity due partly to the quality of climbing but also to the good, sound granite.

French climbers Pierre Allain and Jean Leininger were the first to climb the South Face. Allain was an excellent free rock technician who trained consistently on the boulders of Fontainebleau close to his Paris home. I recall from 1960 the long, unprotected pitches and a feeling of grudging respect for the Frenchman's ability to climb at this level, on a first ascent, in 1936! Allain, Gervasutti and Cassin were well in the front of world alpinism in the 1930s and '40s. However, it was Gervasutti with the Frenchman, Lucien Devies, who pioneered the greatest of the classic hard routes of their time. The North Face of the Olan (1934), the Pic Gaspard by the south-south-east ridge (1935) and the North-West Wall of the Ailefroide (1936) were all first ascended by this pair and to this day the Ailefroide route is still known as the 'Walker Spur of the Dauphiné', respected for its high level of mixed and rock climbing. Gervasutti led the route whilst suffering two broken ribs from an accident early on the day of the climb, and a pitch of grade VI led by this past master is still hard today.

To descend the N91 via the Col du Lautaret towards the fortress town of Briançon is a delight. To the left lies the limestone country of the Massif des Cerces, a walking paradise but with rock climbing a highly attractive possibility when the high peaks are out of condition. Details of all the outlying climbing around Briançon and the Durance valley are contained in a locally produced and available guidebook, *Escalades du Briançonais*, written by J-J Rolland and Suzy Péguy.

The massif can also be entered from Briançon via the Clarée valley, which has good provision for the visitor by way of camp sites, *gîtes d'étape* and other standard types of accommodation. This is a good family base which also offers scope for white-water canoeing, cycling and pony trekking. In spring it is popular too with nordic skiers.

Briançon is the highest town in France, built by Vauban in the latter half of the seventeenth century. It is part of a nationwide development which included not only the fortified towns of Mont Dauphin and Chateau Queyras in the Durance and Guil valleys of the Hautes Alpes, but ports as well. One might compare Vauban's output to that of Telford's but it must be admitted that Vauban's achievements and influence are probably superior. The old town of Briançon has been extensively rebuilt and maintained in recent years and it is well worth a day of any visitor's time. The new town, below the ramparts, has good shops, sports facilities and a few reasonable restaurants.

Downstream from Briançon is Argentière la Bessée, a rail stop and the point of access to the village of Vallouise where three valleys, each from a different glacial system, meet.

Ailefroide (1500m), is the summer hamlet which provides superb camping, two modest hotels and *gîte* accommodation. From mid-June to the first week of July the plant output of two seasons is compressed. Only as more visitors arrive does the commune mow meadows of thigh-deep flowers to make way for tents.

Rock climbing and bouldering around the village must rank among the best in Europe. The *écoles d'escalade*, or practice crags, are well equipped by the Guides Syndicate with anchor points and grading marks. These tend to be more akin to gritstone savagery than Alpine equivalents. It is in this valley that Patrick Edlinger spent his youthful summers and he returns frequently to his roots.

The classic climb of the camp site is the 300 metre *Fissure d'Ailefroide*, which goes at British VS on two pitches with most of the climbing in the Very Difficult to Severe bracket. The line is a single cleft which widens, narrows, overhangs and lies back to give a thoroughly good route. More modern climbs abound, taking the ridges and slabs which descend from the Pelvoux. Fact sheets and topos are available from the Bureau des Guides at a very small cost.

The guides of l'Oisans are generally more open, friendly and supportive than their colleagues elsewhere. Their names may be less well-known than the Burgeners, Simonds, Ravenals or Carrels, but families such as Engilberge, Estienne, Giraud, Turc and Paquet from Vallouise and the Val Vénéon, together with the Gaspards, figure largely in the explorations of both Golden Age and modern times.

Guides offer an honest service and in Dauphiné must work hard in a region where there is only one cable car (at La Grave) and the major classic climbs start from points in different valleys as much as ten hours apart on foot. Perhaps it is this very style of working that sets the guides of l'Oisans apart. Not for them the quick descent by *téléférique* to their families; guides must often stay at huts or move with their clients about the massif in order to 'collect' summits.

This partnership between guide and client often spans generations, such is the bond and trust which develops. This last summer, I was descending in a storm from the Pelvoux traverse with three French clients, to be held up by another party who had dodged the summit as the storm broke. The leader left his rappel rope in place for my party to use. 'Leave it at the Engilberge hotel, or we'll see you there for a drink if you're quick.'

This sharing awareness typifies Dauphiné and it has much to do with politics and religious tolerance. The French Resistance was particularly strong throughout the region. Vercors suffered horrendously at the hands of the Germans in the 1939-45 war and many refugees were given sanctuary in the mountains. This attitude goes back for centuries when persecuted Italians fled to l'Oisans from the Inquisition to be given security by the French King Louis XI, for whom the valley was immortalised as Val-Louise. Names of these refugee families live on as de Bardonneche, from Bardonnecchia, Molinatti and Gaucci.

This generosity of spirit is seen throughout and is one reason why efforts to preserve and conserve the natural beauty must be steadfastly sustained. The ski world has already encroached upon the peripheral areas but, as yet, the Massif des Ecrins remains intact.

The Barre des Ecrins (4102m), first climbed by Edward Whymper in 1864, is the highest peak of Dauphiné. It is not always in condition but its neighbour, the easy Dôme de Neige (4015m) which shares the same approach, is, and is justifiably popular. Perhaps the best expedition on this north flank of Les Ecrins is to climb the Couloir de Barre Noire (AD), a very safe ice/snow climb, then traverse the ridge, north-east to south-west to the summit of the Barre des Ecrins and descend by the normal route on the North Face, which is usually well marked. The difficulty of the ridge varies according to annual and seasonal snow/ice cover.

The original traverse, south to north, starts from the Val Vénéon and the Temple Ecrins Hut. It is less popular now than twenty years ago but it remains a classic, if at times tortuous, route.

The South Pillar of the Barre des Ecrins rises in three sections from the Glacier Noir. First ascended by Jean Franco and his wife in 1944, this 1100 metre climb rises untidily for the first 300 metres or so until it meets the best and steepest of the rock. This wall, known as the 'Bastion', contains climbing of sustained interest and numerous variations of line, mostly more difficult than the original. After the 300 metres of the Bastion, the terrain becomes mixed and easier, leading mainly up snow/ice gullies to the summit. Although the rock is not always good, the South Pillar still remains one of the historical milestones of alpinism in l'Oisans.

Before moving to the next group of peaks, mention must be made of the relatively easy summits and climbs which rise from the Glacier Blanc. Roche Faurio, Pointe Louise, Pic de Neige Cordier, Pic du Glacier Blanc and the Pic du Glacier d'Arsine offer pleasant excursions from either refuge. The views from all of these modest summits (between 3400m and 3600m) are wonderful. Mont Blanc and the Pennine Alps are clearly distinguishable to the north-east. Monte Viso, highest peak in the Cottian Alps, stands remote as one looks down the glacier to the south-east. The Agneaux peaks lie directly behind the Glacier Blanc Hut. They rise at the lower end of the glacier and expeditions often include a traverse of the Dôme du Monetier to descend either to Pelvoux, via the Lac de l'Echauda, or Monetier les Bains-Serre Chevalier, by well-used paths and with breathtaking views all around.

One of the greatest views in all l'Oisans is from just below the Glacier Blanc refuge at points close to the first hut to be built in the region. Refuge Tuckett, nestling beside the tarns and streams descending from the Agneaux, looks out at a 7 kilometre chain of jagged peaks, icy couloirs and hanging glaciers which are amongst the grandest north-facing panoramas in Europe. From 1900 metres at Cézanne or Pré du Madame Carle, the walls tower to almost 4000 metres. Closest to the hamlet and junction of the glaciers Noir and Blanc is Mont Pelvoux. Its highest point, Pointe Puiseux (3946m), was probably first climbed in 1828, with the first confirmed ascent by the Rev. W A B Coolidge and the Almers in 1881, taking the broad couloir on the south flank which bears his name today.

Pointe Durand is only slightly lower at 3932 metres. The two other peaks of the group, the Petit Pelvoux (3754m) and the Trois Dents du Pelvoux (3882m), are sited on the true right bank of the Glacier du Pelvoux, which changes name somewhere along its descent to become the Glacier des Violettes. The ascent of Pointe Puiseux followed by a traverse of the glacier and an airy descent of a most remarkable rake to Ailefroide, is the most varied and rewarding expedition in the valley. A slightly harder route to the summit may be taken using a short, steep and enclosed couloir, found just to the right of the Col Est du Pelvoux. Climbed in 1907 by Henri Mettrier and two local guides, E Estienne and J P Engilberge, this delectable little ice gully gives a Scottish-type climb of around grade III (Scottish) or AD (Alpine).

North Face climbs offer long, serious ice and mixed routes, the hardest being the 500 metre slit of the Couloir Chaud on the Trois Dents and the longest, the central ice slope between Pointes Puiseaux and Durand.

To catalogue the climbs along the chain on the flanks of Pic Sans Nom, Pic du Coup de Sabre and the Ailefroide would be a major issue. Classic routes lie alongside climbs made as recently as 1988 and of the more serious levels of difficulty. Rock climbs on Pic Sans Nom are climbed lightweight in rock slippers, with a descent by abseil on fixed bolts. By contrast the 1988 ice route on the Ailefroide by two British guides, Lew Hardy and Nick Parks, ranks grade 6 on the Scottish scale (the hardest grade), and the descent is by the south flank to the Sélé valley; a committing climb.

Before climbing out of the basin of the Glacier Noir, Pic Coolidge must be recommended for its ease of access and the views from its summit. The great Walter Bonatti climbed the North Face in 1953. It is of middle grade difficulty but has the disadvantage of catching the sun early in the day so that both speed and an early start are vital.

Crossing the Col de la Temple between Pic Coolidge and the Ailefroide requires care, but the technical difficulty is not great. Views of the North-West Buttress of the Ailefroide are chillingly beautiful. From here one also sees Les Bans above the Pilatte Glacier, with its fluted ribs and couloirs beckoning to the climber. To descend from the col to La Bérarde and the Val Vénéon is to enter a colder, more harsh environment. There are few trees, though the grassy pastures about the Plan du Carrelet are pleasant enough.

La Bérarde is the hub of the Massif des Ecrins wheel. Inhabited only in the summer season it caters solely for the mountaineer and climber. St Christophe, birthplace of the Gaspards, Paquets and Turcs, lies some ten kilometres downstream. It is the highest village of the valley. Approaches to La Meije and the Etançons valley, the range to the west and to the head of the river streaming from the Pilatte and Chardon glaciers, radiate from La Bérarde.

Les Bans is special by virtue of its position between three valleys. It is also a climb of character from every aspect, ridge and couloir. By its isolation the 360 degree panorama from the summit repays all effort.

La Meije has been detailed earlier in the chapter, which leaves me clear to introduce what is perhaps a transported form of Chamonix granite aiguille into l'Oisans: the Aiguille Dibona. When climbing up the steep and enclosed path from Les Etages, some three kilometres downstream of La Bérarde, one is suddenly confronted by the dramatic spear of the South Face. The sun plays games of light throughout the day so that it is never the same picture. Rock climbs thread, cross and sinuate all flanks of this dream of a peak, while the small, privately run hut at the base of the face offers the highest level of accommodation. However, many people bivouac, and as many again walk in from the valley bottom to climb at all times of the day without hindrance from glacier approach or descent. Sticky-soled rock boots, shorts and chalk tend now to be the order of the day, and many a mature climber can be seen revelling in the modern idiom of rock climbing in an Alpine situation.

Across the Vénéon river and to the west run the sombre, north-facing valleys whose head walls support the Pic du Vallon des Etages, Tête de l'Etret, Tête de Laurenoure and La Muzelle, the summit closest to Bourg d'Arud and Bourg d'Oisans. These relatively low peaks offer rock climbing in the main, but the North Face of the Pic du Vallon des Etages is rarely climbed and the Tête de l'Etret boasts a couloir of some steepness and difficulty.

All of these valleys are pleasant and rewarding walks. Plants, animals, wild and managed, and picturesque chalets for the shepherds present a warmer ambience than their north-facing aspect suggests. From cols along the head walls the Val Jouffrey and Val Gaudemar can be reached.

From Les Bans the south ridge leads to the refuge of the same name, the valley of Entre les Aigues and Vallouise, a full circle.

This same circumnavigation of l'Oisans may be made at lower altitude by taking the GR54. From Entre les Aigues the path outflanks to the south the massive bulk of Le Sirac (3440m), then swings rightwards to enter Val Gaudemar. By connecting paths, passes, glacier and woodland, this grand route offers superb mountain experience without the need for much skill, but a measure of stamina and organisation. The Park Authority and bookshops carry detailed guidebooks and waymarked maps to help the long-distance traveller.

The GR54 can be linked to the GR541 close to Argentière la Bessée, the railway-served small town in the Durance valley downstream of Briançon. The GR541 then crosses the Durance to enter the last regional park in Dauphiné, Queyras.

The scenery actually changes below Vallouise as limestone replaces igneous rock. Mont Brison, which is poised above Vallouise and Les Vigneaux, together with the Fréssinières and Fournel valleys once again give contrast to the region and the Massif des Ecrins. The Durance valley and all the country to the east is limestone based. White cliffs, which offer rock climbing in summer and winter climbing on the frozen waterfalls, border the main and contributing river valleys. At Mont Dauphin, yet another link in the Vauban chain of fortified towns, one enters the Guil river valley. Passing through the busy market town of Guillestre the road climbs gradually to Chateau Queyras, again placed strategically by Vauban in the jaws of the valley to protect the great alpine passes of the Izoard and Vars to Briançon and Barcelonette respectively. Above the castle a vast cwm spreads out and upwards towards the Italian border. At St Véran, the highest commune in Europe, one can view the whole wooded pastureland which is so popular with summer walker and winter ski tourer alike. Apart from the village there appears to be no crowding. Rural life continues in ageless tradition, farmer and craftsman cheek by jowl in an idyllic world, as yet scarcely affected by modern pressures.

Taken in all, Dauphiné is like a mini kingdom, rich in variety, rich in history and culture. It is so magnificent in all its facets and so friendly by nature, that all tastes and needs can be met. The Massif des Ecrins is under constant pressure, as are several other 'honeypot' centres, but with a little conscious thought that pressure could be spread to preserve this jewel box for the future.

C DOUGLAS MILNER
Mont Blanc

This tremendous range stretches from near Martigny in Switzerland to St Gervais in France, some 50 kilometres away, and lies as a great frontier wall 15 kilometres wide and nearly five high, between France and Italy, with a small part in Switzerland, all in French speaking districts.

The Alpine chains of Europe have many individually splendid peaks, great glaciers and steep rock walls, yet nowhere can be seen in a single massif such a combination of all these things as is found here. Frison-Roche tells us that the Mont Blanc range has some 400 summits and over 40 glaciers.

The dome of snow which, at 4807 metres, is the highest point in Europe west of the Caucasus, is perhaps the least interesting of all, though it was the first of the high Alps to be ascended over two hundred years ago. But its attendant peaks: Mont Maudit, Mont Blanc du Tacul, the Aiguilles de Bionnassay and Peuterey can compare with the best of Swiss peaks—the Eiger or Jungfrau, the Matterhorn or Weisshorn. The only rivals of the long steep rock faces of the aiguilles that flank the Mer de Glace or the Val Veni are those of the Dolomite cliffs.

The Glacier du Géant, from its source between Mont Maudit and the Tour Ronde, supplemented by the Glacier de Leschaux, forms the Mer de Glace. This ice stream is finer in its detail and its setting than the most famous of the Oberland glaciers, the Aletsch.

But the range is more varied than these paragraphs of superlatives might suggest, for at each end of the chain as well as on its flanks are smaller, less formidable areas accessible to walkers or to mountaineers who do not seek the highest standards of difficulty, yet who enjoy good viewpoints, easy glaciers and ridges. Everywhere the rock architecture, in massive brown, ochre and grey granite (protogine) is of the utmost boldness and variety. Moreover it has a solidity of hand and foothold, a feature especially commendable to British climbers accustomed to that quality on their native crags.

Prior to the first ascent of Mont Blanc, there had been little interest in the high tops—*Les Montagnes Maudites,* as they were known to the peasants of the valleys. Indeed, as we have seen, the term 'alp' or 'alpage' really relates to the summer pastures above the tree line and below the snow line. In the snows, only crystal seekers (such as Balmat), chamois hunters or smugglers crossed the high cols.

But there was some interest at lower levels near the Mer de Glace which attracted visitors from Geneva. As early as 1741 Pocock and Windham made what was thought

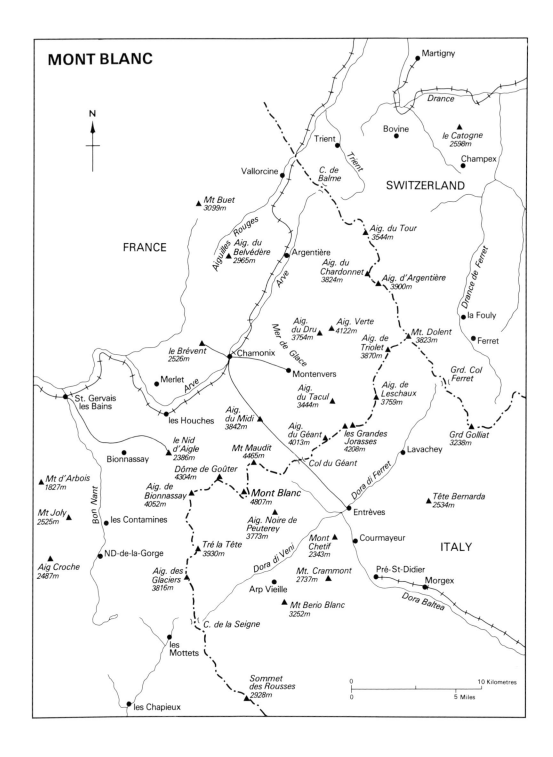

MONT BLANC

N

Martigny

Drance

Bovine

le Catogne
2598m

Champex

Trient

C. de
Balme

SWITZERLAND

Vallorcine

Mt Buet
3099m

FRANCE

Aig. du Tour
3544m

Aiguilles Rouges

Aig. du
Belvédère
2965m

Argentière

Aig. du
Chardonnet
3824m

Aig. d'Argentière
3900m

Drance de Ferret

Arve

la Fouly

Ferret

Aig.
du Dru
3754m

Aig. Verte
4122m

Mt. Dolent
3823m

Aig. de
Triolet
3870m

le Brévent
2526m

Chamonix

Mer de Glace

Grd. Col
Ferret

Merlet

Arve

Montenvers

Aig.
du Tacul
3444m

Aig. de
Leschaux
3759m

St. Gervais
les Bains

les Houches

Aig.
du Midi
3842m

Aig.
du Géant
4013m

les Grandes
Jorasses
4208m

Grd Golliat
3238m

le Nid
d'Aigle
2386m

Mt Maudit
4465m

Col du Géant

Lavachey

Bionnassay

Dôme de Goûter
4304m

Dora di Ferret

Mt d'Arbois
1827m

Aig. de
Bionnassay
4052m

Mont Blanc
4807m

Tête Bernarda
2534m

Mt Joly
2525m

les Contamines

Bon Nant

Aig. Noire de
Peuterey
3773m

Entrèves

Courmayeur

ITALY

ND-de-la-Gorge

Tré la Tête
3930m

Mont
Chetif
2343m

Pré-St-Didier

Aig Croche
2487m

Aig. des
Glaciers
3816m

Dora di Veni

Mt. Crammont
2737m

Morgex

Arp Vieille

Dora Baltea

Mt Berio Blanc
3252m

C. de la Seigne

les
Mottets

Sommet
des Rousses
2928m

0   10 Kilometres

0   5 Miles

les Chapieux

to be a dangerous journey to the 'Vale of Chamouni', being fully armed, with sumpter mules and camping gear. They were hospitably treated by the villagers and they made the journey to the Montenvers. There a stone marked with their names can still be seen a short distance below the hotel. Later in the eighteenth century, more travellers visited the village, and such painters as Francis Towne drew the 'Source of the Arveiron'. In 1802 J M W Turner (an R A at 27) came there and made many studies later published in his *Liber Studiorum*. (One of his finest watercolours is that of the Mer de Glace, now in the Mellon Collection and last seen in London in 1972).

The first man to make a detailed study of the region was the Genevese scientist, Horace Benedict de Saussure, who made the first Tour of Mont Blanc, on muleback, by what then would only have been tracks or country roads. It has been said that 'It is mainly due to him that we can count Alpine travel among the pleasures and consolations of life.'

After de Saussure had offered a reward to those making the first ascent of Mont Blanc, this was achieved in 1786 by Balmat and Dr Paccard, via the Grands Mulets. During the first half of the nineteenth century the ascent was repeated about forty times, usually with a large party of 'guides' carrying great amounts of food and drink—so much so that the affair fell into disrepute.

Nowadays the route is classified by *Vallot* as 'easy'. So it is, technically. But it can be dangerous in adverse weather or snow conditions. It is a long slog up snow and ice, and a journey that few will undertake more than once. In clear conditions the view from the summit is tremendous. Leslie Stephen said of it '. . . everything has been so arranged as to intensify the sense of vast height and an illimitable horizon. The effect is perfectly unique in the Alps, but it is produced at a certain sacrifice. All dangerous rivals have been removed to such a distance as to become apparently insignificant . . . a block, big as a pebble, is the soaring Jungfrau, the terrible mother of avalanches . . . the grim Matterhorn shows its angular dimensions of infinite minuteness . . . .' It can be added that in clear conditions, through a telescope, the great water spout on the Lake of Geneva can be seen, 87 kilometres away. (In the reverse sense it is interesting to know that a telephotograph of the mountain was taken from Geneva as long ago as 1892.)

A far better way to the summit is from the west, via the Aiguille and Dôme du Goûter. In fact this approach as far as the Dôme was made before 1784 by two men from St Gervais. The route continues via the Bosses du Dromedaire with good views on both sides of the ridge. If conditions are poor, then a quick descent can be made to the Grands Mulets but otherwise a line may be taken on the slopes of Mont Maudit and Mont Blanc du Tacul to the Vallée Blanche, and so downhill to the Requin Hut.

It was not until the latter half of the nineteenth century that mountaineers left their cols and glacier walks to attain summits. In 1864 first ascents of Mont Dolent and the Aiguille d'Argentière were made and in 1865 there were three great routes devised. First, the Grandes Jorasses from the Courmayeur side, and then the Aiguille Verte; both by Edward Whymper and his guides a few weeks before his tragic ascent of the

Matterhorn. A day after this climb another party made the first ascent of the old Brenva route.

In the same year the Verte was climbed by the Moine ridge—a safer route than that of Whymper—and also the Aiguille de Bionnassay. The ascents were made by British amateurs employing mainly Swiss guides and it was to be many years before guideless climbing was generally practised, or even approved.

It has been suggested that this Golden Age ended in 1865 but I regard it as having continued at least to the end of the century because some years after these routes were made, mainly on snow and ice, the following rock peaks were attempted:

The Aiguille Noire de Peuterey (3773m)—Lord Wentworth in 1877.
The Grand Dru (3754m)—Clinton Dent in 1878.
The Grépon (3482m)—Mummery in 1881.
The Requin (3422m)—Mummery, Slingsby, Hastings and Collie in 1893.

This last was the only guideless ascent, and it was a great privilege and pleasure for me, as a young man in 1939, to talk with Professor Collie about this peak which I had ascended in 1938. (He was at that time living in retirement at the Sligachan Hotel in Skye.)

Twentieth century pioneering was no longer the near monopoly of British parties and the 'owners' were moving in, the most eminent being the Duke of the Abruzzi. His attempt in 1901 on the Dames Anglaises, with four guides and five porters, was a very odd affair, for attempts were made to fire a rope over the summit by means of a rocket. This failed and the Duke suggested the ultimate use of a seal gun! Due to his support the Courmayeur guides were establishing themselves as greatly superior to those of Chamonix, many of whom were really muleteers. But in 1908, with the opening of the Montenvers railway, the use of mules began its inevitable decline.

Yet a few fine routes were still made by the British; especially by Winthrop Young and his friends, led by the Swiss guide Josef Knubel. In particular the traverse of the Grandes Jorasses in 1911, the great ascent of the Mer de Glace Face of the Grépon in the same year, and then the Pointe Isolée of the Dames Anglaises (without rockets or seal guns).

Perhaps the last climbs before the modern age were those on the Brenva flank of Mont Blanc de Courmayeur inspired by Graham Brown and described by him in his book, *Brenva*. They were the Sentinelle Rouge in 1927, the Route Major in 1928 and the Pear Buttress of 1933. Each can be well seen from the Tour Ronde.

The formation of the *Groupe de Haute Montagne* in France after the Great War was the initial cause of the considerable advances made in the district. The *Groupe* admitted both amateurs and guides to form a *corps d'élite*. It was not restricted to Frenchmen, though, and it had many Swiss, Italian and even British members. It was due to the GHM that guideless climbing became the regular thing and guides would often climb together as amateurs. The group has been responsible for the detailed *Vallot* guidebooks and hundreds of new routes and variations have been devised. If one of them is repeated a few times it is accorded the status of a 'classic'.

In the inter-war years the 'owners'—French, Swiss and Italian—did not have things all their own way. German climbers made the first ascent, in 1930, of the South Ridge of the Aiguille Noire de Peuterey, which has been called the finest rock climb in the Alps, being some 1100 metres in length. To be fair, sections of this route had been attempted since first tried in 1913 by the Austrian, Mayer, with his Dolomite guide, Angelo Dibona.

Another German victory was on the forbidding North Face (Central Spur) of the Grandes Jorasses to the Pointe Croz (4110m) in 1935, while the Italian party of Cassin, Esposito and Tizzoni reached the summit of the ridge, the Pointe Walker (4208m), by the same face (Walker Spur) in 1938. It should be noted, however, that these North Face routes are rarely in climbable condition.

Long ago John Ruskin declared that the best views in mountains were from places accessible to '. . . the child, the cripple and the greybeard.' In that he was only half right, yet around the range are viewpoints easily attainable without any walking or climbing. Even without those disabilities, there are many visitors who come just for the scenery and the mountain air. Here I refer to the many cable cars and, in two cases, railways.

Foremost is the ascent to the Brévent where the whole northern slopes of Mont Blanc can be seen, with the commanding summit clearly standing above all else in a way that cannot be appreciated from the streets of Chamonix, where it seems lower than either the Dôme du Goúter or the Aiguille du Midi. Even in the early days the Brévent was reached on foot or on muleback and it is amusing to recall the young John Auldjo's comment, on his 1827 ascent of Mont Blanc, when through his telescope he saw on the Brévent '. . . some female forms, which renewed our courage and incited us to still greater efforts than before.'

Another journey that must be made, by rack railway, is to the Montenvers for the splendid sight of the Drus, with the Aiguille Verte beyond, and across this sea of ice to some of the rock aiguilles.

From Les Bossons below Chamonix starts the wonderful cableway, first to the Plan de l'Aiguille and up to the Midi, and finally in a great arc across the upper glaciers to the Col de Géant. It is estimated that over a season about a quarter of a million tourists use this route and in the high season it may be necessary to wait an hour or two before a numbered ticket indicates that one's turn has come. Fortunately there is a good restaurant at the foot of the *téléférique* where a meal helps to pass the time.

I have in mind the fact that many people take this trip without previous experience of conditions at high altitude, especially the incandescent glare from the glaciers. Dark glasses are essential, as well as protective cream for the face. However hot the valley, outer clothing such as an anorak should be carried.

Further down the valley to viewpoints below the snow line are three cables from Les Houches to Prarion, Bellevue, and the Col du Mont Lachat. Lastly from St-Gervais, the 'Tramway du Mont Blanc' takes us by rack railway to the Col de Voza

Aiguille du Midi and Mont Blanc. (Photo: C Douglas Milner.)

for another fine view of the Glacier and Aiguille de Bionnassay.

On the Courmayeur side, facilities are not so extensive but the Col Chécrouit and the Col du Géant can be reached in the same way. For active greybeards, such as myself, there is no need to walk uphill, but a compromise is to walk down.

Having made a few suggestions for the great majority of visitors, it is now time to deal with the hopes of walkers and climbers, for whom this book is primarily written. These fall into four categories:

1) The walkers and back-packers, primarily interested in the famous Tour of Mont Blanc, with a few useful travels not included in the tour.

2) The climbers of modest experience who wish to reach good viewpoints inside the range, for whom some suggestions can be made.

3) The greater number of alpinists, either guideless or with a guide, who undertake the classic climbs of the region, some more than a century old, yet worthy of repeating.
4) At the end of the scale, the modern 'hard' men who are devoted to the latest routes, mostly devised over the last thirty years, in the top category of difficulty. During this period much use has been made of pitons, bolts and wooden wedges. One of the hardest, in the *Vallot* classification, has no fewer than 200 such aids.

The Tour of Mont Blanc is reputedly the finest walk in the Alps. It involves no glacier travel and has been followed for two centuries since devised by de Saussure. The modern route avoids what are now busy roads by variants, well marked on the Didier and Richard map, which also shows the staging posts *(gîtes d'étape)* which are either plain refuges or hotels.

The whole walk can be done in about a week but most people will prefer to take longer, especially if bad weather hinders progress. The walk is splendidly described by Andrew Harper in his guidebook, in which he recommends starting at Les Houches. Here I venture to differ from him and suggest a base is first established at Argentière, either at an hotel, or what experienced friends of mine have called the best camp site in the Chamonix valley. The walk can then either be taken north-east via the Col de Balme and Champex to Courmayeur, or south-west via the Val Montjoie, the Col du Bonhomme and so to Courmayeur. In either case, if shortage of time or bad weather makes it necessary to cut the journey short, a quick return can be made by coach through the Tunnel.

If you are not disposed to do even the shorter tours, there are sections which should on no account be missed. From Argentière the walks to Les Cheserys, the Lac Blanc and La Flegère all afford views of the Chardonnet, Argentière and the Verte. From Chamonix an ascent can be made to Plan Praz, then a walk through the woods to Merlet, with a view of the Aiguille du Goûter—especially worthwhile for the evening light. Also, though not included in the Tour, is a steep ascent up the Montagne de la Côte, between the Bossons and Taconnaz glaciers, perhaps as far as the Gîte à Balmat, to see the formidable séracs of the Bossons Glacier.

On the Courmayeur side, take the walk from Dolonne to the Col Chécrouit then through the woods to Lac Combal, with remarkable views of the Aiguille Noire de Peuterey, with its two ridges enfolding the Fauteuil des Allemands (the Gothic Chair).

On the east side, the ascent to Mont de la Saxe and the Tête Bernada (2584m) with a return via the Col Sapin and the Trou des Romains, is part of the Tour with views to the Jorasses.

Having dealt with non-walkers and keen walkers, the next stage is to consider opportunities for those parties with good British rock experience and some practice in glacier travel, implying the use of rope and crampons. I suggest four objectives:
1) The Moine from the Couvercle Hut.
2) The Aiguille du Tour from the Albert Premier Hut.
3) The Petits Charmoz and Aiguille de l'M from the Montenvers.
4) The Punta Innominata or Aiguille Croux from the Monzino Hut.

The Moine (3412m): The way to the Couvercle Hut from the Montenvers is easy and safe during the season when the glacier is 'dry' (ie wet!). The route crosses to an area called Les Moulins where streams flow into the ice, then a steep rocky part, Les Egralets, with steps cut into the rock and wire handrails fitted. The hut is a fine modern building (with showers!) and should be avoided at weekends as it can be very crowded.

The ascent of the Moine is not difficult and the pleasure of the climb is enhanced by the sight of the dawn light on the great cliffs of the Grandes Jorasses. The Drus and the Verte are also well seen.

The Aiguille du Tour (3542m): This is classified in *Vallot* as the easiest rock route in the region. It can be scaled from the Albert Premier Hut, but the Trient Hut of the Swiss Alpine Club is just as convenient. The view is of the Chardonnet with the Verte behind, and Mont Blanc beyond that.

This climb can usefully be combined with the traverse of the Three Cols; the Col du Tour, Fenêtre de Saleina and the Col du Chardonnet with a descent to the Argentière Glacier.

Petits Charmoz (2867m) & Aiguille de l'M (2844m): These short rock climbs are easily reached either from the Montenvers, or from the *camping sauvage* a few hundred metres from the Plan de l'Aiguille. The Petits Charmoz have a good view towards the Verte and the Moine, whilst from the 'M' we can look down to Chamonix, or across the valley to the Aiguilles Rouges.

Punta Innominata (3730m) & Aiguille Croux (3251m): These rock peaks are in the centre of the most famous amphitheatre of Mont Blanc de Courmayeur. The views are awe-inspiring. The eye sweeps from the Col Emile Rey at left to the Col de Peuterey at right, then to the Aiguilles de Peuterey and Dames Anglaises. The ridge, high above us and rising from the Col Emile Rey, is the classic Brouillard route, whilst ahead of us is the great Innominata buttress.

This area has been celebrated for many challenging climbs and in recent years fine routes of a high level of difficulty have been made on the Pillars of Brouillard and those of Frêney. I don't want to harrow readers with details but more men have been killed here than elsewhere on Mont Blanc.

First we must reach the Refuge Monzino, another excellent modern hut, replacing the old Gamba Hut which was certainly the most primitive in the region. The hut can best be approached shortly beyond La Visaille, where there is a car park and the start of the cable available for hoisting sacks to the hut. From there we walk or scramble up to the hut, the steeper parts having wire cables.

Finally a few comments about the classics, not only those mentioned earlier but numerous others detailed in *Vallot,* especially the 4000 metre peaks. This guide is indispensable but it must be realised that Alpine weather in the last few years has caused some change in snow and ice conditions and enquiries for up-to-date conditions should be made, for example, at the Office de la Haute Montagne, Chamonix.

Some very able climbers are liable to mountain sickness at high altitudes, and for them the low level routes described in the *Topo* guide will be a consolation.

But whether we think of sightseers, in the comfort of good hotels; walkers or climbers in their *gîtes* or alpine huts, or the hard men in their high bivouacs, the range can offer something to them all.

As they might say in Chamonix, Champex or even Courmayeur, *'chacun à son goût'*.

Ben Lomond from the shores of Loch Ard in the Trossachs – Scotland. (Photo: Cameron McNeish.)

Above: Looking towards the hills of Ben More Coigach from Stac Pollaidh – Scotland. (Photo: Cameron McNeish.)

Below: Rydal Water from Loughrigg Terrace – The Lake District. (Photo: Walt Unsworth.)

Climbers on Grey Crag, Buttermere – The Lake District. (Photo: Walt Unsworth.)

Climbers on Snowdrop, North Wales, a grade IV route on the Trinity Face of Clogwyn y Garnedd—Snowdon's summit cliff. (Photo: Steve Ashton.)

The classic Direct Route on Tryfan's Milestone Buttress – North Wales. (Photo: Steve Ashton.)

Above: The Mourne Mountains – Ireland. (Photo: Joss Lynam.)

Below: Glendalough—County Wicklow, Ireland. (Photo: Joss Lynam.)

Prelude (VS) on Twin Buttress, Glendalough – Ireland. (Photo: Joss Lynam.)

Climbing the slabs of Knutsholstind above Svartdalen – Norway. (Photo: Hamish Brown.)

Above: The summit of Glittertind (2454m)—Norway's second highest. (Photo: Hamish Brown.)

Below: The ice-scoured Jotunheimen; a view of Memurutind from Leirhoë – Norway. (Photo: Hamish Brown.)

Grand Pic de Bellonne above Lac Blanc – Dauphiné. (Photo: Serge Coupé.)

Above: Barre des Ecrins – Dauphiné. (Photo: John Barry.)

Below: Evening light on Mont Pelvoux from near the Tuckett Hut – Dauphiné. (Photo: John Brailsford.)

Above: The Verte and Drus from Col des Montets – Mont Blanc. (Photo: C Douglas Milner.)

Below: The classic view above Montenvers, looking along the Mer de Glace to the Grandes Jorasses – Mont Blanc. (Photo: C Douglas Milner.)

Above: Aiguilles Dorées – Mont Blanc. (Photo: C Douglas Milner.)

Below: Aiguille de Géant from the Col – Mont Blanc. (Photo: C Douglas Milner.)

Above: The Mischabel peaks, with the Dom (centre) separating the valleys of Zermatt and Saas – The Pennine Alps. (Photo: Kev Reynolds.)

Below: The Moming Glacier in the wall of peaks linking the Weisshorn and Zinalrothorn – The Pennine Alps. (Photo: Kev Reynolds.)

Above: The largest glacier in the Alps, the Grosser Aletsch, drains a mass of peaks on the south side of the Oberland crest – The Bernese Alps. (Photo: Kev Reynolds.)

Below: One of the loveliest of all Oberland mountains, the Jungfrau shines above the meadows of Wengen – The Bernese Alps. (Photo: Kev Reynolds.)

Above: Bernina (left) and Piz Morteratsch, from Diavolezza – Bernina/Bregaglia. (Photo: Kev Reynolds.)

Below: At the head of Val Bondasca the granite spires of the Sciora aiguilles offer superb climbing – Bernina/Bregaglia. (Photo: Kev Reynolds.)

KEV REYNOLDS
The Pennine Alps

This dramatic and scenically spectacular range of mountains contains the greatest collection of 4000 metre peaks in all the Alps—including ten of the twelve highest summits. Among them are some of the best-known and most easily-recognised of any mountains in Europe: the Matterhorn, Monte Rosa, Ober Gabelhorn, Dent Blanche, Weisshorn, Zinalrothorn, Mont Blanc de Cheilon, Mont Collon, Pigne d'Arolla. Many of its resorts are as popular in winter as in summer, a fact which has inspired a number of great feats of engineering that have laced summits and icefields alike with a veritable cat's cradle of *téléfériques*, thus enabling the skier to gain access to a lofty wonderland of permanent snow all year round, but at the same time devaluing some of the former glory of a once-virgin landscape. Progress in the Alps, as elsewhere, wears two faces.

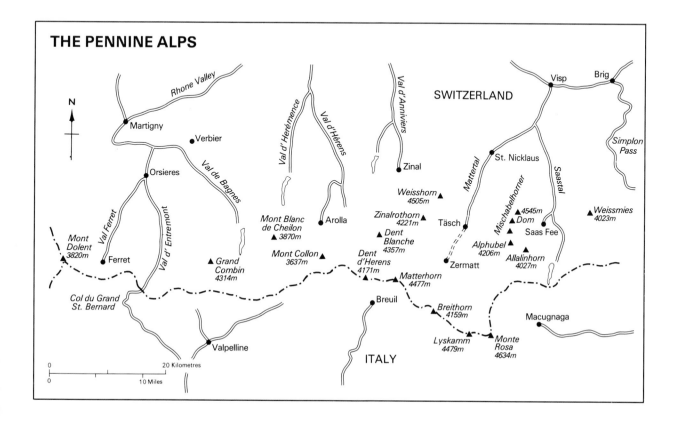

THE PENNINE ALPS

The Pennines, with their jagged peaks and huge glacial basins, extend eastward from the Col Ferret below Mont Dolent—an outlier of the Mont Blanc massif—as far as the Simplon Pass which links the Rhône Valley town of Brig with Domodossola. The range is shared unequally between the Swiss canton of Valais and the Italian regions of Aosta and Piemonte, with Switzerland claiming the lion's share by virtue of a number of extensive spurs and ridges forcing northward from the frontier. Along these spurs and ridges rise many splendid peaks, some even higher than those on the main ridge—including the great wall of the Mischabel which separates the valleys of Zermatt and Saas—while the frontier ridge itself forms part of the main Alpine watershed of the Rhône and the Po, and at the same time acts as an effective divide between Central and Southern Europe. It's a consistently high crest with a great concentration of snowfields and glaciers from which the magnificent array of individual peaks stand out in impressive shape and stature.

On either side of the watershed deep lateral valleys have been carved by intense glaciation into glens of primitive loveliness. They are long, narrow, full of character. Rousseau praised them and their pastoral simplicity in *La Nouvelle Héloïse*. Through them run streams that drain the icefields; those on the southern side watering a lovely series of valleys, those on the northern side flowing down to the vineyards and orchards of the Rhône. But in many of the Swiss valleys these streams have been harnessed early on their journey from the ice by the Grand Dixence hydro-electric scheme, with vast dams now blocking the head of several of the more remote glens. But despite the dams, despite the major tourist resorts like Zermatt and Saas Fee, these Pennine valleys have an unhurried, pastoral charm that is revealed in a basic form of agriculture and in the traditional architecture of its little villages, while high on the hillsides, way above the valleys, tiny alp hamlets with their flower-dazzled meadows announce themselves as much a part of the landscape as are the very mountains.

Two road passes only cross the Pennine Alps from Switzerland into Italy; Col du Grand St Bernard (2469m) and the Simplon Pass (2005m). Both now have tunnels running beneath them, the rail tunnel under the Simplon being the longest in the world at 19.8 kilometres. As for the St Bernard, even before the Romans crossed the Alps it was known to the Celts and through many centuries since has been used by countless thousands of religious pilgrims bound for Rome. Even so a fearful English monk, John de Bremble, prayed in 1178: 'Lord restore me to my brethren that I may tell them not to come to this place of torment.' In May 1800 Napoleon chose the St Bernard for his army's march on Marengo. He brought 40,000 men and dragged his big guns across the snows in hollowed tree trunks. Today the col is better known for its hospice, monks, dogs and brandy, while at the eastern end of the range the first recorded crossing of the Simplon was made in the thirteenth century, and in 1801 Napoleon set in motion the building of a road across it, with a large barracks being established on the summit where the original hospice had stood.

At the head of the Saastal, west of the Simplon, a mule track crosses the Monte Moro Pass (2832m) to Macugnaga in full view of the massive ice-clad East Face of

Monte Rosa—the greatest mountain wall in the Alps. It is an ancient trading route that has been in use for at least seven hundred years, while the route to the nearby Antrona Pass (2838m) leading between Saas Almagell and the Italian Valle d'Antrona, still has sections of medieval pavement visible. The importance of both these passes as trading routes across the international frontier has, of course, been superseded by the ease of modern road and rail access via the neighbouring Simplon, although for mountain walkers they have still an undeniable attraction.

Whilst a hard-won livelihood is still achieved by a peasant agriculture, by far the most important industry—on Italian slopes as well as the Swiss—is that of tourism. In winter crowds flock to the Pennines for some of the finest downhill skiing in Europe; in summer the valleys are busy with walkers, day-trippers, flower-lovers; the glaciers and peaks with climbers. It was, after all, mountaineers who initially brought the Pennine range its fame and mountaineers who continue to be attracted to the snow, ice and rock of the district.

By the mid-nineteenth century the pioneers of mountaineering had temporarily been distracted from the heights of Savoy by the major Pennine summits, and during the so-called 'Golden Age', which culminated in Whymper's oft-told ascent of the Matterhorn in 1865, all the major peaks in the range were climbed. With so many high and attractive mountains available it is understandable that the region should have borne the brunt of so much activity, but of course climbing—and the search for new routes—did not come to an abrupt halt with the winning of the Matterhorn, despite the loud voices of condemnation which followed the tragedy marring this ascent, for there were still other summits to gain, and after the summits, the ridges. The Matterhorn's twisting Zmutt Ridge was claimed by Mummery in 1879; the Viereselgrat of the Dent Blanche in 1882 by Stafford Anderson; the lovely Weisshorn's Shaligrat in 1895.

Prior to the First World War Geoffrey Winthrop Young frequently climbed with the St Niklaus guide, Joseph Knubel, and together they made numerous difficult ascents in the Pennines, including the South Face of the Täschhorn on which they joined forces with V J E Ryan and the Lochmatter brothers in 1906, a climb whose telling is one of the best things in the classic memoir, *On High Hills*. Ryan, according to Winthrop Young, was the 'comet of the alps', and he and the Lochmatters—Joseph and Franz—were responsible for the long East Arête of the Dent d'Hérens in the same year as the Täschhorn climb, in addition to the Santa Caterinagrat on Monte Rosa's Nordend, while Winthrop Young developed a route on the Breithorn that was subsequently named after him (the Younggrat), and later climbed all three faces of the Weisshorn—again with Joseph Knubel.

In the two inter-war decades particularly hard routes were developed on the remaining faces of major peaks, almost all of them by guideless parties. Willo Welzenbach from Munich, a brilliant climber on rock as well as ice who was to lose his life on Nanga Parbat, came to the Pennine Alps and put up some very adventurous direct lines on the North Face of the Lyskamm and the 1300 metre ice-clad North Face of the Dent d'Hérens (with Eugen Allwein) in 1925. This last-mentioned was the most difficult ice face then climbed, and it remains a serious test piece even today. Welzenbach, who evolved a sixfold numerical grading system for rock climbs, was one of the most daring mountaineers of his day, and one of the greatest ice climbing pioneers of all time, and it was his home town of Munich that also bred the Schmid brothers who had plans for the spectacular, yet objectively dangerous, North Face of the Matterhorn.

At the end of July 1931 Toni and Franz Schmid cycled from Munich to Zermatt heavily laden with all their climbing equipment, camped at the foot of the Matterhorn's Hörnli ridge, then spent two days storming the snow-plastered North Face. After 33 hours on it they reached the summit in atrocious conditions, then descended to the Solvay Hut where they shivered their way through two nights and a day before escaping down to Zermatt in drifts of fresh snow. It was a remarkable achievement and one that remains among the finest of all mountaineering feats in the region's history.

There were two faces left to be climbed on the Matterhorn, the South and the East. These were also won in 1931, but by Italian parties, and in the very same year the French rope of Lagarde and Devies pushed a hard line up the icy North-East Face of the Signalkuppe on Monte Rosa (4554m).

Since the war major new routes in the Pennines have been somewhat limited, although mention should be made of the East Face of the Zinalrothorn, climbed in 1945 by André Roch. Mostly the emphasis has been on variations of existing lines, or new routes on lesser peaks and the repeat of major summer routes under winter conditions—or solo ascents in both summer and winter of the major faces and ridges. Unlike the superb granite of the Mont Blanc range the rock here often leaves something to be desired. As a consequence there are few pure rock routes of note although the mixture of snow, ice and rock on big peaks combine to make the Pennine Alps a wonderland of classic-style mountaineering.

France, Switzerland and Italy meet on the summit of Mont Dolent north-east of the Grandes Jorasses. Below it the south-east ridge, which bears the international frontier, dips to the twin saddles of the Petit and Grand Cols Ferret from which soft green valleys spread north and south into Switzerland and Italy. Both are known as the Vals Ferret. Both these valleys are walled to the west by aiguilles of the Mont Blanc massif, while off to the east stretch the Pennine Alps.

The first peak of note is the easy Mont Vélan (3731m) which rises at the end of the south-westerly spur of the Grand Combin at the head of the Val d'Entremont. Usually climbed from the Valsorey Hut, it received a very early first ascent (in 1779) and is justifiably popular today on account of the magnificent panorama its summit affords. Detached from the main block of mountains it has superb distant views, as well as a close study of the great southern cliffs of the Grand Combin plunging into a tributary of the Valpelline.

The Grand Combin itself is a bold and snowy massif consisting of several worthwhile summits on projecting ridges that contain great terraces of ice in the northern cirque. The Pannossière Hut, which stands among the moraines of the Glacier de Corbassière and is reached in four hours from Fionnay, is the base for numerous climbs in the massif. Combin de Corbassière, across the glacier from the hut, is often linked by a short ridge walk with the Petit Combin (3672m). From both peaks the billowing ice cliffs that hang from the Grand Combin are seen to intimidating effect, while the ascent of the main peak (4314m) makes a fine day's outing. It was first climbed in 1859 by C Deville with D, E and G Balleys and B Dorsaz. In spring the district abounds with fine ski-mountaineering possibilities, but to the north, and some way along the Val de Bagnes, the resort village of Verbier has become something of a Mecca for the downhill enthusiast.

Immediately below the Grand Combin to the east Cabane de Chanrion occupies a charming site among pastures and little tarns. Glaciers curl towards its basin and act as highways to the peaks which rise all around. The route up the Otemma Glacier and the crossing of the Col de l'Evêque to the head of the upper Arolla Glacier is one of the classic ice tours of the district.

Above the hut to the north stands La Ruinette (3875m) which was climbed by Whymper just nine days before his ascent of the Matterhorn. But whereas the Matterhorn was won only after a long campaign, La Ruinette fell at the first attempt. 'There is not, I suppose, another mountain in the Alps of the same height that can be ascended so easily,' he wrote later. 'You have only to go ahead: upon its southern side one can walk about almost anywhere.'

As has been said with regard to Mont Vélan, so may also be said of the views from La Ruinette; they are magnificent. The Grand Combin naturally assumes a senior role in the panorama but it is backed by the great mass of Mont Blanc, while eastwards the Matterhorn dominates the scene, even to the extent of dwarfing the nearer Dent d'Hérens.

South of Cabane de Chanrion the frontier ridge dips and grows with easy cols and minor summits, while most of the important mountains of the region rise on the Swiss side of the frontier; Mont Blanc de Cheilon and Pigne d'Arolla being the most accessible although these would more often be approached either from the Cabane des Dix or from Arolla.

Before leaving the Grand Combin region the week-long Tour of the Combins Massif deserves to be mentioned, for it's a stimulating walking route for the fit mountain trekker. Martigny, on the sharp bend in the Rhône Valley, is the usual starting point for this tour but as a circuit it could equally, of course, be started at almost any point in the Vals de Bagnes or Entremont.

The Vals d'Hérémence and d'Hérens drain a great number of glaciers. In their upper reaches secondary glens cut into the mountains as the Val des Dix and Val d'Arolla. At Le Chargeur in the former valley an enormous dam holds back the waters of Lac des Dix. To the west of it stands Rosablanche (3336m) which overlooks the quietly unsung Val de Nendaz, but a long ridge runs south from Rosablanche to La

Parrain and Le Pleurer, and from there to Mont Blanc de Cheilon (3870m). This, in turn, throws out a ridge south-westwards to the peak of La Ruinette.

Seen from the north Mont Blanc de Cheilon is a vast, triangular wedge of a mountain with a second face spreading out to the east like a great fan of stone and overtopped by a graceful fold of cornice. Glaciers pour from every side of this noble yet often dismissed mountain, and its ascent is a rather more demanding affair than that of the nearby snow plod of Pigne d'Arolla or the Tête Blanche or, indeed, the stroll up La Ruinette.

Pigne d'Arolla stands amid a sea of ice and is easily climbed from the Vignettes Hut, from which point it is often ascended in a couple of hours as a ski expedition in the spring, followed by a delightful run down to the Cabane des Dix. It is generally considered to be the easiest of the snow peaks accessible from Arolla, and another of those from which an immense panorama may be gained. Coolidge reckoned it to be one of the most famous panoramic points in Switzerland.

This broad summit dome is seen roughly as the central marker of the Pennine Alps; mid-way between the Col Ferret and the Simplon Pass; the half-way point on the Haute Route, that classic ski-tour which leads from Chamonix to Saas Fee.

Arolla has held a special place in the affections of British climbers for a very long time. A small village, it sits among the pines and steeply sloping pastures at the head of the western branch of Val d'Hérens—which forks at Les Haudères—here known as the Val d'Arolla. Opposite the village a lofty wall of mountains, punctuated by the sharp needle of the Aiguille de la Tsa, blocks all view of the Dent Blanche which dominates the eastern branch of the valley.

Mont Collon impresses itself on Val d'Arolla. Not a particularly difficult mountain it is, nevertheless, a graceful one which stands a little forward of the main frontier ridge. Between it and the ridge is the higher nub of L'Evêque, first climbed within a week of Mont Collon, although by different parties, in the summer of 1867.

Petit Mont Collon and Pigne d'Arolla are its nearest neighbours to the west, the wall of the Dents de Bertol and Bouquetins to the east. But just below L'Evêque on the watershed two glacier passes (Col de L'Evêque and Col Collon) lead to the wild Comba d'Oren which runs south into the upper reaches of the Valpelline at the village of Prarayer. Col Collon offers the easiest route between Arolla and the Valpelline (or vice versa), but another high pass to the east of it, Col de Tsa de Tsan (3243m), leads from the upper snowfields of the Glacier d'Arolla, down to Alp de Tsa de Tsan and then directly into the head of the Valpelline. The long, deep trench of the Valpelline, of course, flows down to Aosta, and is the last of the western valleys on the Italian flanks of the Pennines.

East of the Bertol-Bouquetins wall a great swirl of glaciers radiates from the Tête Blanche; the glaciers of Mont Miné, of Ferpècle, of Tsa de Tsan and Stochji. One flows south into the Valpelline, another joins the Zmutt and Tiefmatt glaciers to drain eastward to the hydro-electric works above Zermatt, while the Mont Miné and Ferpècle glaciers flow northward into Val d'Hérens. Tête Blanche is easily reached from several glacier passes and by virtue of its lookout over as fine a collection of climbers' peaks as one could wish, it featured in a number of adventures—and journals—of the Victorian pioneers.

Heading up the eastern branch of Val d'Hérens the green pastures of Ferpècle lead to the deserted alp of Bricola, a rough belvedere overlooking an estuary of ice with Tête Blanche crowning the horizon. But rising from Bricola to the east is the great savage tooth of Dent Blanche (4357m) climbed first in 1862 by T S Kennedy and W Wigram with J-B Croz and J Kronig.

It's a fine peak, one of the most challenging and visually satisfying of all, with four great ridges spreading like a cross from the summit. The South Ridge was the route of the first ascent; the East Ridge, climbed by Stafford Anderson twenty years later, became known as the *Viereselgrat* after the comment made by Ulrich Almer on reaching the summit following an epic on crumbling rock: 'We are four asses!' It was on the West Ridge, seen so closely from Bricola, that Owen Glynne Jones fell to his death in 1899, while the North Ridge was the last of the great Pennine ridges to be claimed. This was won by Joseph and Antoine Georges leading Dorothy Pilley and I A Richards on their honeymoon in 1928.

Not only is Dent Blanche visually inspiring above the Val d'Hérens, it is also a cornerstone of Val de Zinal at the head of Val d'Anniviers. In many respects this is *the* Pennine Valley *par excellence*. Its pedigree speaks for itself. The western wall rises to the Grand Cornier—which overlooks the cascading glaciers at the head of the small Val de Moiry. Grand Cornier in turn drops to a col and rises again to Dent Blanche above long sheets of ice. Round now in an amphitheatre to Pointe de Zinal, Mont Durand, the magnificent Ober Gabelhorn, Wellenkuppe, Trifthorn and the spike of Zinalrothorn, often hidden from the valley itself. The horseshoe then projects northwards to form the eastern wall of Val de Zinal, separating it from Zermatt's valley. Pointe Sud de Moming is lost among cornices. Then there's the Schalihorn and, best of all, the Weisshorn.

Zinal is the unpretentious centre for climbing here. Although the village is inevitably growing, by comparison with some resorts in neighbouring valleys it appears to make few concessions to modern tourism. As a base for middle-mountain walking excursions it has few parallels, while the big peaks hovering nearby are of the utmost appeal to the climber enchanted by a classical mountaineering approach. Many of the great Victorian pioneers were active on these peaks during the Golden Age; Tyndall on the Weisshorn in 1861, Leslie Stephen on the Zinalrothorn in 1864. The same year Hornby and Philpott made the first ascent of the Schalihorn with Christian Almer and Christian Lauener, and Whymper made the first dangerous crossing of the Moming Pass with A W Moore. The following year Whymper was back to tackle the Grand Cornier, first of his Pennine summits in a season which was destined to end so tragically on the Matterhorn.

It is a region of much loveliness, with hanging valleys and high mountain terraces affording the most memorable of views. There are several SAC club huts situated in dramatic surroundings, none more so than that of the Grand Mountet in the very heart of the glacial cirque which so effectively contains the head of the valley. Of it G D Abraham wrote: 'From the massive, monstrous form of the Dent Blanche, around the easterly ice-hung screen of peaks and over the tapering snow-cone of the Ober Gabelhorn, to the graceful, bepinnacled crest of the Rothorn, the eye wanders untiringly.'

The Mattertal and Valtournanche strike deep ice-cut swathes north and south of the snowy world of the frontier crest and watershed. Both drain perpetual winter; one to the broad vine-clad valley of the Rhône, the other to the teeming valley of Aosta. The two are linked by one of the easiest and most frequented glacier passes in the Alps, the Theodule (3317m) which is now laced with a series of *téléfériques*, and from both valleys one is drawn irresistibly towards the Matterhorn.

Probably no mountain is more symbolic of the Alps than this. Recognised by a far wider public than just the mountaineering fraternity, it is not perhaps surprising that it should be so. Its solitary position gives it an air of superiority and a suggestion of even greater elevation than the spot height on the map reveals. Its climbing history has passed into folk lore, and its classic profile is everything the mountain architect could design. 'It has no rivals in the Alps,' wrote Whymper, 'and but few in the world.' A close acquaintance, however, shows its true nature. The Matterhorn is a lofty pyramid of loose rubble and crumbling rock.

It is unnecessary to relate fully the story of its first ascent on 14 July 1865, of the rivalry between Whymper and Carrel or of the broken rope and the deaths of four of the party of seven on the descent. All this has long passed into popular history and become one of the most controversial of all mountaineering stories. Success, and the consequent tragedy, came as the culmination of a five-year series of attempts by the young artist who had become obsessed with the desire to be first man on the summit. That summit has since yielded to countless thousands of others; climbers, one-summit-only tourists dragged up by the guides, by the blind, by the one-legged and by others on two artificial limbs, and even by a cat named Mitza who lived for a time at the Solvay Hut. The Matterhorn long ago became 'an easy day for a lady', and the Hornli Ridge has actually been climbed in an amazing 63 minutes.

Between the Matterhorn and Breithorn the watershed dips to the saddle of the Theodule Pass, but the frontier ridge remains high after the Breithorn, running on to Pollux and Castor, Lyskamm and the great dome of Monte Rosa, a glacial gateau with a number of individual peaks shared between Italy and Switzerland. First of its summits to be reached was that of the Parrotspitze (4432m) in 1817, the last being Nordend (4609m) in 1861. The main summit, the Dufourspitze (4634m) is the highest summit in Switzerland and its ascent in 1855 by a British party is seen by some as the start of serious mountaineering in the range. Later Tyndall, drifting between scientific duty and the joy of climbing simply for the sake of it, made a solo ascent of Monte Rosa fortified only by a flask of tea and a ham sandwich.

If Dufourspitze is the highest point in Switzerland, Monte Rosa itself is only part

East Face of the Matterhorn, from Rotenboden. (Photo: Swiss National Tourist Office.)

Swiss, but it is the Dom (4545m) which is actually the highest mountain entirely under the flag of the white cross. As part of a grand wall of peaks, collectively known as the Mischabelhorner, which runs to the north of Monte Rosa and forms the great divide between the valleys of Zermatt and Saas, the Dom and its neighbours offer face climbs of some severity and a lofty traverse of the ridge which overtops them all.

The Pennine Alps offer something for every taste. For the climber there are long, classic mixed routes that have a special charisma on account of the colourful history of the range's exploration and development. There are snow routes and easy summits accessible to the first-time alpinist, and tempting arêtes for the more experienced mountaineer.

For the mountain walker there are ample opportunities to roam through charming valleys, or to link one alp hamlet with another along the 'middle-mountain' paths that have been used for centuries by peasant farmers going about their daily labours. There are high, glacier-free passes in the northward-projecting ridges to enable exhilarating journeys to be made from one valley to the next. There are circuits of some of the western massifs and a long multi-day traverse of the range which is rewarded by some of the finest mountain views in all of the Alps.

And of course the downhill ski enthusiast has so many resorts to choose from, on both sides of the frontier, while the ski mountaineer comes into his own here. The *haute route* from Chamonix to Zermatt (or Saas Fee) is *the* classic ski tour of Europe and one which seems to have lost none of its appeal in all the decades of its popularity.

All in all the Pennines have so much to offer the active mountain lover. And when time has worked its malevolence to the extent that memories have to replace dreams and plans for the future, then the great peaks, wrapped in their armoury of ice and snow, will remain as symbols of glory shining above the deep-cleft valleys.

KEV REYNOLDS

The Bernese Alps

It is difficult not to get carried away with superlatives when writing about the Bernese Alps. It is, of course, among the loveliest of all the mountain ranges of the Alpine chain, its individual peaks compelling in their splendour, yet forbidding too with some huge north faces rising out of the pastures and drawing savage storms across the lowlands of north-west Europe and the chequerboard Swiss plain.

The cold facts are impressive. Stretching from the Grimsel Pass in the east, to the slopes that sweep down among vineyards on the shores of the Lake of Geneva in the west, its great snow-crowned massifs represent the longest continuous range of mountains in the Alps. Nearly forty of its summits top 3600 metres. Extensive ice-sheets are spawned among them, including the largest glacier in the Alpine chain (the Grosser Aletschgletscher) which flows south of the main crest towards the Rhône's great sunny trench. Lofty waterfalls shower into deep, ice-carved valleys. In

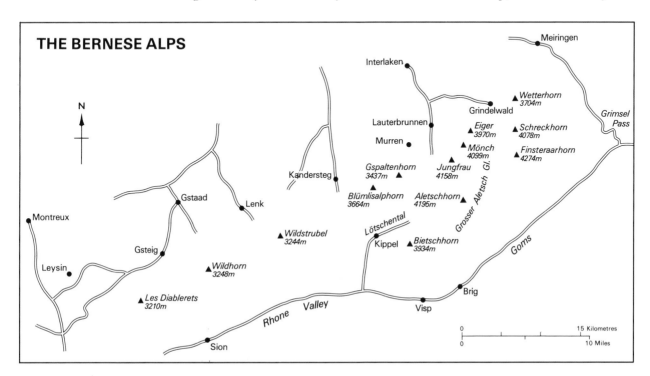

THE BERNESE ALPS

certain of these valleys and on their green hillsides nestle some of the best-known resorts in all of Switzerland: Grindelwald, Kandersteg, Wengen, Mürren, Lauterbrunnen, Adelboden, Lenk and Gstaad. On the southern flanks, however, there are villages seemingly untouched by tourism and utterly charming for all that with their air of simplicity and isolation.

These mountains contain no political frontier, but the wall of the Bernese Oberland is a major watershed, for to the north streams drain into the Aare (a tributary of the Rhine) and off to the North Sea. Glaciers and rivers on the south side flow into the Rhône which, of course, works its way to the Mediterranean.

Between the Rinderhorn and Wildstrubel the Gemmi Pass (a walker's route but with mechanical aid to it coming from the south), crosses the watershed and makes a convenient division. On the northern side lies Kandersteg. To the south, Leukerbad. But the mountains to east and west of the pass are of contrasting natures. To the east rise the major peaks of the region, among them those that are instantly recognisable even to the non-climbing fraternity. They include the Wetterhorn and its neighbouring peaks, the fabled triptych of Eiger, Mönch and Jungfrau. There are, however, many more equally impressive summits clustered around, if largely unknown to the layman.

West of the Gemmi the mountains are mostly of a minor order by comparison. Ideal for newcomers to the Alps, these are peaks to give a taste of high adventure without the full commitment required further east, although there are, of course, exceptions to this rule. Apart from its many lesser peaks the western district boasts three major massifs: the Wildstrubel and its great glacial bowl of the Plaine Morte, the Wildhorn, and Les Diablerets, whose northern slopes are laced with cableways.

Whilst the crest of the Bernese Alps holds the majority of major summits, there is a great knot of peaks tangled behind the mountains that so dramatically dominate Grindelwald's chalet-strewn pastures; a knot of peaks rising out of a vast plateau of ice like a displaced polar ice cap. These mountains are some of the shapeliest of them all: the Schreckhorn and Finsteraarhorn being especially worthy of note. And on the southern side of the crest runs the magnificent Lötschental, from which there soars the Bietschhorn.

The Bernese Alps played a significant part in the history of mountaineering. Even before the so-called 'Golden Age' began, Swiss explorers were active here and two of the most prized peaks fell to the Meyer brothers of Aarau (the Jungfrau in 1811 and Finsteraarhorn in 1812). While they and others were actively laying the foundations of mountaineering, the glaciers of the region were being studied by such men as Louis Agassiz (1807-73), the Swiss geologist whose theories startled the scientific world of the nineteenth century, and James David Forbes (1809-68) from Scotland. The Unteraargletscher was the main base for their glaciological observations and from living on the ice at his rough shelter amusingly called the Hôtel des Neuchâtelois, Agassiz learned invaluable lessons for moving safely among the inner recesses of the mountains and began to visit summits not solely for scientific reasons. In 1841, Agassiz and one of his regular helpers, Edouard Desor, climbed the Jungfrau (thirty years after its first ascent), and a year later Desor attempted the Schreckhorn. 'The ambition of hoisting the first flag on the Schreckhorn, the one big Bernese summit which was still untrodden,' he wrote later, 'was far too obvious for us to resist.' He failed, however, but reached the secondary summit of the Lauteraarhorn (4042m) instead.

When Alfred Wills climbed the Wetterhorn in 1854 it was by no means the first ascent of the mountain, nor was it even the first 'sporting' ascent, for Agassiz had reached the summit ten years earlier, and others had been there even before him. Yet Wills' account of the climb (recorded in his book, *Wanderings among the High Alps*) made such an impact that his ascent came to be seen as a cornerstone of the Golden Age of Mountaineering.

The Wetterhorn overshadows Grindelwald and is the first of the major peaks to be seen when approaching form Meiringen. As you rise through the Reichenbach valley towards the Gross Scheidegg, the great limestone cliffs soaring above the pines are first those of the Engelhörner, then of the Wellhörner, and finally those of the Wetterhorn's north flank. But it is not until you drop down towards Grindelwald that its distinctive shape becomes apparent. A handsome mountain, it is, with a coronet of summits; the *Peak of Tempests*.

When Wills set out to climb it during his honeymoon, his party included guides from Chamonix—much to the chagrin of the Grindelwald men, who resolved to climb the mountain too, and to plant 'a young fir tree, branches, leaves and all' on the summit alongside Wills' 'Flagge'. These Grindelwald men were Ulrich Kaufmann and Christian Almer (1826-98), the latter destined to become the most famous of all Oberland guides.

On the final part of the ascent the two parties joined forces and having hacked a way through the cornice that guards the summit (of the Hasli Jungfrau—3701m), one by one they stood on the narrow crest. 'One step, and the eye took in a boundless expanse of crag and glacier, peak and precipice, mountain and valley, lake and plain.' Wills wrote, 'The side we had come up was steep, but it was a gentle slope compared with that which now fell away from where I stood. A few yards of glittering ice at our feet and then, nothing between us and the green slopes of Grindelwald, nine thousand feet beneath.'

Today the Wetterhorn is a popular mixed climb for alpinists of some experience based at Grindelwald. There are several approaches to the summit, using either the Gleckstein or Dossen huts, all quite steep and none altogether straightforward or particularly easy. As with many of the peaks in the region there is some stonefall danger, particularly when climbing from the Gleckstein Hut on the south flank.

The Gleckstein Hut is perched above the Oberer Grindelwald Glacier, seen cascading from the icy amphitheatre out of which rise not only the Wetterhorn but also the Bärglistock, Schreckhorn and Kleine Schreckhorn. Highest of them all, and looming over the Nässihorn, the Schreckhorn (4078m) is a superb fang of a peak, the so-called 'Peak of Terror', first climbed by Leslie Stephen in 1861. Its northern side is mostly ice but the south and west flanks are rocky and best approached from the

Schreckhorn Hut.

The Schreckhorn is not only a good-looking mountain but a serious one with some classic routes; some mixed and some on good-quality rock which is a light brown gneiss, while the North-East Face offers a fine ice climb at an average angle of 53 degrees. Ice adorns this splendid peak. As Leslie Stephen said in *The Playground of Europe*: 'Four great glaciers seem to radiate from its base. The great Oberland peaks—the Finsteraarhorn, Jungfrau, Mönch, Eiger and Wetterhorn—stand round in a grim circle, showing their bare faces of precipitous rock across the dreary wastes of snow.'

The Schreckhorn Hut, tucked against the rocks at the base of the south-west ridge, replaces the Strahlegg refuge which was destroyed by avalanche in 1977. Formerly, fit parties could attempt the Finsteraarhorn from the Strahlegg Hut (8–10 hours by the Agassiz Ridge), but with the new location of its replacement this is an even longer proposition without a bivouac. Most parties use instead the Finsteraarhorn or Oberaarjoch huts to the south and east.

The Finsteraarhorn projects a shapely fin on a long ridge overlooking one of the largest and most remote collections of icefields in the Alps. At 4274 metres it is the highest of the Bernese Alps and was first climbed by the south-east ridge. But it is the great North-East Face of the mountain that impresses most. Rising for 1050 metres above the Finsteraar Glacier it is one of the classic north walls of the Alps, if one of the least publicised. First attempted by Gertrude Bell with two guides in 1902, the face is notoriously prone to stonefall. Miss Bell, a noted Arabian explorer and archaeologist, was forced to retreat by a combination of bad weather and danger from falling stones, and endured two bivouacs before escaping unscathed—after 57 hours of effort. (An Arab chief is reported to have remarked of her: 'And this is one of their women! Allah, what must their men be like?') The face was climbed two years after Gertrude Bell's attempt by Gustav Hasler and Fritz Amatter, who emerged at the top of the North-East Rib after fifteen hours. Today the route is still considered both difficult and dangerous, whilst the East Rib by comparison has little objective danger to contend with.

As stated above, the Finsteraarhorn stands amidst a veritable sea of ice, the greatest glacial highway in Switzerland. To the west, beyond the ridge that sweeps from the Fiescherhorn to the Grünhorn, and another leading from the Fiescher Gabelhorn to the Kleine Wannenhorn and beyond, a clutch of icefields come together at Concordiaplatz and from there grind on as the huge arctic stream of the Grosser Aletschletscher.

Concordia is most conveniently reached either on foot or by ski from the Jungfraujoch, the saddle between the Jungfrau and Mönch at 3475 metres. This lofty and scenically spectacular place is the terminus of Europe's highest railway (and probably the most expensive too), the result of an astonishing feat of engineering completed in 1912. The railway leaves Kleine Scheidegg and burrows through the Eiger and Mönch before depositing the hordes in a landscape of dazzling snow and ice.

Since completion of this railway the 'hinterland' of the Bernese Alps has been made accessible not only to mountaineers and skiers, but to ordinary tourists too, though few enough of these stray far from the station and complex of entertainments. From the *joch* the Jungfrau and Mönch, snow climbs both, can be climbed in two hours, given good conditions, and it is by no means uncommon for a party to bag both summits in the same day. A convenient hut stands an hour's walk away from the Jungfraujoch on the Mönchsjoch.

Returning for a moment to the green pastures of Grindelwald, it is worth noting the tremendous range of excursions available to walkers based in the town. There is something here for everyone; gentle riverside promenades, steep but straightforward hillside walks, and longer and more demanding traverses to be made of a series of green ridges and modest summits among the minor ranges to the north. One of the best leads from Schynige Platte (reached either by steep path or railway from Wilderswil), a belvedere with a simply glorious view of the great Oberland wall to the south. A path then heads along an easy ridge to the Loucherhorn, then on to the Faulhorn and down to an exquisite lake with a view—Bachsee, which gazes out to the Wetterhorn, Schreckhorn and Finsteraarhorn—before descending through the woods to Grindelwald.

The Oberland Wall—Schreckhorn, Eiger, Monch and Jungfrau. (Photo: Swiss National Tourist Office.)

Bussalp is a vast green bowl of hillside below the Faulhorn. Peasant farmers graze their cattle and make cheeses there throughout the summer, with another memorable view towards the Eiger spreading its dark shadow over the meadows of Alpiglen. Reached by Postbus, this too makes a starting point for some lovely walks.

In Grindelwald, as at Kleine Scheidegg, telescopes are forever trained on the dark looming face of Europe's most notorious mountain, a mountain that has had more journalistic ink spilled over it than any other, save perhaps for the Matterhorn. That mountain, of course, is the Eiger.

There are no easy routes to the Eiger's summit, but the one which is climbed most often is by way of the south-west flank, the route of the first ascent in August 1858, by Charles Barrington with Christian Almer and Peter Bohren. As with most other lines on the mountain, this is subjected to stonefall. One of the most satisfying routes is the Mittellegi Ridge which rises from the north-east. Having repelled a number of early attempts, it was finally won by the Japanese Yuko Maki in 1921, with the guides Fritz Amatter, Fritz Steuri and Samuel Brawand. Amatter, who had been with Gustav Hasler on the Finsteraarhorn, had already attempted the ridge before and on this successful occasion he led throughout. He also made the first winter ascent in February 1934.

As for the brooding Nordwand, its individual free-climbing pitches are seldom graded higher than IV+, but given the poor condition of the rock, the unpredictable nature of the upper icefields, the daily bombardment of stones and the unwelcome habit which the face has of attracting sudden savage storms, it is an extremely serious proposition. Its tragic history, objective dangers and great length have given it a charisma that attracts many of the world's foremost climbers. Since its first much-publicised ascent in 1938, several routes have been developed up the face, and it has now been climbed hundreds of times; in winter, solo, by siege tactics and in less than a day from the meadows of Alpiglen to the corniced summit. Whilst it may not be strictly true to call the Eigerwand 'An easy day for a lady', it has lost some of its horrors—though not so for the non-climbing tourists who still find themselves peering through the telescopes of Grindelwald and Kleine Scheidegg with grim fascination at the black shadowed wall of the mountain called 'The Ogre'.

The Jungfrau, by comparison, is very much the glamorous young lady, hung about with glimmering snowfields and glaciers, the lovely white wave of the Silberhorn jutting from the face and the western wall plunging into the deep trench of the Lauterbrunnen valley. Walking from Grindelwald to Lauterbrunnen footpaths cross the easy saddle of the Kleine Scheidegg (or, better still, the transverse ridge of Männlichen) directly below the Jungfrau, and as you come out of the dark green woods on the outskirts of Wengen, so this magnificent white bride of a peak is seen at her best, contrasting her snows with the flower-flecked pastures.

Lauterbrunnen's valley is headed by another great wall of peaks: Gletscherhorn, Ebnefluh, Mittaghorn, Grosshorn, Breithorn and Tshingelhorn—all well over 3500 metres and the first two in excess of 3900 metres.

The ice-clad north faces of these peaks, collectively known as the Lauterbrunnen Wall, contain some very fine ice climbs that are associated particularly with the name of Willo Welzenbach, who was active here in the early Thirties. But most of these summits may be reached with rather less commitment from the Lötschental, the seductively colourful valley which forms a moat to them on the southern side. Also from the Lötschental, a great prize is the Bietschhorn (3934m), that noble mountain first climbed by Leslie Stephen and his guides in 1859 and considered among the most difficult of all the big peaks of the district.

The western wall of the Lauterbrunnen valley rises steeply to a soft terrace of meadowland, and on this terrace sits the resort of Mürren, birthplace of downhill skiing. This is another wonderland for the hill walker who may wander for hours through pastures with cattle grazing and with dreamlike views demanding homage every step of the way. One such path leads into the Sefinental under the nose of the Gspaltenhorn; another wanders beneath the Schilthorn and crosses the Sefinenfurke (2612m), a steep pass from which you look south-westward to the crusted ice-faces of the Blümlisalp massif.

Take the Gspaltenhorn first; a lovely limestone mountain, 3437 metres high, with one of the longest north walls in Switzerland and some fine ridges that contain bristling, savage gendarmes. The South-West Ridge (the Rote Zähne) affords a magnificent rock climb with pitches up to grade V. At the time of its first ascent by Geoffrey Winthrop Young and his party in 1914, it was considered to be the last great Bernese ridge to be won. *On High Hills* contains a moving account of this climb.

The North Face blocks the head of the Sefinental. It is an extremely impressive wall, wild and remote, and as consistently steep as that of the Eigerwand. A connoisseur's face, there are a number of lines on it that drew the attention of Welzenbach and his companions in the Thirties.

South-west of the Gspaltenhorn the Rote Zähn sweeps down to the pass of Gamchilücke but beyond this rises the mass of the Blümlisalp, steep-walled to the south-east, ice-clustered to the north-west. The traverse of the ridge, from the Blümlisalphorn to the Morgenhorn, crossing the Weisse Frau on the way, is one of the finest of the classic routes to be made here. The ridge is consistently high, at well above 3500 metres, with some delicate cornices to be wary of.

Below to the north-west gleams the tourist honeypot of the Oeschinensee, an overprized lake trapped in a pot of mountains. Daily throughout the summer visitors by the hundred swing their way out of Kandersteg on a chairlift, and amble along the dusty paths that lead irresistibly to this lake. Walkers based in Kandersteg who prize peace among their mountains will, however, find greater harmony by wandering into the charming valley of the Gasterental, where a choice of high passes offers the possibility of crossing over the ridge and down into the Lötschental. (The railway makes a faster journey through the Lötschberg Tunnel leading from Kandersteg to Goppenstein—but it does not have the splendour of extensive views.) Rearing over the lower levels of the Gasterental are the Balmhorn and Altels, both over 3600 metres, whose traverse is a classic expedition (PD+) in a grand setting.

To the south-west of Kandersteg a long walk will bring you to another high lake, the Daubensee, which lies just below the Gemmi Pass. And to the west of this rises the charming Wildstrubel (3244m), an easy mountain reached from either Kandersteg, Adelboden or Lenk. This massif has a number of regular summits barely rising above its south-eastern glacier, while the Plaine Morte is a vast snow-filled glacial basin stretching from the Schneehorn in the east to the Gletscherhorn and Weisshorn (not to be confused with the better-known Weisshorn in the Pennine Alps) in the west. The Wildstrubel gives mixed climbing and easy to moderate snow routes, but overlooking Lenk there are more technical climbs on rock and snow or ice, graded AD/D.

To both north and south cableways service the ever-popular winter ski trade, whilst there are dozens of pleasant, easy walks (and challenging walks too) to be made from Adelboden and Lenk. One especially fine outing takes the walker from Lenk up into a delightfully gentle green valley through which the Wallbach stream comes chuckling, and up to the Trüttlisberg Pass (2038m). This flower-rich saddle lies between the Simmental and the Lauenental and is well to the north of the main crest of the Bernese Alps. As such it gives a wonderful panorama of the distant peaks across a succession of soft folding ridges. To the south rises the snow-draped Wildhorn (3248m), a superb viewpoint with some interesting climbs. A minor classic is the Wildgrat (the north ridge, maximum grade IV on a variant near the start). Once on the summit an enormous panorama shows not only the full extent of the Pennine Alps across the Rhône Valley but the Mont Blanc range too. A memorable view indeed.

Running parallel with the Lauenental is the busy valley of the Saane. Gstaad blocks the junction of three valleys but in the upper reaches of the western branch, Gsteig gives access to a cluster of minor peaks, while the mass of Les Diablerets (3210m) looks impressive when seen from the Col du Pillon. The northern slopes are laced with cableways; grey rock towers and a clutch of ice. To the east cower the Zanfleuron chalets and the Sanetsch inn, base for the start of one of the normal routes. Other huts exist to the north (Refuge de Piereedar in the cirque of the Creux de Champ), and Cabane des Diablerets, reached more easily from Col du Pillon. There are routes, too, to be made from the south, routes that emerge onto the west ridge which is then followed to the summit.

To the south lie masses of boulders that have fallen over the centuries from Les Diablerets. R L G Irving, in his book *The Alps* (Batsford, 1939), tells how one massive rockfall in 1714 trapped a peasant in his chalet that was built against a cliff. Although the chalet was buried by the rockfall, it was not destroyed by it and as the peasant had a store of cheeses, and a stream filtered through the rocks to give him a steady source of water, he managed to survive and slowly tunnel his way out. It took him three months!

Les Diablerets represents the last of the major massifs of the Bernese Alps. Between it and the sharp bend in the Rhône Valley leading north to the Lake of Geneva there's the small chain of mountains containing the Grand Muveran and Dent de Morcles, and north of these the playground of peaks around Leysin, home of one of the best-known mountaineering schools in all of Switzerland. Beyond them, terraced vineyards and cheek-by-jowl developments along the waterfront of Lac Léman. Another world.

KEV REYNOLDS

Bernina/Bregaglia

To the east of the Bernese Alps lie a number of lesser-known groups of mountains frequented more by local Swiss than by foreign visitors; among them the Lepontine and Rhaetian Alps. The former is one of geographical importance since it forms the nodal point of the whole Alpine chain, while the latter group provides a link between the Lepontines and the Ortler and Otztal Alps; a group of mostly ice-free mountains through which there runs the great sunlit trench of the Engadine Valley in south-east Switzerland. Its major peaks, though small by comparison with those of Mont Blanc or the Pennines, are nonetheless full of snowy majesty: Piz Bernina, Piz Palü and Roseg among them.

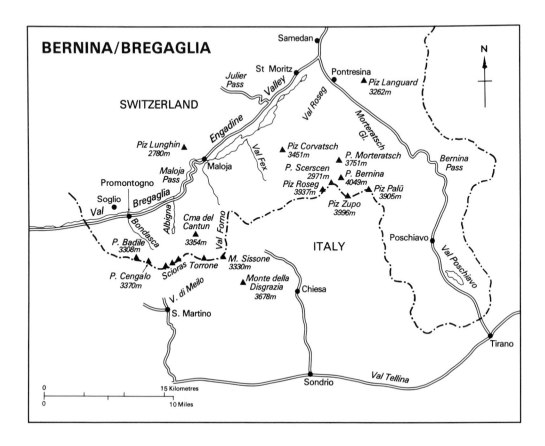

The River Inn springs from a cold tarn on the slopes of Piz Lunghin just below the saddle that is one of the most important of Alpine watersheds, and dances its way to the valley near Maloja where it then flows north-eastward into a succession of lakes, and all the way through the Engadine, eventually to drain into Austria. Behind Maloja the upper reaches of the Engadine have been stolen by the Mera, a river that has carved a glorious steep-walled valley running south-westward, full of the flavour of Italy and with the soft warmth of Tuscany trapped in its bed, but a suggestion of Alpine savagery in its upper glens. This is the Bregaglia, home of a small cluster of granite aiguilles and broad north-facing slabs: the Scioras and Piz Badile, Cengalo and Trubinasca.

Between them the Bernina and Bregaglia offer sport of immense charm, one giving snow and ice in abundant quantity, the other providing first-rate rock routes in a magical setting. In truth these neighbouring mountains are topographically of a single group joined at the Muretto Pass, but their features are of such contrasting and individual characteristics that they are invariably treated as separate districts. To them should be added a third major mountain, the distinctive Monte della Disgrazia (3678m), an outlier of the Bregaglia but standing entirely in Italy a little to the south of the Muretto Pass, which is itself reached from Maloja.

Italy's frontier outlines the crest of the mountains of both Bernina and Bregaglia and follows all along the eastern wall of the Engadine. The Engadine, of course, is Swiss and downstream of the bustling winter resorts of St Moritz and Pontresina the country's only National Park is located on the right bank of the Inn; a series of relatively short, but deeply cut valleys devoid of development where Man the intruder plays a very subordinate role to the demands of Nature.

Much of the charm of the Engadine region comes from its feeder valleys; Fedoz, Fex, Bernina, Roseg and Susauna being representative of those which either flow into the Upper Engadine, or are accessible from it, while the Lower (or Unter) Engadine is enriched by such side glens as Val Tuoi behind Guarda, and Val S-charl cutting away to the south of Scuol.

Although the Lower Engadine has few really high summits, it borders the mountains of Austrian Vorarlberg and Tirol to the north, with peaks like the Silvrettahorn, Piz Buin, Dreilanderspitz and Fluchthorn all accessible from the valley and notable for their ski-touring prospects. On the southern side of the Inn rise several modest peaks of Dolomitic limestone, culminating in Piz Pisoc (3174m) which guards the entrance to the Val S-charl. Perhaps the finest outing for the climber on these peaks is that which leads directly behind the village of Tarasp, climbs the north ridge of Piz Lavetscha and continues along the linking ridge to Piz Pisoc—a route of about ten hours.

But the Lower Engadine is really a walker's country. Flower meadows adorn every corner. Footpaths and ancient mule trails lead up to easy passes, into side valleys or along a hillside terrace in places 400 metres above the foaming River Inn to link some of the most exquisite villages in all the Alps. Some of these villages, stone-walled and with cobbled alleyways where the ancient Romansch language is still spoken and taught in the local schools, are almost like outdoor art galleries with their splendid displays of *sgraffito* ornamentation which delight the visitor with traditional scrolls and patterns round windows and doorways. In the square at old Scuol some of the finest examples are to be seen. Farther up-valley Guarda is considered the best of Engadine villages with its determined hold on traditional values; Ardez has the famed 'Adam and Eve House'; Tarasp's alleyways look onto geranium-bright houses with the castle looming over all.

Rising steeply behind Lavin is Piz Linard, a soaring pyramid of a peak, at 3411 metres the highest on the north side of the Lower Engadine. This makes for an interesting, though not difficult, scramble and is worth giving a day's holiday to, for from its upper reaches one gains a true perspective of this modest, yet utterly charming district.

Up-valley among the Albula Alps, Piz Kesch (3418m) makes another popular outing. With its little glaciers and jutting peaklets, it offers as good an introduction to the Alps as any in this corner of Switzerland. There are huts to both north and south of the mountain, thus making a traverse—or even a circuit—a tempting prospect.

A short distance upstream of Piz Kesch the Engadine becomes a broad flood-plain where the Val Bernina sweeps in from the south-east. Samedan is the valley's 'capital' and from the edge of this little town eyes are drawn across the Inn and along Val Bernina to the gleeming, triple ice-decked buttresses of Piz Palü (3905m). Distinctive, much-loved and memorable to all who gaze upon it, it is a truly graceful mountain; its high summit crest boasting three tops linked by a narrow corniced ridge that has a somewhat macabre history of accidents.

In 1879 a well-known lady climber, a Mrs Wainwright, tackled Piz Palü with her brother-in-law and two of Pontresina's top guides, Hans and Christian Grass who, incidentally, had made the first traverse of the three summits in July 1868. One of the guides and both amateurs broke through an overhanging cornice on the north side of the summit ridge (the Swiss/Italian frontier runs from the Central Peak to the West Peak), but their fall was arrested by the quick-thinking Hans Grass who leapt to the southern side of the ridge and alone held the rope. His brother Christian then untied, climbed back to the ridge and helped Hans rescue their clients.

Seen from Berghaus Diavolezza the mountain's three great pillars rise directly from the Pers Glacier and are divided one from another by billowing folds of hanging glacier. Each of the pillars gives superb mixed climbing, the most difficult being the Bumillergrat which is the central buttress, while to the left of this a difficult ice route has been made up the hanging glacier below the East Peak, where the final pitch can be as much as 90 degrees and the overhanging cornice sometimes impassable.

It is not certain who made the first ascent of Palü but it is known that the East Peak was climbed in 1835 by Oswald Heer, Meuli and P Flury, with Johann Madutz and the so-called 'King of the Bernina', the chamois hunter, Gion Marchet Colani. As you stride along the white crest from one peak to the next a glorious panorama unfolds.

Piz Palü and Bellavista, with the Morteratsch Glacier draining towards Val Bernina. (Photo: Swiss National Tourist Office.)

First comes the long ridge of Bellavista, then the sharp point of Piz Zupò (3996m)—second highest of the Bernina Alps—then Crast' Agüzza and beyond that, Piz Roseg to the left and Bernina to the right. Piz Scerscen punctuates the ridge between Roseg and Bernina, while farther still to the right stands Piz Morteratsch above a jumble of ice-cliff and glacier.

The traverse of the three peaks of Piz Palü is a classic outing, not very difficult but with care required to avoid breaking through the cornices. The ridge leading over Piz Roseg, Scerscen and Bernina, on the other hand, is a strenuous and serious expedition, and one of the best of its kind in the Alps. It was first completed by Walter Amstutz with Walter Risch in September 1932.

Piz Scerscen is serious from every side and on its north-west spur the Eisnase is a magnificent ice route of six to seven hours from the Tschierva Hut near the head of Val Roseg. This same hut is normally used as the base for the classic Biancograt on Piz Bernina (4049m)—the most easterly 4000 metre peak in the Alps. The Biancograt, or Crast' Alva, is the north ridge of Bernina, a graceful snow arête that leads to a rock-crusted finale; one of the most prized of the modestly-graded routes in the Alps. The great Austrian climber Hermann Buhl once completed the Biancograt and returned to the Tschierva Hut within six hours in order to win a 200 franc wager that enabled him to extend his stay in the area!

Some outstanding climbs have been made in the cirque of mountains above the Tschierva Hut where hanging glaciers create a savage yet awe-inspiring scene. It's a region where one name stands out, that of the greatest guide the Engadine has known—Christian Klucker.

This is all Klucker country of course. In the soft tranquillity of Val Fex, a high and intimate little glen cutting back from Sils Maria just to the west of Bernina, he was born in 1853, and lies buried there in the little churchyard. It was Klucker who was responsible for developing numerous routes in the Bregaglia, and who achieved some notable expeditions among the snow and ice peaks of the Bernina. Active throughout the Alps he was still climbing in his seventies and actually made the first ascent of the east arête of Torrione del Ferro at the age of 74.

With L Norman-Neruda he made routes on the north faces of both Piz Scerscen and Piz Roseg. On the latter, where a broad 60 degree ice-filled gully had to be crossed, Norman-Neruda calculated that Klucker needed seventy strokes with the axe for each step. Klucker wrote modestly: 'When one is bent on a job like this one has no time to count strokes.' Two days later Klucker and his client were caught by a storm on the Biancograt. 'The wild battle of storm, hail and snow, the glaring flashes of lightning, and the mighty thunderclaps, threatened to confound our senses,' he wrote in *Adventures of an Alpine Guide*. 'There was a roaring vibration round my hat all the while, such as a strong wind makes passing through a feather, and sparks were sometimes hanging from its brim, though the hat was loaded with a quantity of snow and hail.'

To the east of Piz Roseg, and between that peak and Piz Scerscen, the gap of the

Porta Roseg gives access onto the fearsome ice wall that leads down to the Tschierva Glacier. In 1898 Klucker made the first descent of this wall, letting himself down over the bergschrund by a rope doubled round a wooden club used for stirring polenta!

Val Roseg gives the walker a fine intimate view of icefalls, moraines and snow peaks. There is a hotel halfway along the valley approached from Pontresina by track or woodland path. Happily the track (and the valley itself) is closed to motorised vehicles although horse-drawn sleighs in winter ply a regular trade to and fro. In winter Val Roseg makes a rewarding, if easy, excursion on cross-country skis, while in summer one of the best walks of the district leads behind the hotel and climbs the western hillside to Fuorcla Surlej, a saddle below Piz Corvatsch giving access to the Engadine near Silvaplana. The head of the valley is blocked by the Sella peaks; Piz Sella, La Sella, Ils Dschimels, Cima Sondrio and Piz Gluschaint, all over 3500 metres except for one of the Dschimels 'twins' which is only three metres below. These snow and rock peaks rise above a heavily crevassed turmoil of glacier which can cause problems for climbers approaching from the Coaz Hut, while the southern, Italian, approach is straightforward. A glacier pass takes you down from here into the pastoral glen of Val Fex.

Above Pontresina in the mouth of Val Bernina and directly opposite Val Roseg, ibex can often be spied among the high crags and boulder slopes around Piz Muragl, Piz Albris and Piz Languard, the latter at 3262 metres being one of the easiest 3000 metre summits in the Alps, and one that gives a magnificent panorama of the big Bernina peaks to the south. For generations Piz Languard has been either lauded for its accessibility and view, or treated to the scorn of those whose ambitions lie in sport of a more challenging nature. But although Languard's summit has become hackneyed (Baedeker even gave it a double panorama), those with modest intentions would find a night spent in the privately-owned Georgyhütte just below the summit worth sampling for the opportunity to catch sunrise on Piz Palü and the Bernina group.

Val Bernina continues south-eastwards, rising gently to the rather barren lip of the Bernina Pass, an ancient crossing which takes you out of the sterile wastes of snow, ice and ice-scarred rock, and down to the lush warmth of Poschiavo, a finger projection of Switzerland into Italy. Italian architecture dominates the villages. Italian voices are heard in the streets. Italian names are given to village, pasture and mountain, and it comes as no surprise at all to find that the Italian Valtellina runs at a right angle to it. This is no mountaineering centre but there are delightful walks in the Val Poschiavo (or Puschlav as it is also known), and when bad weather haunts the Bernina group and sends climbers scurrying to sunnier levels, it can make a tempting place to rest for a few days in the warmth and calm of flower meadows and beside the jewel of its lake.

In the high western wall of the Poschiavo valley the Passo Canfinale (2628m) is a walker's pass which presents an opportunity to make a southerly loop round the Bernina towards Monte della Disgrazia—all in Italy—then back to the Engadine via the Muretto Pass. There are high remote alps lodged just below the glaciers that cream down from Piz Palü, Zupò, Bernina and company, and superb full-frontal views of

Disgrazia, the 'Mountain of Ill Omen'. One of the finest views of all is from the easy summit of Monte Motta (2336m) above Lake Palü, where Disgrazia stands almost due west rising nobly out of the depths of Val Malenco.

Val Malenco too offers plenty of scope for a walking holiday, with abundant wild camp sites, mountain huts and villages to satisfy a variety of accommodation needs. One of the best walks here is the Alta Via della Val Malenco, a high-level tour of the valley using huts along the way, with Monte della Disgrazia dominating the whole district.

This is another elegant, shapely mountain, 3678 metres high and with a splay of glaciers draped down its flanks. The north wall is particularly fine with its curtain of ice holding some difficult routes; the icy north-east arête is another classic but there are many more. Leslie Stephen and his favourite guide, Melchior Anderegg, achieved the first ascent of Disgrazia in 1862, while both Tuckett and Freshfield failed, the first through rain, the latter because of a doubting guide. Today it is a surprisingly forgotten mountain but with a variety of routes to attempt.

A long ridge links Disgrazia with Monte Sissone (a classic viewpoint) above the Forno Glacier. Monte Sissone marks the international frontier; Switzerland to the north, Italy to the south. To the west rise the Bregaglia peaks, to the north-east the snow mountains of Bernina.

The walker making his way by the southerly loop round Bernina swings north-westward through (or above) Val Malenco to cross back into Switzerland at the Muretto Pass. Descending towards Maloja initial rough slopes give way to alpenrose, larch and pine. The stony wastes of the Forno valley curve in from the south-west, desolate grey moraines gradually being transformed into a natural rock garden. This Forno valley is one of the main arteries of the Bregaglia region. From the Forno Hut perched on the bank of the glacier, a wide choice of rock routes—some modest, some desperate—await the climber. But the main attractions are to be found at the head of Val Bondasca, two valleys to the west.

To gain Val Bondasca from Maloja entails dropping into Val Bregaglia and travelling a short distance down-valley as far as either Promontogno or Bondo at the very mouth of the Bondasca glen. Postbuses regularly run through Bregaglia from the Engadine but there is a splendid high-level walk to be made way above the valley on its northern flanks. A switchback of a path links several lonely alp hamlets, with stunning views to the south, until you begin the steep descent from Plan Vest to the valley bed by way of Soglio—one of the loveliest of villages in all Switzerland.

Deep in the bed of Val Bregaglia will be found lush chestnut woods, but as you progress into Val Bondasca, so vegetation levels change and you climb higher and higher into a region of stark profiles, of huge ice-scraped boulders, dashing streams and small icefields. Piz Cengalo (3370m) and Piz Badile (3308m)—'the grey twins'—loom overhead. Cengalo with a wonderful north face giving almost 1200 metres of hard climbing on rock, with a number of surprisingly complex icy gullies to contend with. (Seen from the Bondo Pass it looks rather different. Freshfield described it as 'as weird a pile of granite as I have seen in many a long day's wanderings.') But it is Badile that reigns supreme here, with its massive sweep of unbroken rock giving its north-east face a compelling attraction. This is listed as one of the Alps' six classic faces.

Riccardo Cassin put up the first route on the north-east face in 1937, sharing his rope with Esposito and Ratti. At the same time two young climbers from Como, Molteni and Valsecchi, were also attempting the first ascent. The two parties joined ropes and after two bivouacs and 52 hours spent on the face Cassin led through to the summit in atrocious weather conditions. With a blizzard raging both Molteni and Valsecchi perished from exhaustion and exposure. It was eleven years before a second ascent was made. Nowadays Badile's north-east face is part of the repertoire of all ambitious rock climbers in the Alps. It has been climbed hundreds of times and even soloed in less than three hours! In the summer of 1987 Cassin returned to the face and repeated the climb—fifty years after his first ascent.

While Piz Badile guards the Trubinasca cirque, it is Piz Cengalo that leads the eye towards the head of Val Bondasca and the jagged teeth of the Sciora aiguilles.

As with practically every other peak in the Bondasca, it was Klucker who had the lion's share of pioneering here, much of it in the unhappy employ of the Russian, Anton von Rydzewski. Rydzewski came late to climbing but he quickly grew ambitious beyond his capabilities. Klucker had the ability and enthusiasm to pioneer new routes and although he attempted to steer other employers with whom he had a greater rapport towards the Bondasca peaks, it was the difficult and ungracious Rydzewski who urged Klucker to lead him on first ascents of the Ago di Sciora, Punta Pioda di Sciora, Sciora di Fuori, the first crossing of Colle della Scioretta, Fuorcla di Sciora, Colle del Cengalo and Colle dei Gemelli, of Piz Cacciabella and Pizzi Gemelli and several more. One of Klucker's notable 'failures' was on the classic north buttress of Piz Badile when, scouting a route for Rydzewski in 1892, he climbed solo and in stockinged feet to a point less than 150 metres from the summit. He turned back convinced that Rydzewski would be unable to follow his lead, and, one assumes, hoped for another opportunity to complete the route at a later date.

Between the Bondasca glen and that of the Forno valley lies the Albigna cirque with a huge dam hiding its secrets from the casual observer in Val Bregaglia. This is a high, rocky little glen, a monochrome landscape by comparison with Bondasca but with plenty of climbing of all grades on the spiky horseshoe of peaks that enclose it. The Albigna Hut holds 90 in its dormitories and in the height of summer every one of those beds will be needed.

So much for the northern, Swiss flanks of the Bregaglia. The Italian slopes are equally as charming, the amphitheatres that block Valle di Mello and Valle di Bagni which sprout from Val Masino are both impressive. Their walls are a paradise for climbers, especially to the south of the ridge that divides Albigna and Forno where the little Allievi cirque holds some excellent routes. Italian climbers systematically worked at these walls in the Twenties and Thirties, including the great Gervasutti, Molteni,

Bramani and Count Aldo Bonacossa. But as with all these mountains the pleasure of climbing them is in no way devalued by the numbers of hands and feet that have also used their ledges and crannies, any more than the glorious scenery is devalued by the eyes of men and women who have strayed here in the past and similarly gazed at them with a sense of wonder.

Both Bernina and Bregaglia manage to draw a special glow of affection from those who know them best.

CECIL DAVIES

The Austrian Alps

If variety is the spice of life then every taste of the Austrian Alps will whet the appetite for more, for Austria is like Cleopatra: Age cannot wither her, nor custom stale her infinite variety.

Within their comparatively limited compass these mountains offer almost every mountaineering experience: snow and ice, rock climbs of all grades and lengths, an incomparable system of paths and huts, protected scrambles, lakes, waterfalls, gorges, lush valleys, lonely alms, meadows and forests, animals and flowers. Every mountain group has its own distinctive character, every valley and village its own unique features. The visitor can find a new area every year for half a lifetime, or fall in love with one and return to it time and again. There is always something new to be discovered even in a part one knows well. The claim of the Tirol to be *Das schönste auf*

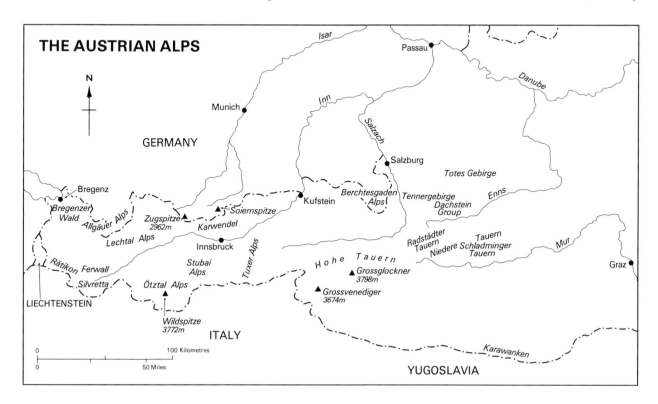

der Welt is hard to refute, though any mountain area of Austria might equally well be described, in its own inimitable way, as the most beautiful in the world.

The principal ranges of the Austrian Alps take the form of two roughly parallel chains of mountains, each approximately 400 kilometres in length, running from west to east and divided from each other by the valleys of the Inn, the Salzach and the Enns. Of the more northerly chain, the *Mittelgebirge*, much of which forms the Austro-German frontier, only one summit, the Parseierspitze, exceeds 3000 metres, while the more southerly, the *Hochgebirge*, has large areas over 3000 metres and its highest peak, the Grossglockner, misses the 4000 metre class by only 203 metres.

Travelling from Britain and entering Austria near Bregenz at the eastern end of the Bodensee, we first discover the Bregenzerwald where deep, well-wooded valleys divide green, pastoral ridges grazed by the cattle of prosperous farms. Gentle walking offers extensive views north into Germany and west across the valley of the upper Rhine to Swiss mountains, while to the south the Rätikon group, with the Sulzfluh, Drusenfluh and the glaciated Schesaplana, provides a serrated skyline. There is drama too, in deep limestone gorges like the Rappenlochschlucht, and excitement on the knife-edge ridges of the Hoher Freschen (2004m). The north-south route over this fine top is part of the European long-distance footpath E4. Alpine flowers abound and part of the Bregenzerwald is a Nature Reserve. Austrian Alpine Club huts are few and far between, but warmly welcoming.

The undulating hills of the Bregenzerwald are, however, only a prelude and untypical of what is in store. Due east, the Allgäuer Alps bound the southern-most tip of Germany. Along their bare and rocky ridge runs a high-level route, the Heilbronner Way, protected in part by fixed ropes. There are a number of accessible summits; the Muttlerkopf and the Krottenkopf (2657m), for example, both reached from the Kempter Hut at 1846 metres. This lies on the E5, the long-distance route from Lindau via Bolzano to the Adriatic, and is consequently much frequented. Very different is its nearest neighbour, the Waltenberger Haus, perched on a tiny spur above a dramatic path to Einödsbach, the most southerly permanently inhabited place in Germany. The Allgäu group also offers innumerable rock climbs of all grades.

South from the Heilbronner Way the land drops some 1500 metres into the depths of the Lechtal, a valley so steeply sided that hay-makers there sometimes need to wear crampons. Beyond the valley rise the Lechtal Alps, forming a magnificent panorama from the Valluga (2809m) to the Parseierspitze (3036m). The Valluga is disfigured by ski-machinery from St Anton in the Rosanna valley, but otherwise the Lechtal Alps, with nearly 500 peaks of over 2000 metres, nearly fifty mountain lakes and several small glaciers, are among the wildest and also the most attractive in Austria, with so complex a structure that a geological map of the area has been described as resembling a painting by Kandinsky. The complete hut-to-hut walk from Lech to Nassereith, the so-called Kalkalpen Traverse, is a worthwhile two-week expedition. Despite its steepness and crumbling castellations, this group has points of access from every quarter of the compass: from Lech in the west, from the Rosanna/Inn valley (St Anton to Imst) in the south, from Nassereith in the east and from the villages of the Lechtal itself in the north. The Lechtal villages have their own interest too, such as the elaborately decorated house facades in Holzgau and Bach, or Anton Falger's *Dance of Death* in the churchyard chapel at Elbingenalp.

The walker in the Lechtal Alps will enjoy picturesque rock scenery, sculpted foregrounds, mountain vistas to the south, and sudden revelations such as that of the Hintersee when crossing the Kridlonscharte. But he will also encounter damp, demanding traverses of precipitous ground, such as the Theodor Haas Way across the Jochrücken between the Kaiserjoch Hut and the Ansbacher Hut (the E4 again). Even some walkers' paths, such as the Augsburger High-Level Path, the direct route between the Ansbacher and Augsburger Huts, are very serious and not to be attempted by anyone lacking high alpine experience and technique. As might be expected, the best climbs in the area are of high technical grades on sound, compact, steep rock. There are, on the other hand, many easy summits but loose rock and stonefall are all too common hazards. One of the easiest and most rewarding of the major summits is the Muttekopf (2777m), the *Hausberg* of Imst. It can be climbed from the Muttekopf Hut with a fixed rope in one section: fine views south towards the Pitztal and Kaunergrat.

About 16 kilometres north-east from Nassereith as the alpine chough flies, the Zugspitze, exactly on the frontier, is the highest mountain in Germany at 2962 metres, though older maps give its height as five metres higher than this, and Walter Pause ironically suggests that it has been worn down by the feet of visitors (the majority arriving by cable-car) and that the 'cement barons' of Garmisch-Partenkirchen therefore built the hotel on top to prevent further erosion! The ascent without cable-car remains a serious proposition involving exposure, fixed ropes and, if the Höllental route is taken, the steep Höllental Glacier.

Different again in character is the Karwendel, four roughly parallel mountain chains running between the Isar valley and the Achensee. Of these the most southerly is known as the North Chain (Nordkette) because the inhabitants of Innsbruck see it to *their* north! Although now a mere hour's drive from Munich, this area, until comparatively recently *terra incognita*, is still one of the largest, as well as one of the most beautiful, unspoiled regions in Central Europe. Though the Karwendel is built largely of brittle and crumbly types of limestone and dolomite, its rocks have been called an alpine school for extreme rock climbers, and above all, the North Wall of the Laliderer Spitze, towering some 700 metres above the Falken Hut, presents the hard climber with severe challenges. For the walker there is the classic valley crossing from Scharnitz to Pertisau, the more picturesque approach to the heart of the area, the Kleiner Ahorn Boden, from Hinterriss, the ascent of the highest summit, the Birkkarspitze (2749m) from the finely situated Karwendel House, and a wealth of other routes and variations.

In the Kleiner Ahorn Boden stands the memorial to Hermann von Barth (1845-1886), the principal explorer of these mountains. Here he climbed 88 summits, including many first ascents, at a time when alpinism was in its infancy. Born within sight of the Karwendel, he died of fever when exploring Angola.

Just over the German border lies a virtually independent massif, the Soiern group, a horseshoe enclosing a deep basin with a lake. This provides a superb round walk over five 2000 metre summits with extensive views in every direction. The hut which is the base for the walk was built in 1866 as a royal hunting lodge by Ludwig II, the tragic King of Bavaria, Wagner's patron.

Further to the north-east, beyond the Achensee and the Rofangebirge, lies the town of Kufstein, from whose grim fortress a giant organ, the *Heldenorgel* (Organ of the Heroes), placed in one of the towers, peals daily over the surrounding countryside in memory of the dead of two World Wars. Above Kufstein rises the Kaisergebirge with its celebrated climbing routes on the Fleischbank, the Predigtstuhl and above all the Totenkirchl, which boasts some eighty routes to its summit. But the Kaisergebirge has much more than rock climbs. There's easy walking on the Zahmer Kaiser, a magically hidden valley, the Kaisertal and, in the Wilder Kaiser, the *Eggersteig*, one of the earliest of the *vie ferrate* or *Klettersteige*, up the Steinerne Rinne, a vast 'groove' between the Fleischbank and the Predigtstuhl where fixed ropes enable adventurous and experienced walkers to share the thrill of climbing amid this glorious rock scenery. At the top, the Ellmauer Tor (Ellmau Gate) opens a splendid vista to the south, the distant horizon dominated by the huge bulk of the Grossvenediger. The Hintere and Vordere Goinger Halt (2195m–2243m) above the Ellmauer Tor, and the Scheffauer at the western end of the chain, are summits accessible to the mountain walker.

Still further east three sister groups, the Berchtesgaden Alps, the Tennengebirge and the Dachstein group, are all characterised by extraordinary ice caves—limestone caverns whose glistening fairy-tale palaces are decorated not with stalagmites and stalactites, but with fantastic creations of pure ice.

Berchtesgaden, notorious as the country seat of Adolf Hitler, is the centre of a mountain-ringed German basin almost wholly enclosed by Austria. Although many of the summits are too easily accessible by roads and lifts, others reward the effort of ascent. The finest within the German area is the Watzmann (2651m), rocky-ridged and with a view to the south of the Hochkönig away in Austria.

Eastward again, beyond the wild Tennengebirge, is the Dachstein group, the most richly compact of the *Mittelgebirge*. Broadly, it has two principal geomorphological features: a great crescent of rocky peaks culminating in the Hoher Dachstein (2993m), the second highest summit in the northern limestone Alps, embracing the Halstätter Glacier; and an incredibly jagged 'comb', the Gosaukamm, otherwise known as the Salzburg Dolomites. In the heart of the crescent, overlooking the tongue of the glacier, is the Simony Hut, named after the Dachstein's nineteenth century explorer. The northern approach to this sanctuary is from Halstatt, perhaps the most beautiful lakeside town in Europe, while the southern approach is from Schladming in the Enns valley. It is from this side that summer skiers are mechanically lifted to pursue their sport.

The Gosaukamm, as well as offering high-grade climbs on its airy pinnacles, provides a high-level round walk (one of Walter Pause's *100 Best Walks in the Alps*) and, in the Grosser Donnerkogel (2054m), an outstandingly dramatic walkers' summit. The view from the dam (available even to motorists) of the Gosausee and the high peaks beyond, is a classic for painters and photographers alike.

Further north-east, beyond Bad Aussee, is a vast, barren limestone plateau, a giant Ingleborough—the Totes Gebirge, the Dead Mountains. Walled on most sides by stupendous cliffs with impressive rock routes, this great wilderness is tilted from north-east to south-west, its high point being the Grosser Priel (2515m) in the north-east corner. The bare and stony desert is pock-marked with innumerable sink-holes or *Dolinen*, death-traps for the unwary, and in bad weather skilful navigation is essential. The Pühringer Hut by the Elmsee in the very heart of the plateau is a welcome and welcoming haven for the walker caught in a snowstorm. Further west, where it is lower, the land is greener and rather less forbidding: here the Albert-Appel House is a refuge for the wanderer.

East of the Totes Gebirge the mountain groups become gradually lower, but they must not in any way be underestimated; they are often extremely steep and rugged and such a route as the Peternpfad up to the Peternscharte in the Gesäuse demands determination and endurance.

Having traced Austria's *Mittelgebirge* to its eastern extremity, we return to the west in order to follow the course of the greater *Hochgebirge* and start in the Rätikon, south of Bludenz and lying on the frontiers of Leichtenstein to the west and Switzerland to the south.

One of the nineteenth century explorers of this area was John Sholto Douglas, a British industrialist and engineer whose name is honoured in that of the Douglass Hut on the rock-lip of the now dammed Lünersee. The original hut was built on his initiative in 1872, the very first Alpine hut to be built by the German Alpenverein. The highest of the principal mountains here, and the most westerly high mountain in Austria, is the Schesaplana. Almost 3000 metres high, it is a snow mountain, not technically difficult from the Douglass Hut but to be taken seriously nonetheless. From its summit the eye can follow the fine series of rock mountains that form the Austro-Swiss border, above all the Drusenfluh (2827m), one of the most massive of the Austrian limestone alps.

The walk along the whole of the Rätikon from here to Gargellan is as delightful as one could wish. The Sulzfluh near the Tilisuna Hut is an easy but most rewarding summit, while the experienced scrambler can include two of the Three Towers above the beautifully-situated Lindauer Hut.

To drive up the Silvretta Strasse from Partenen at just over 1000 metres to the Silvretta Stausee at 2030 metres, is an alpine experience in its own right, and the Wiesbadener Hut, a 6 kilometre walk away at the head of the Ochsental, is practically encircled by glaciers and peaks, several of which are accessible to experienced alpine walkers. Even the celebrated Piz Buin (3312m) involves only easy rock climbing and a simple glacier crossing. The combination of considerable glaciation and rugged summits makes the Silvretta one of the most spectacular of Austria's mountain groups, especially when viewed from the Hohes Rad near the Wiesbadener Hut. Its high-level route (*Höhenweg*) from Gargellan to Ischgl is a serious one-week expedition, and even the alternative Silvretta walking route (*Silvretta-Wanderweg*) is in no sense easy.

The Ferwall group to the north of the Silvretta lies, on the map, in the latter's crescent 'like the old moon in the new moon's arms'. These are solemn mountains of darkly coloured rock, with steep flanks and corries filled with stony rubble. Ice-filled gullies line the cliffs and grass grows but sparsely in the high valleys. Yet this austere setting holds not only dozens of mountaineering rock routes, mostly of grades II-V, but also excellent walking routes over high passes of some 2700 metres, and to lonely summits with splendid views north to the Lechtal Alps and south to the Silvretta. The highest mountain in the Ferwall, the Kuchenspitze (3170m), and the most finely shaped, Patteriol, can both be climbed at grade II, while the second highest, the Hoher Riffler has a walkers' route. The Ferwall abounds in scattered lakelets. One area of wide tarn-bedecked passes, the Winterjöchle, is the actual watershed between tributaries of the Rhine and of the Danube. A quiet region, where the loneliness encourages marmot and chamois, and where there is peace to be found on the shores of little lakes reflecting the dark mountains.

South of Imst the Pitztal, deep and narrow, runs some thirty or so kilometres into the heart of the mountains between two great north-south ranges: the Kaunergrat and the Geigenkamm. Once completely unspoiled, it has been considerably developed in the last twenty years, but its bounding walls of steep slopes and ridges help to preserve its pristine character. This is true mountaineering country where the Hohe Geige (3395m) on the east, faces the stunningly conical Waze or Watzespitze (3533m) across the gorge-like valley. To climb the latter by its splendid East Ridge (grade III) and descend by its two hanging glaciers makes a memorable Alpine day, while from the valley head where the Taschach Glacier and its icefall resemble a landscape on the moon, the Wildspitze (3772m) can be reached by glacier routes from the Braunschweiger Hut or the Taschach House, by any mountaineer who wants to avoid the more popular route from the Breslauer Hut above Vent in the Venter Tal.

But the Pitztal has not given its name to a mountain group, and all these are part of the Otztal Alps, a huge area of high tops and extensive glaciers culminating in the awesome chain of snow summits from the Weisskugel to the Hoch Wilde, and beyond to the Timmelsjoch which forms the frontier between Austria and Italy, with views to the south as if from Austria's natural battlements. Back in the 1960s, a time of political tension over the future of South Tirol long since resolved, strange things could happen up here. In the night of 29–30 August 1966, the warden of the Hochwildehaus (2883m) went out about 10.00 pm and played the Last Post on a bugle; an impressive performance in that context. About midnight one of our party went downstairs to relieve nature and surprised a group of people, dressed for going out, who flashed torches at him and scuttled away. Smugglers? Saboteurs? Had the Last Post been a signal? We never knew. But the sound of gunfire was heard several times during our stay.

Despite skiing developments at Obergurgl and Vent, the Otztal Alps are probably still the best introduction to high Alpine mountaineering in Austria. If the weather precludes the big stuff, the Otztal has many lesser tops and other fascinations, such as the long, lonely Polles Tal, a hanging valley above Huben, or the Hauersee, high under the 3000 metre peaks of the Geigenkamm. (The Hauersee Hut is without a guardian and requires a special key.)

East of Otz the mountains are not classed with the Otztal but with those of the Stubai. Kuhtai, a rather dreary ski resort, gives access to the north-west Stubai up the beautiful Finster Tal and over to rocky, lightly glaciated country where the Gubener Hut, and above all the Winnebachsee Hut, occupy positions of remote and barren beauty. But the main peaks and ranges are best approached through the Stubai valley itself, the round of whose head from the Nürnberger Hut to the Franz-Senn Hut is one of the most satisfying in the whole country, though the Dresdner Hut is now accessible by lift for summer skiing and the basin containing the Sulzenau Hut seems to be under constant threat from hydro-electric schemes. For experienced walkers a snow and rock summit such as the Wilder Freiger (3418m) can be included: this, like the great Otztal peaks, lies on the Italian border.

Moving east along this frontier we cross the summit of the Brenner Pass and reach the grand frontier mountains of the Zillertal Alps: the Hochpfeiler, Grosse Mösele, the Schwarzenstein and the Grosse Löffler. These peaks, all well in excess of 3300 metres, are linked by a magnificent hut-to-hut route which joins the heads of the parallel valleys that come from Mayrhofen. It keeps north-west of the chain of summits, usually at a little over 2000 metres, but once, at the Schönbichler Scharte and Horn, between the baronial Berliner Hut and the Furtschagl Hut, it reaches 3133 metres—a bonus for the modest walker, for here we are really on the sharp north ridge of the Grosse Mösele and can feel ourselves to be as it were involved in that great mountain.

But the Zillertal Alps do not only offer high tops (as a whole the most serious we have yet encountered), but also the variety of its valleys. The most romantically picturesque is the Floitengrund. The most westerly, the Tuxer Tal, has been heavily developed by the ski industry. Although Mayrhofen has now the feeling of a resort rather than of an Alpine village, it has produced some of Austria's greatest climbers, such as Peter Habeler, one of the first pair to climb Everest without oxygen.

We have now travelled all too swiftly through the Austrian *Mittelgebirge*, much of it lying on or close to the frontier with Germany, and have followed the *Hochgebirge* along the Swiss and Italian frontiers. The Italian frontier now falls away to the south where it follows the line of Austria's Southern Alps. These begin to share Italian characteristics, as a name such as that of the Lienz Dolomites witnesses, while further east the Karawanken on the Yugoslav frontier is linked with the Julian Alps. Thus the most easterly sections of the main chain of the *Hochgebirge*, the Hohe Tauern and the Niedere Tauern, the majestic climax and magical coda of Austria's mountain symphony, are left lying wholly within Austria.

A crown of ice, some 30 kilometres in circumference, extends further tentacle-like glaciers on all sides and is topped by a mountain of 3674 metres with its attendant peaks and rock islands—this is the core of the Venediger, the most westerly mountain group of the Hohe Tauern.

From every direction involving an extensive glacier crossing, the ascent of the mighty Grossvenediger is nevertheless easier than that of the Grossglockner, but is vastly rewarding. The Venediger-Höhenweg skirts this great ice dome in a huge semi-circle on the south, crossing massive spurs on high passes in its exhilarating march from hut to hut. Below it to the south lies the delightful, and as yet unspoiled Virgental, and to the east the Tauerntal, which leads north from the charming little town of Matrei-in-Osttirol into the high-alpine Gschlösstal, with its rock chapel, 'glacier path' and the approach to the Neue Prager Hut, base for the easiest route up the Grossvenediger.

The Virgental is bounded on the south by the Lasörling group, up which rewarding walks lead to splendid views of the main Venediger massif. The Tauerntal is bounded on its east and north-east by the Granatspitz group, linking the Venediger and Glockner groups. Here the most interesting features include the Sudeten-Deutsch Höhenweg from the Kals-Matreier Törl to the Sudeten-Deutsch Hut; the Kleiner and Grosser Muntanitz, both perfect viewpoints for the Grossglockner and Grossvenediger; and the beautiful 'Three Lakes' walk, past the Green, Black and Grey Lakes to the St Pöltener Hut on the inhospitable Felber Tauern. This is a windy, harsh pass which, from prehistoric times until the Felber-Tauern Tunnel was opened in 1967, was the easiest route across this part of the Alps.

So far we have seen the Grossglockner (3798m) as a titanic church spire dominating the eastern skyline from the more westerly Hohe Tauern summits. To approach it more nearly, we drop down from the Kals-Matreier Törl to the village of Kals and from here take bus or car to the Luckner House at about 2000 metres. From the big car park here the South Face of the Grossglockner is impressive. Leaving the Luckner House and passing the Luckner Hut (both said to be expensive), follow the mountain track to the Stüdl Hut, built at his own expense in 1868 by Johann Stüdl, a Prague businessman and one of the founders of the Alpenverein.

At this busy spot guides meet their clients. With a guide or as one of an experienced party, you leave the hut, climb a broad, dull, stony shoulder, cross the tip of a glacier to a mini pass, and after a longer glacier crossing and a rock ridge, suddenly arrive at the famous Erzherzog-Johann Hut on the Eagle's Rest (Adlersruhe) at 3454 metres. This, the highest hut in the Eastern Alps, is often very full, not only with mountaineers pleasure-bent, but also with large parties of Austrian soldiers who use the mountain for training in mountain-warfare. Though the ascent from here is not difficult, it is exposed, especially on the narrow ridge of the Kleinglockner and on the tiny snow ridge in the Obere Glocknerscharte between the Kleinglockner and the summit. In good summer conditions it can also be extremely crowded and one literally has to queue for the 15–17 metre descent into the 8 metre wide gap. Be that as it may, when you reach the cross you can get no higher in Austria and the scenery, both in the depths below and in the wide views beyond, is glorious.

Non-climbers who tell you they have 'done the Grossglockner' have simply driven over the high Alpine road of that name, at the southern end of which lies Heiligenblut, a village which, from the first ascent of the Grossglockner (in 1800) until 1855 was the sole starting point for climbing the mountain.

Too many mountaineers regard Heiligenblut as the eastern terminus of the Alps. Conway in 1894, and David Brett in 1981, both ended their west-east traverse of the Alps (which both called *The Alps from End to End*) here. It is not to belittle the achievements of these men to point out that the Alps do not end at Heiligenblut. The Hohe Tauern itself continues eastwards with a number of not inconsiderable mountains, such as the Hoher Sonnblick, the Ankogel and the Hockalmspitze (3360m). And slightly to the north of the eastern end of the Hohe Tauern, there begins the Niedere Tauern, a largely unspoiled mountainous region some 120 kilometres long from east to west, and varying between 30 and 50 kilometres from north to south. Its

Untere Klafferscharte in the Schladminger Tauern. (Photo: Cecil Davies.)

heart, the Schladminger Tauern, is still (1989) untouched by through-roads, hydro-electric schemes and, except on its edges, by the apparatus of downhill skiing—a gigantic jewel situated almost exactly in the centre of Austria.

The most westerly group of the Niedere Tauern is the Radstädter Tauern, and though small in area, it rejoices in a series of fine tops joined by a good high-level path, a lonely tarn (the Wildsee), and a friendly hut, the Südwiener Hut. This is reached by a choice of picturesque paths from the Tauernpass, east of which we enter the Schladminger Tauern where every eastward step reveals new beauties: the quiet Oberhüttensee, the two Kalkspitzen, north and south of the Ahkarscharte, the Ignaz-Mattis Hut by the lovely Unterer Giglachsee. From the Rotmannlspitze the Dachstein massif rises proudly beyond the Enns Valley and after a steep and tricky descent from the Krukeckscharte (2303m), the Zechmann family gives a hearty welcome at the Keinprecht Hut. From the next hut, the Landwirsee Hut (the only one on this route that cannot be reached simply by the varied and photogenic valley routes from the north) the highest mountain of the Niedere Tauern (Hochgolling: 2863m) is a most shapely and challenging wedge-like formation which can be climbed via the Gollingscharte without technical difficulty. From the summit ridge the drop of some 1400 metres into the Göriachtal is most impressive and much of the route already traversed and still to come can be seen. Beyond the Gollingscharte we descend into the Gollingwinkel, locally claimed to be the largest natural amphitheatre in the world; and so to the Golling Hut.

Between this and the Preintaler Hut we pass, after climbing and descending from the Greifenberg, through the great natural wonder of the Niedere Tauern, the Klafferkessel (the Gaping Cauldron), formed out of two huge merged corries like a crucible of the gods, filled with innumerable lakes and tarns (about forty being of significant size); a veritable labyrinth that calls for careful navigation if visibility is at all poor. It contains a memorial plaque to Hans Wödl, pioneer explorer of the area, whose name is also honoured in that of the hut in the Seewigtal.

From the Preintaler Hut, weather and snow conditions permitting, we cross the potentially dangerous Neualmscharte (2347m). The steep and sometimes difficult descent from this into the Seewigtal passes the Obersee, the Hüttensee (with the Hans-Wödl Hut) and finally the Bodensee, at least as beautiful as the larger and better-known Bodensee last seen at the far western end of the Austrian Alps.

C DOUGLAS MILNER
The Dolomites

The Dolomites are among the strangest and most beautiful rock peaks in the world. They are neither vast and high like the rock peaks of the Himalaya, the American Rockies or Andes, or even the Swiss Alps. Nor are they so minute by world standards as the crags of the British hills. There are about fifty summits reaching 3000 metres, yet often about a third to half that height is occupied by massive rock walls and towers with large areas of continuously vertical cliff. Their strangeness lies not only in their steepness or the many fantastic pinnacles, but also in their colouring of golden yellow and grey, streaked and flecked at times with black and purple and red, with dazzling white scree slopes at their feet.

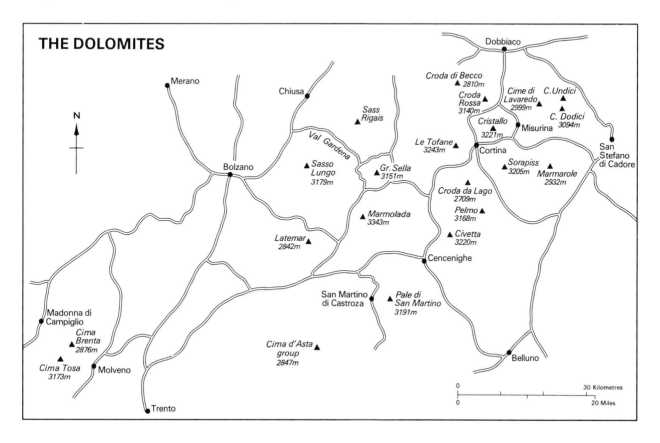

In parts they seem bare and desolate by comparison with the mossy and richly tinted crags of Britain and their effect of ruined masonry is, in its detail, less attractive than the sweeping sculptured lines of granite peaks.

Sometimes in the glare of noonday, such eccentric creations can look less like mountains than the residual bleached skeletons of mountains that long ago have died, ghostly and terrible in their arid silence. No streams run through the upper glens, there is no grass or tree growth; no sound is to be heard, and only the walker or climber who loves both solitude and bare rock can be fully at ease among them.

Yet the dramatic lines of the outer bastions exist for all to enjoy as they rise swiftly from the hillslopes above the green forests and flowery alpine meadows at their feet, to sparkle against deep Italian skies. Above all they react to fine conditions of atmosphere and weather. They are a superb stage setting for the beauty created by the light of dawn and sunset, by the march of a storm, by the windblown mists and by the round of the seasons.

All limestone is distinguished by its boldness of form. But dolomite is a special kind of limestone, containing magnesium as well as calcium, and so it is much harder and more colourful than 'mountain' or carboniferous limestone. It seems to stand midway between limestone and marble in its incipient translucence and the polish it can acquire.

The Dolomites are a very small part of the eastern limestone Alps, which in all are spread over an area as large as Switzerland, stretching from the shores of Lake Constance to the Raxalpe near Vienna in the east, from Bavaria in the north, to the Julian Alps of Yugoslavia.

Most of these mountains are concentrated in a rectangle of north-east Italy between the valleys of the Adige in the west and the Piave in the east, bounded on the south by the Val Sugana and on the north by the Val Pusteria. One other compact group is just outside this rectangle: the Brenta, west of the Adige, which some visitors think is the finest of all.

Before proceeding to a detailed description of these areas it is interesting to look briefly at the history of the region. The earliest accounts are those of the campaigns of Drusus two thousand years ago, when he established the Roman colony of Rhaetia, which included the Dolomites and Eastern Switzerland. The language spoken there was a form of Latin, and although 1500 years have passed since the fall of the Roman Empire, this patois, called Ladin, has survived mainly in the north (Val Gardena) as it has in Switzerland in the Grisons (Graubunden), along with an associated patois, Romanche.

In the Middle Ages, as part of the great Venetian Republic, such towns as Trento, Bolzano, Belluno, Caprile and Cortina were of importance. Also significant was the great highway from Innsbruck over the pass of Brenner through Bolzano to Verona. The conquering Visigoths 'teutonised' the northern part of the region around Bolzano, but further south in the Trentino this was not the case. The enclaves in the lateral valleys such as the Val Gardena and Ladinia were unaffected.

An interesting survival was the name of one village between Bolzano and Trento; Welsch Metz. Welsch meant foreign in German and the word has come into our language, via the Saxons, for the Celtic people of Wales!

The various groups of mountains are separated by good roads, the most important of which is that linking Bolzano with Cortina. Other useful roads are those leading from the Brenner, from Ora north of Trento east to San Martino, from Ponte Gardena to the Val Gardena, over the Sella Pass to join the Bolzano-Cortina road.

It is convenient to identify the groups of peaks accessible from the valleys:

Val Gardena	Sciliar, Sasso Lungo and Cir/Odle
Val di Fassa	Catinaccio and Marmolada
Val d'Ampezzo	Monte Cristallo, Tofanas, Sorapis, Anteleo and Pelmo
Val di Landro	Cime di Lavaredo and Sesto peaks
Val Cismon	San Martino group and the Peaks of Primiero
Val Campiglio	The Brenta group and the Tosa group

The Brenta group can easily be reached from Bolzano via La Mendola, and also from Trento through Stenico and Pinzolo. All these roads are well served by motor coaches. But the motorist has advantages, especially if he is prepared for car camping. There are numerous camp sites in the area and with a decent-sized tent for comfort, the saving over hotel or even hut costs largely compensates for the extra expense of motor-rail. On the other hand, the visitor with plenty of time may well prefer to spend a few days driving through Switzerland, reaching Italy by way of the Stelvio Pass. Another way is through Germany to Innsbruck and down the Brenner road.

Though this book is primarily for walkers and climbers, the motorist 'pure and simple' can derive much pleasure from travel through the old and beautiful towns and villages, with their many castles and churches. Of the former, two examples will suffice: Schloss Tirol near Merano, and Schloss Wolkenstein in the Val Gardena.

As has already been noted, there are perhaps 200 huts or refuges, mostly well appointed with reasonable food and wine. The walks, either from hut to hut or just daily excursions, are numerous in each valley, and a full fortnight's holiday could be well spent in many of them, especially the Val Campiglio. But let us begin with the Val Gardena, best suited for anyone making a first visit to the Dolomites.

Above Ortisei and Santa Cristina, the villages of the Val Gardena, is the vast Siusi alp, a stretch of woodland and pasture with the background of the Sasso Lungo, giving pleasant walking country. Monte Sciliar can be reached from its southern end and offers a splendid panorama. To get the best from this viewpoint it is well worth having binoculars.

Another repaying walk from Santa Cristina leads up the great hollow between the Sasso Lungo and the Sasso Piatto, into a wilderness of scree up which the path zig-zags to the col between the Sasso Lungo and the Cinque Dita (five fingers), whose cluster of pinnacles is as Gothic as the spires of any village in the area. From here we see the Pordoi, with the famous trio of the Sella Towers as a prominent feature. Then we can either walk down or take the cable which reaches the Sella Inn.

Not far away is the Col Rodella and from there several paths lead to the Val di Fassa in rolling alp and woodland. This is a very good area for alpine flora. The view of the Fassa valley is interesting in that the rock changes from dolomite to porphyry, the foundation on which the whole area is laid. But since our immediate objective is a return to the Gardena valley, we take a track north under the great cliffs of the Sasso Lungo leading down to our valley.

Also from Ortisei we can walk north towards Le Odle still along pleasant country paths.

As to other areas, a few special features ought to be mentioned. From the Val di Fassa we can easily get into the range of the Catinaccio. (Incidentally, this awful name has been given by the Italians to what was formerly known as the Rosengarten—the Rose Garden of the Goblin King Laurin, where the roses bloom at dawn and sunset.) However, they have made some amends in the Croda del Rey Laurino, a part of this splendid group. The best approach is by the Val di Vajolet to the refuge of that name, where we have a superb view of the Vajolet Towers.

Near the head of the valley we can go via Penia to the Contrin refuge, and so to the Ombretta Pass with the awesome cliffs of the Marmolada in profile.

The peaks of the Val d'Ampezzo are spread out over many kilometres but visitors based on Cortina should certainly go up to the Tre Croce pass, from which walks can lead into the margins of Sorapis, with Cristallo looking its best. Then on to the Lago di Misurina—a beautiful lake unfortunately cluttered by several hotels and shops. It has a good camp site not far away. From here a two-hour walk takes us to Monte Piano, with a vast panorama even better than that from Sciliar.

We can also motor or walk up to the refuge just below the Tre Cime di Lavaredo and follow a horizontal path round these famous pinnacles to the Locatelli Hut. From here another path takes us to the Zsigmondy Hut in the heart of the Sexten peaks. These are the Elfer, Zwolfer and Einser; so-named because the sun is over each summit at 11, 12 and 1 o'clock, from Sexten (Sesto).

Purists may query my allocation of these peaks to the Val di Landro or Sesto. They can certainly be reached from the village of Sesto, or by a beautiful track through the woods of the Val Rinbon leading from the Lago di Landro to the Locatelli Hut. But the most convenient is that already mentioned, from near the Tre Cime.

The Val Cismon is best approached over the Rolle Pass from where we have a striking view of the Cimon della Pala, rightly called the Matterhorn of the Dolomites. The wall of peaks from here to the Cima Cimerlo includes the Pala di San Martino, the Rosetta, and at the end the towers of Sass Maor and Cima della Madonna. (There are no dolomites on the other side of the glen but lower tops of red porphyry.)

The wall faces west and when the sun is low it takes on the rose glow that rivals that of the Catinaccio. Before the Great War, Guido Rey, the famous Italian climber, wrote of the sunset light here:

'The mountains are aglow with their own light . . . at the supreme moment the wondrous forms of the ancient towers, palaces and temples appear as if by

Cristallo. (Photo: C Douglas Milner.)

magic; the dead castles come to life again, the battlements are crowned with shining breastplates . . . the blind loopholes are endowed with sight and the deep caves reveal their treasures.'

San Martino is the patron saint of innkeepers and he has certainly done well for his protégés here, for this very popular summer and winter centre was completely rebuilt between the wars. Although it is the best base from which to walk or climb, it is in itself far less interesting than Primiero further down the valley, which is an old village with the unusual feature of a Gothic church. This and other old buildings date from the Middle Ages when the population was mainly German silver miners. Equally attractive are the neighbouring villages of Tonadico, Siror and Ormanico.

What should not be missed is the walk through Tonadico to the Val Canali, for the remarkable sight of Castel la Pietra standing like an eagle's nest on a great crag guarding the enchanting view of Count Welsperg's park. Leslie Stephen wrote of this with enthusiasm:

> 'The stream which watered it flows through a level plain of the greenest turf, dotted occasionally with clumps and groves of pines. Contrasting it with the mighty cliffs that enclosed it on every side, it was a piece of embodied poetry.'

Along with the Brenta, the Val Cismon is the most southerly of the Dolomite area, and below Primiero are slopes that look to the sun and grow maize and corn, chestnuts and vines. The hills themselves are rich in alpine flora. 'Ordinary' walks are less numerous than in other areas but the Val Pradidali is worth a visit as are the lower porphyry hills west of the valley.

The Brenta Group are aloof from the main Dolomites some kilometres west of the Adige, between Molveno and Madonna di Campiglio. They are distinctive for their larger glaciers, ice couloirs and snow slopes. The great ice couloir of the Cima Tosa, 900 metres long, is unequalled in the Dolomites.

On the other hand, at lower levels, we can walk through pleasant woods rich in flowers. In the Vallesinella there are great carpets of Alpine Roses, whilst the rare Ladies Slipper Orchid is occasionally seen; it should be photographed, not gathered. Similarly the Edelweiss, that essential Alpine symbol, has declined in number owing to undue collection.

Near to Campiglio are two beautiful little lakes within easy walking distance. The main huts, the Tosa, Brentei and Tuckett, all in the centre of the group, can be reached by using convenient cable cars for part of the way, and if we take that to Grosté, a track leads almost horizontally to the Tuckett Hut, thence by a snow slope to the Bocca di Tuckett, leading down to the Val delle Seghe, with the massive cliff of the Croz del' Altissimo near the route.

Yet perhaps the finest prospect is from near the Brentei Hut with the great Crozzon di Brenta rising in all splendour of orange and light brown rock. On the other side of the valley we see the most impressive line of pinnacles in the region—the Torre, the Sfulmini, the Campanile Alto, and the Basso (formerly the Guglia) and the Brenta Alta. The Guglia is the most famous of all the Dolomite spires and was the last to be climbed.

Thus far we have described only the fine views and the straightforward walks among the peaks. Today there are hundreds of rock climbs in every area. It was different in the mid-nineteenth century when little rock climbing was done and the main routes to alpine peaks were by snow and ice slopes where steps could be cut by guides. Apart from the glacier of the Marmolada, such others in the Dolomites were small and offered nothing of interest to alpine travellers.

The first peak to be ascended was Monte Pelmo, by John Ball in 1857. In 1860 he ascended the Marmolada as far as the summit ridge and he also climbed the Cima Tosa thinking it too was a first ascent, but it transpired that a party of Italians had preceded him. But the real impetus to exploration of the region came from the publication in 1864 of *The Dolomite Mountains* by Gilbert and Churchill, one of the finest travel books ever written. Other contemporaries of John Ball came to the area, often with Swiss or Chamonix guides, and in 1870 the Cimon della Pala was climbed, one of the guides being the great Santo Siorpaes. (The second ascent of that peak was made by him with five other guides leading the local landowner, Count Welsperg.)

The period of real rock climbing can be thought to have begun with the ascent of the Sass Maor by C C Tucker in 1875. The German and Austrian Alpine Club was formed in 1874 and the year previous to that saw the creation of the Trentine Alpine Society. These clubs led the way in the establishment of alpine huts, giving impetus to exploration by German and Austrian climbers such as Purtscheller and Zsigmondy, whose skill and vigour of approach led to many brilliant ascents. There also emerged an adequate corps of good guides under the steady patronage of foreign (i.e. British) amateurs.

One by one the inaccessible towers had been conquered, until last (and best of all) the Guglia di Brenta was climbed in 1899.

The use of pitons had already become common among all the limestone crags, because they lacked the natural spikes and bollards of the granite cliffs. They were thus useful as belays, and also as abseil points. In the early days the karabiner had not been introduced and climbers on an ascent had to unrope at a piton—a very nerve-racking procedure. Their use was not immune from criticism, however, and Dr Paul Preuss in particular urged that they should only be used in an emergency. He was a famous 'solitary' climber and his ascent of the East Wall of the Guglia in 1911 without pitons was, and remains, inimitable. Today that route is over-pegged.

Also the twentieth century saw attention to the big walls. In 1901 two San Martino guides led Miss Beatrice Thomasson up the South Wall of the Marmolada, still one of the classic climbs of the region. Then in 1905 the rib, or arête, of the Crozzon di Brenta had been traced by the Austrians and this climb was even longer than the Marmolada route.

By 1914 guideless climbing, mainly by the Germans and Austrians, was well-developed, as was the creation of elegant new climbs by the élite guides, especially the Italians. Highly regarded in this sphere was Sepp Innerkofler from Sexten.

In 1915 Italy declared war on Austria and the region became a theatre of hostilities. The Austrians occupied the Marmolada and achieved a first by the descent of the South Wall. Trench warfare was seen on Monte Piano and in other parts but the most interesting was on the Sexten peaks, the Elfer, Einser and the Paternkofel. Innerkofler, though 50 years old, enlisted in the Jäger with his two sons. One of his exploits was the night ascent of the Klein Zinne by his eponymous route of the North Wall, to lay a telephone line to an Austrian outpost on the summit. His last venture was to ascend the Paternkofel with five companions, under covering fire from a machine gun team on the Innicher Riedel. He was killed when his figure was seen on the skyline and the official account says this was due to the Italian post on the summit. They buried him on the mountain with full military honours and after the war his sons brought the body down for re-burial in Sexten.

At an evening meeting of the Alpine Club in London in 1916, regrets were expressed at his death—technically our enemy, yet with many old friends there. Just after the last war I called on his son, Sepp II, at his farm, and he told me that his father had been shot in the back by the machine gunners, not by the Italians.

When the war ended the Trentino was ceded to Italy, and a few years later the province of Alto Adige was established. The Italian Alpine Club took over the former German and Austrian huts and rebuilt those destroyed in the fighting. Though German visits declined, at least one fine route was made by them in 1928; the Steger on the North Wall of the Einser Kofel (or, since the wholesale renaming of the peaks, the Cima Una).

Though guidebooks in German continued to be produced, the eventual issue by the Italian Alpine Club of their splendid series of guides, together with the 1:50,000 maps of the Italian Touring Club, did much to promote tourism between the wars.

The continued use of pitons, now with karabiners and other aids, led to pioneering in a higher gear. The ultimate was attained in 1933 by Comici and his friends in the ascent of the North Wall of the Grosse Zinne. It was reported that 550 metres of rope, 90 pitons and 50 karabiners were used. The formidable Colonel Strutt said in the Alpine Journal that 'the expedition was reduced to the piteous level of a repulsive farce'. Yet that was only the beginning of climbs in that extreme category. Not only have many top level climbs been done in the last fifty years, but even medium grade classics tend to be heavily pegged, and to climb by using them is today called 'traditional'. The explosive Colonel must be turning in his grave!

The Dolomites were spared damage in the Second World War, Italy being on the side of the Austrians, and aerial bombing was confined to the railways. After the war *il turismo* was quickly re-established and continues unabated.

Finally, mention must be made of the *vie ferrate,* or protected paths, which offer a middle course between normal walks and the rock climbs. On these paths, with some ladders and wire ropes in parts, and steps cut in the rocks, the walker can have much of the thrill of real rock climbs in safety. *Via Ferrata—Scrambles in the Dolomites* is a translation by Cecil Davies of two books in German and is an excellent guide listing some 50 climbing paths of varying degrees of difficulty.

These paths were begun, mostly in the Thirties, by the German and Austrian Alpine Clubs and have been continued by the Italian Club. There is one distinguished exception: the *Sentiero delle Bochette,* or Path of the Gorges, in the Brenta. This was made by the Trentine Alpine Society and is, perhaps, the best of all these routes.

Also worth a mention is the tunnel of the Paterno, made in the first war and only a few years ago reopened to allow an ascent of the mountain. Just across the valley is the Strada degli Alpini, originally a military track on the Elferkofel (Cima Undici) and now very popular. It is said that each summer around 2000 walkers use it.

The Dolomites have something to offer all visitors, whatever their age or inclinations. The not-so-young can walk pleasantly through the vineyards, chestnut groves or orchards, especially around Bolzano; use the many chairlifts to the hills with the easy option of walking down, often through woodland, clearly waymarked. They can botanise, photograph or paint. They can stay at a comfortable *albergo* in a village away from the main tourist centres, and benefit from the extensive network of motor coaches to get around.

At the other end of the scale, young walkers can go from hut to hut, or take one of the high level treks, two of which are detailed in the book *Alta Via,* whilst climbers find ample outlets for their skills and energies in the top grades of route. In this, the development of climbing on mountain limestone in Britain, with the more general use of aids, is a valuable training for the vertical rigours of the dolomite cliffs. Moreover it is an advantage, by comparison with the High Alps, that there are virtually no glaciers to deal with, and 2 am starts are not necessary.

Somewhere in the middle of this age range are the experienced climbers who are content to climb the classic routes, and if they wish to do so with a guide, experienced men can be engaged in any valley.

One word of advice to all . . . remember the Italian proverb: *Chi va sano, va piano, Chi va piano, va lontano.*

DUDLEY STEVENS

The Julian Alps

When we first wanted to go to the Julian Alps the Iron Curtain had only recently been drawn aside and hardly any Britons had visited these mountains since the special envoys who contacted the Partisans during the war. Today the Julians are still the least known part of the Alpine chain—to Britons. And in spite of developments they are very much the same as we found them then.

We spent a year trying to research the area. There were no books in English still in print, though we read records in old Alpine Journals and were proud to possess one of Julius Kugy's classic and inspirational books in an English translation. *Son of the Mountains* and *Alpine Pilgrimage*, both translated from the German by H E G Tyndale, are set in the period before the First World War. Eventually one of our correspondents told us of another book, *Beautiful Mountains* by F S Copeland, an Englishwoman who actually lived in Yugoslavia, but who had not been heard of since the war. By then she would have been over seventy, if still alive, and her address unknown.

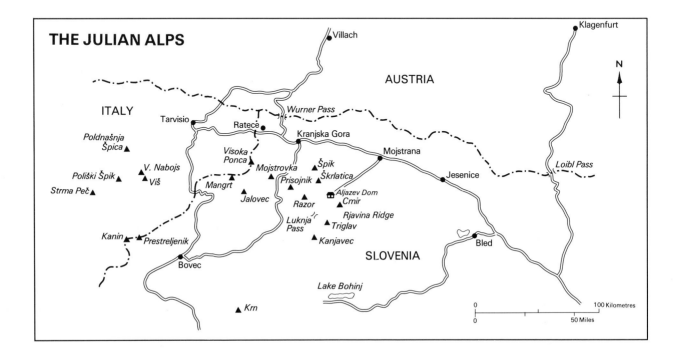

At this stage we gave up hope of learning what to expect, but were even more determined to go. We packed everything we should need to camp completely independently for two weeks whatever might befall us, and bought tickets on the train to the Middle East, for we had spotted a connection to a little town just inside the Yugoslav frontier, which is where the Julian Alps are situated. On an old Austrian map several valleys were marked which appeared to lead into the heart of the mountains. We picked the Vrata, not knowing then that it meant 'the gateway'.

In a few days we were settled on an island in the glacier-blue river amongst the meadow flowers and from our sleeping bags looked up to a ring of fantastic spires and turrets shining white in the sunshine, almost close enough to touch, but hundreds of metres above. We had seen it often, but in books of fairy tales.

It was not until later that we wandered up the valley and found we had camped within a few minutes of a hotel, with waitress service and hot meals. But even this was part of the fairy tale; a graceful wooden chalet with people sitting out on the balcony enjoying drinks and right behind it the great North Wall of Triglav, 1200 metres high and nearly 3 kilometres long.

This combination of beauty, excitement and approachability is the hallmark of the Julian Alps.

The Julians are the most distant part of the Alpine chain—beyond the frontiers of Austria. The Eastern Julians, forming the larger area, are in Slovenia (the northernmost state of Yugoslavia), and the Western Julians in Italy. This presents no problem to a British visitor nowadays, though it is not long since the frontier ridges and even their adjacent valleys were forbidden territory.

The journey from England is simple. The airport is near Ljubljana, capital of Slovenia, which is south-east of the mountain area. From there you travel north-east by coach to Kranj, and then west to Lake Bohinj to reach the southern slopes, or further north to the industrial town of Jesenice for a northern approach. From Jesenice the motor road runs westwards from just inside the Austrian frontier, through the villages of Mojstrana (for the Krma, Kot and Vrata valleys) and Kranjska Gora (For the Vršič pass) to Tarvisio in Italy (for the Montaz group). From Ljubljana to Kranjska Gora, allow two hours by bus.

By rail you can catch the Belgrade train in Paris, with couchettes, and next morning enjoy views of the Austrian Alps before changing at Swarzach St Veit and then leave the train just inside the Yugoslav frontier at Jesenice, or carry on further to Bohinj. Once inside the country you can reach any town by bus.

If travelling by car you can drive through Austria to Villach or Klagenfurt. The former gives a direct approach to the mountains by the 1-in-4 Wurzen Pass (a lot of work was done to improve this road in 1988), and the latter leads to the Loibl Pass—also steep on the Austrian side but giving easy access to Ljubljana, and even to a motorway which passes the famous Postojna caves. But for easy driving go via Villach and detour just a little westwards into Italy over the Tarvisio road and then easily back.

Package holidays are organised by JugoTours. Camping and caravanning are both possibilities but I would personally go unencumbered by all such gear and rely on staying at the huts which are found both high and low in the mountain areas.

The Slovenes love their mountains and have worked to make them enjoyable for everyone. Journeys over and between most of the main summits are open to adventurous walkers and huts are well-placed, well-equipped and welcoming. On the other hand, certain large areas have not been so equipped and remain accessible only to climbers.

In winter skiing is both a sport and the only means of access to the mountains. Even the main road may be under as much as 4 metres of snow, and to reach a familiar pass becomes an adventure. However, some of the lower huts, as well as the hotels, remain open (higher huts are open from July to September), and ski lifts are beginning to proliferate. 'Downhill' is well catered for and there are wonderful opportunities for ski touring.

In the spring each 'marked way' is checked by the climbing club responsible for that district and where sections of the route have slipped into the valley a new path is explored or the bad sections bridged by the use of iron pegs or wire ropes. Some of these may be ignored by rock climbers in good weather but they are life-savers when a storm comes down. And they make it possible for the general mountain lover to enjoy the thrill of long journeys through superb mountain scenery, coupled with hair-raising scrambles.

The mountains are formed mostly of karst limestone, a beautiful but sometimes unstable white rock which is enticing for photographers and exhilarating for mountain walkers but suspect in places for climbing. There are other reasons, however, why rock climbing in the Julians is less well known than in the Alps further west.

The history of mountaineering here followed a timetable similar to that of the Western Alps but was much less intensive. British pioneers reached that far-off range with much less frequency and while Switzerland, France and Austria were being over-run, Slovenia remained very much the country of their dreams. (To Longstaff between the wars, the Julians were 'a goal of greatest desire'.) After the last war for some years Yugoslavia was trapped behind the Iron Curtain. But even when the country as a whole began slowly to attract tourists, the mountains were still treated as a potential Maginot Line; not only the frontier ridges, but the adjacent valleys too were forbidden, and since their own Partisans' exclusive knowledge of the mountains had been so invaluable in the war, the authorities made no new maps.

During the period of my own activities in the range, climbs up to grade VI were plentiful, and many of the classic routes are today indicated in Robin Collomb's guidebook, *Julian Alps* (published by West Col). But Slovenian climbers are both numerous and strong, so there is constant development and grades of new climbs can only reliably be obtained from the horse's mouth. British climbers serious about the area are recommended to contact the Slovenian Alpine Association in Ljubljana. Membership is not open to foreigners but help is generously given.

In the districts which have not been developed for tourists, there are *bivacs* (tiny huts) open only to club members—but foreign climbers may be able to borrow the key by arrangement. Bivac II is particularly beautiful. From your bed, through the doorway, you gaze at Triglav. (For the key contact the Jesenice Planinsko Društvo.) However, since the routes to them are in no way marked, foreigners may not find their way to these bivouacs. Another idea is to write in advance to the Planinsko Društvo in Ljubljana and ask for a mountain guide; this is usually possible to arrange although the guiding system is not so well developed here as it is, for example, in Switzerland.

In short, the Julian Alps offer a wealth of opportunity not only for those climbers who wish to see classic routes which are new to them, but also for those who wish to take part in development. A few districts of special interest are mentioned here as samples.

On Triglav's North Wall a large number of routes and combinations of routes have been identified. The wall stretches for some 3 kilometres, is 1200 metres high from the valley floor and leads directly onwards to the summit pyramid of the highest peak in the Julians, thus totalling about 1500 metres of climbing. There is also a fine traverse. Some of the routes are easy in good weather but it is not uncommon to be stopped by bad weather and forced to bivouac one or even two nights.

Climbs here are performed in full view of binoculars at the Aljažev Dom, but other climbing regions tend to be secluded.

The Martuljek is a circle of mountains visible from the main road to Kranjska Gora. On arrival travellers, straining to see what sort of region they have come to, are mostly frustrated by the low hills bordering the road, but at this point they catch a glimpse which is likely to make an indelible impression.

And a glimpse is all they will get. There are no marked ways leading into the Martuljek clusters but the whole area has a wealth of high quality climbing routes and four *bivacs* to make them accessible. From the Martuljek (northern) end the ridge runs south to Škrlatica, the second highest peak of the Eastern Julians passing, on the way, through Špik—unmistakable for its immense triangular peak. There *are* two marked ways on this mountain—to the summit. But not up its 950 metre North Face.

Iof di Montasio, also known as Poliski Špik (2754m), is the second highest peak in all the Julians and forms part of a group stretching nearly 8 kilometres along fine ridges and through numerous summits topping 2000 metres. Its northern face holds the snow and is noted for route-finding problems.

A unique feature of the Julians is the chance they give to the mountaineer—the person who, not necessarily an experienced rock climber, has a deft foot, a head for heights, a love of exploration and a sense of fulfilment in the mountains.

Reference has been made to 'marked ways', and these are the key. These routes are skilfully constructed and their developers are as well-known as the first ascenders of a climbing route. They are marked on maps by red lines and on the ground by a system of red circles on the white rock. These markings are almost always clear and easy to follow, though I have seen even a main route obliterated by snow and all the mountain features disappear in a white-out of dazzling and frightening cloud. Only a close familiarity with the area, and long perseverance, enabled us to emerge on the right route—and this when a party of eighteen primary school children with inadequate clothing (yes, it sometimes happens in Yugoslavia too) had trustingly chosen to follow our lead.

All mountains are potentially dangerous. The Julian Alps may not be as high as their Swiss counterparts (they are all under 3000 metres), and on the whole may be lacking in snow and ice, but they have storms, sheer cliffs, crumbling pinnacles, knife-edge ridges 300 metres above the valley floor, and vistas of mountains crowding each other for 16 kilometres before the next motor road or village can be reached.

Through this daunting region the marked ways can be safely followed by any responsible, sensible mountaineer. They give access to all the main summits, each with a different grandeur and beauty, and—for those who wish it—hair-raising ascents up routes especially pioneered for their excitement.

Take, for example, the Okno route up Prisojnik (2541m). This mountain is an immense mass of rock with a vertical-seeming North Face and a vast hole (Okno) near the top through which one can look right through the mountain from north to south. You begin by taking a gentle walk of a few hundred metres from the hut, then rounding the corner you step off into space. Anyone who dislikes this start should return to the hut and play chess, because the rest is very much the same.

Trusting to iron pegs driven into the rock, you must traverse across a face which drops away sheer below and finally escape over an awkward, overhanging bulge. Higher up there is a chimney pitch about 9 metres high, quite vertical and just too narrow to climb from within, so that you are obliged to climb up its outside edges using a bridging technique. Here iron pegs and steel ropes abound but it is still an airy interlude. A second chimney ascends diagonally and you have to push your rucksack while you squirm and thrust yourself upwards to its exit.

After this an hour of good standard rock scrambling gives access to the floor of the Okno, which at close quarters is revealed as an immense gash in the mountain, with the roof far overhead almost too high to crane your neck for, and the floor composed of appallingly rotten rock where deviation off the marked route is most inadvisable. You ascend at an angle of about thirty degrees to the steep slab exit pitch at the top of the chasm. Then one final step and you are out in the sunshine—and on the summit ridge.

This is said to be the most exposed marked way in the Julian Alps.

Other airy routes are the North Wall of the Mojstrovka; the Bamberg way up Triglav; the direct route up the North Face of Prisojnik; the traverse of the face of Kanjavec on rotten rock; the North Face route (in Italy) up Mangrt—one of the most demanding (secured) routes in all the Julians; Rjavina and the Vrbanova Špica . . . all too varied to describe in a single chapter. The Slovenes have gone to town on these routes. To celebrate the sixtieth anniversary of the Alpine Club, what did they think of? Why, to create a rather special one: the Jubilee Route, a traverse of the full length of the Prisojnik ridge through *both* the 'windows'.

In general the weather is sunny and hot. The best plan then is to start at 5.00 am, finish the journey by noon or 1 o'clock, and spend the hot afternoon outside the hut with a refreshing drink in hand, marvelling at the fantastic scenery or playing chess on one of the boards from the hut. Like most mountains the Julians do tend to gather clouds in the afternoons and occasionally there will be several days of thunder, lightning, hail and rain storm.

Little snow lasts through the summer, although it can come down thickly at any time. There is a permanent snowfield on Triglav and an ice axe may also be useful to approach the North Wall of the Mojstrovka, and crampons too if you want to approach Kanin from the Rifugio Divisione Julia-Nevea in Italy.

But supposing you do not want hair-raising ascents. Supposing you love travelling over and round mountains, up to the summits and along the ridges with far-reaching views but a certain comfort underfoot—can you still enjoy the Julians? Yes, supremely!

Most Slovenes want to do the same. They have created a network of long-distance routes to open up travel all through the mountain areas, from summit to summit, from high hut to high hut, or from valley to valley. These 'transverse Alpine paths' (or 'trade routes') are specially marked on the maps. More importantly, they are well marked on the ground, for maps can only give an approximation.

Instead of a Duke of Edinburgh Gold, young people 'collect' summits and long mountain expeditions, with their achievements validated by the wardens of the huts, and by rubber stamps and signing-in books which are placed in weather-proof containers on every summit.

For the route to the top of the highest mountain, Triglav, the Alpine Association has created especially secure protection because it is almost a place of pilgrimage. I have encountered a twenty-stone lady high on its slopes between two guides (one pulling and one pushing), who told me that she climbed Triglav every year.

My favourite journey is the high-level traverse from the western side of Prisojnik to the Pogačnikov Dom, taking about seven hours. It begins across wide mountain slopes of juniper and mountain rose, through pine forests and cool fragrant woodland glades where dappled sunlight filters here and there and then, above the treeline, out into the heat, the blinding sunlight and the wild rocky environment of a high valley, out of which the route zig-zags for 360 metres up through the welcome shade of the Razor south-west wall to the saddle.

I think the greatest moment of this traverse is when, all quite unsuspectingly, you reach the rim and peer over the top and are suddenly greeted with a view into an entirely new world. About 300 metres below is a limestone landscape which seems more like the surface of the moon. It is a huge area of completely bare rock, a vast chaotic jumble of scree, towers, outcrops and slabs, carved by erosion throughout aeons of time without any intrusion from mankind.

In this hostile landscape is a hut, solidly built by goodness-knows what ingenuity and effort; a safe haven for exhausted travellers whatever storm they may have passed through. There is one simple exit from this hut, a route 1500 metres down to another

valley system altogether. This is the way the mule train used to supply the hut and take the laundry.

Pogacnikov Dom, a typical Julian Alps hut. (Photo: Hamish Brown.)

But for those who want to continue their mountain journey, a route leads over nearby summits to the Ljukna Pass, set amongst flowery mountain slopes at the head of the Vrata valley, and then up again to the Triglav plateau where there is another world of huts and peaks.

The Julian valleys are beautiful and many of them can be explored by car for at least some distance, as I proved for myself after a severe illness when, although desperately disappointed that I could not reach the tops, I had a marvellous holiday all the same. There are huts offering drinks and simple meals in surroundings which seem a million miles away from city life. Many of the valleys are steep-sided and thickly forested, with meadows in the lower regions. If there is a river, it will be glacier-blue and clear. There are paths in the woods for gentle exploration, and constantly changing insights into the mountain background. The whole area is noted for its mountain flora and some of the villages are full of cultivated flowers. Famous travellers have described the Sava as the most beautiful valley in Europe and the Soča as the most beautiful river.

Where the climber will probably rush straight into the northern approaches, the car traveller may like to go round by the south, setting out along the Sava Valley through Bled, a civilised town surrounding a beautiful lake with a swimming temperature of around 21°C. From here a country road runs westward to Lake Bohinj, with the Hotel Zlatorog (meaning chamois). Starting again from Bled by a more southerly road, it is possible to wander gently round the Triglav massif right to Bovec in the west, a pleasant little place to stay and a good centre.

Across the Predl Pass into Italy it would be a short drive to the Mangrt lakes—two tiny, intensely blue lakes in a circle of mountains, where it is possible to camp—or to Valbruna, Kugy's favourite valley. One can return to Slovenia by going west through Rateče, to the skiing village of Kranjska Gora, and then turn south for the Vršič Pass at 1611 metres (a good motor road, though some cars have to stop to cool the engine), and down the Trenta Valley along the River Soča. Its source is in a cave with a small hut at the roadside nearby and its lower reaches are noted for the blueness of the water and for powerful gorges. It is loved by canoeists.

As well as exploring the valleys the non-climber has ways of reaching some of the heights. For instance it is possible to drive up the Lepena valley (the road is poor in some years) and have a meal at the new little hut of Koča Pri Krnski Jererih just below the summit. From Bovec a cable car in the Kanin range rises to over 2000 metres and from there a gentle walk gives access to the fine viewpoint of Presteljenik in about one hour. And I myself once reached one of the highest huts on the back of a mule from the mule-train which used to carry the supplies.

Slovenia is a magical place for any lover of mountains.

JERZY W GAJEWSKI
The Carpathians

Curving like a bow across the map of Central Europe run the Carpathians, a range of mountains some 1300 kilometres long and between 100 and 350 kilometres wide.

Flying over them one gains a variety of impressions. Passing across their western section, for example from Warsaw to Budapest, you notice a distinct and isolated island of peaks often partly-covered by snow and surrounded by lower mountains that appear from above like small hills. This island of peaks is the Tatra. More to the east, if flying from Sofia to Warsaw, you will be surprised by a very different landscape below; a landscape of greenery with a sea of mountains covered by forest, and understand then why some writers have called this region the 'Forest Carpathians'.

The range acts as a major divide across Central Europe and cradles the Danube valley more or less from Bratislava in the west to Orsova, near Iron Gate Gorge to the east of Belgrade. In fact the small hills on the south bank of the Danube in Austria belong to the Carpathians too, which may be of particular interest to visitors travelling from Vienna. In the north and west the Moravian Gate, the valley of the Morava River and Vienna Dale cut the Carpathians from the Sudets, the mountains of Bohemia and the Alps; similarly in the south the Danube ravine divides the Carpathian range from the mountains of Serbia.

In general these mountains are divided into three distinctive regions: the Western Carpathians, which cover parts of Czechoslovakia, Poland and Hungary up to the Lupków Pass (657m); the Eastern Carpathians which curve towards the south and mostly lie within the USSR and Romania as far as the Prahova valley and the Predeal Pass (1051m); and lying west to east, the range of the Southern Carpathians—known also as the Transylvanian Alps of Romania. In recent times the Eastern and Southern Carpathians have been geographically accepted as one, although the former tripartite partitioning is still widely acknowledged.

The Carpathians were formed in the Cretaceous and Tertiary periods and raised during the same orogenetic movements that built the Alps, although their geology is rather more complex than that of the Alps. They consist of limestones, marl, sandstone and slate, and crystalline rocks such as granite and gneiss.

The outer range has a different formation to that of the inner; it runs all along the north and east rim of the Carpathian bow, from the Danube in Czechoslovakia to the Dimbovita River in Romania, and owes its existence to the Tertiary period. This outer lining is composed mostly of sandstone, marl or slate and includes a number of the smaller ranges with rounded summits like Biele Karpaty (the White Carpathians),

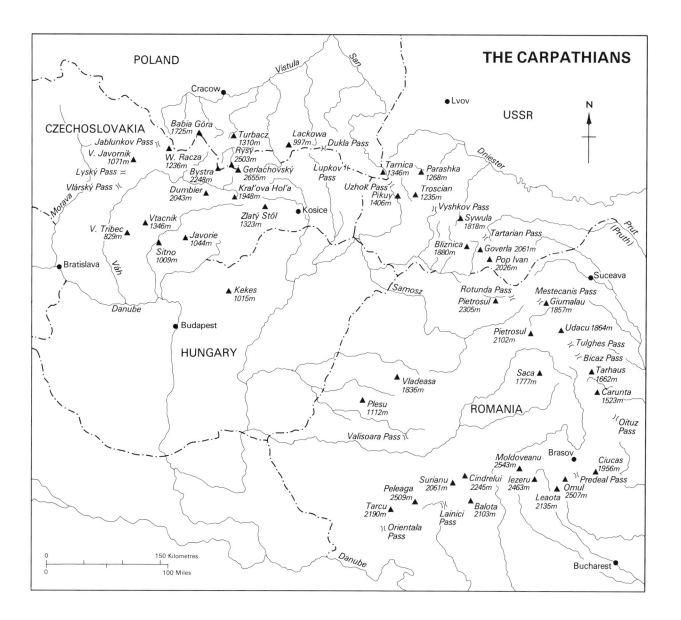

THE CARPATHIANS

Javorniky, Beskidy Zachodnie and Beskidy Wschodnie (the Western and Eastern Beskidys), and Muntii Moldovei (the Moldavian Carpathians). In the Eastern Beskidys minor ranges run parallel one to another and create ridge-and-valley mountains. Similarly in the Moldavian Carpathians, between the valleys of the Bistrita and Buzău rivers, the ranges run from north-west to south-east. The most interesting is that of the Ceahlau with mountains up to 1911 metres, noted for their decaying rocks, and the peak of Mt Ciucas (1956m) in the Buzău Mountains, built of sedimentary rocks.

In the north, on the Polish/Ukrainian side, the lower range of Pogórze joins the outer Carpathians with their low hills mostly reaching between 350-500 metres, but attaining their maximum altitude east of the Wisloka River on Pogórze Dynowskie (672m).

The inner Carpathians however, are composed of older formations like granite, gneiss, crystalline schist, and also dolomite and limestone, but in some areas there are magma intrusions too. In the inner zone essential crystalline parts can be seen with typical high mountain sculpture. This is especially true in the Tatra and Fatra Mountains of Slovakia and the Transylvanian region of Romania (the Rodna Mountains, Southern Carpathians and Apuseni Mountains). On the western side Transylvania is closed by the Apuseni Mountains, of which the Bihor massif reaches 1849 metres.

At the time of the range's creation there were volcanic outflows on the south side. This area belongs to the inner Carpathians and is divided into minor ranges such as the Ptačnik, Matra and Bükk Mountains in the west, and the Gurghiu and Harghita Mountains in the east. But the main part of the range has been shaped by river erosion, while the highest regions (the Tatra, Fǎgǎras or Retezat Mountains) have typical Alpine characteristics, created by the glaciers of the Pleistocene period.

The climate here is typical of the temperate regions, but it is greatly influenced by the higher mountains where precipitation is heaviest in early summer (when rainstorms are notorious) or late autumn. Annual rainfall varies from 600 millimetres (24in) in the valleys, to 1800 millimetres (70in) and more on the summits, and floods occur during early summer in most years. Snowfall is heavy in winter and ice forms to give fine, if harsh conditions for the committed climber in the loftiest regions. Snow cover lasts for about five months of the year but in the highest parts of the Tatra or Fǎgǎras Mountains it may extend for as long as eight months, and snowfall even in August is no rarity. There is some permanent snow in a number of couloirs and shadowed hollows.

There is plenty of evidence of landscaping by Pleistocene glaciers, for there are many glacial cirques and lakes to be found among the Fǎgǎras Mountains (the lakes of Capra, Caltun and Bilea), and in the Tatras where there are almost two hundred, the largest being Lake Morskie Oko. Some of the other, larger lakes in the Carpathians are artificial reservoirs like that of Zywiec in the Western Beskidys, Lake Solina in the Bieszczady Mountains, Lake of Bikaz on the Ceahlau Mountains and Lake of Vidraru in the heart of the Fǎgǎras Mountains.

Forest covers most of the hillsides. Deciduous forests of oak, hornbeam and beech dominate the lower levels to about 600 to 750 metres, but in the Southern Carpathians steppe-plants are common too. In the higher regions, up to 1200 to 1400 metres, lush mixed forests of beech and fir take over, and above this level conifers—mostly spruce—reach to 1800 metres. In the Tatras there are larch and stone pine (*Pinus cembra*), while the dwarf mountain pine (*Pinus mughus*) is found in many high mountain regions where it perfectly complements the rugged scenery. At a similar altitude in the

Eastern Carpathians alders are common.

Crowning the higher ranges is a layer of peak and pasture—pasture being given a variety of regional names. In the Eastern Beskidys these pastures, known as *poloniny*, are seen advancing immediately above the deciduous woodlands and are unique to this region.

The wild life of the Carpathians is not very different from that of other European ranges, but there's a rich population of animals well-known among amateur huntsmen. Symbolic of the mountains are the red and roe deer, wild boar and wolves, as well as chamois and marmot. (The Tatras form the northern limit for chamois—the Carpathian species being the largest of them all.) A surprise confrontation with the European brown bear should not be discounted as a possibility—not only in the Tatra National Park, but also more to the east, in the Eastern Beskidys and in the Southern Carpathians. Naturally any such meeting is a memorable experience!

There is a wide selection of flowering plants too; edelweiss, crocus, gentian and the glorious mixture of wild flowers of the mountain pastures—especially abundant in the Beskidys. In addition to numerous alpines seen in other European ranges (notably those of Scandinavia) the Carpathians boast no fewer than thirty-five endemic species.

Some regions have been given the status of National Parks, like those of the Tatras and the Pieniny Mountains (on both sides of the Polish/Czechoslovakian frontier) and regions in Babia Góra (the highest part of the Western Beskidys); in the Polish section of the Bieszczady Mountains and on the northern hillsides of the Charnogora in the Ukrainian Eastern Beskidys, in the Retezat Mountains of Romania and elsewhere. There are an even greater number of small reservation areas in other parts.

The character and landscape of the extensive Carpathian range varies considerably, as does its accessibility and degree of touristic development. For example, the lower ranges of Malé Karpatry (the so-called Little Carpathians) not far from Bratislava, are visited mainly by local inhabitants of the town. Equally the Silesian Beskidys, divided by the Czechoslovak/Polish border, are the nearest mountains for the residents of the industrial areas of Moravska Ostrava and Katowice. The main ranges of the Western Beskidys on the Polish side are visited at weekends by the townspeople of Cracow and in summer and winter by visitors from all over Poland. (By contrast with Romania and Czechoslovakia, Poland's land area over 500 metres is very small, but within it is concentrated the greatest number of tourists.) The Western Beskidys up to 1725 metres are well developed for walking but their eastern part (the Lower Beskidys), which culminate in Mt Lackowa (997m), retain a reputation for being wild and undeveloped. In fact this wild landscape is at present undergoing change and previously empty valleys are now crossed by new roads, while the numerous wooden Orthodox churches hidden among the hills, as well as the architecture of cemeteries from the First World War (the whole area was the scene of some major battles in 1914/15), adds enchantment to these otherwise modest mountains.

The Bieszczady Mountains, situated more to the east, are typical of the Eastern Carpathians with their wide views over the somewhat empty scenery of the 'poloniny' pastures. Uninhabited mountain ranges are the domain of the Eastern Carpathians of Romania. Huge spaces, broken only by the peaks of the 'Forest Carpathians', accompany hikers who set out to cross the wilderness—a labyrinth of mountain massifs—equipped either for backpacking, or for journeys leading from hut to hut.

By contrast with the Romanian mountains, Czechoslovakia is better developed and more prepared for tourists. Tourist hotels are situated especially among the Vysoké and Nizke Tatry (the High and Lower Tatra), and in the Malá and Vel'ka Fatra (the Little and Great Fatras). The Little Fatra culminates in the Vel'ki Fatranský Kryváň (1709m), but its centre is the Vrátna valley, accessible through the Tiesňavy ravine with a lovely view to the rocky Mt Vel'ky Rozsutec (1610m). The Little Fatra is 50 kilometres long and cut off by the Váh River between Strečno and Vrútka. Confusingly, the Great Fatra (45km) reaches only 1592 metres.

The Lower Tatra Mountains run parallel to the main Tatra chain, the two being separated by the wide valley of the Váh River. Eighty kilometres long, with their highest summit being Ďumbier (2043m), these peaks were formed of crystalline rocks, dolomite and limestone, and are famous for the Demänovské Caves near Liptovský Mikuláš. Similarly the numerous ranges of limestone have created magnificent karst landscapes, especially in the Slovenský kras to the west of Košice.

The rivers Olt, Ialomita and Arges in Romania, and the Horned River in Slovakia, have carved defiles here and there but the connoisseur of picturesque canyons will prefer the Pieniny Mountains on the Polish/Czechoslovak border. The beauties of the Dunajec River there can be observed equally from the 'Falcon Trail' (a marked footpath running above the valley), as from the river itself where trips can be made by wooden raft to Szczawnica-spa through an infinite variety of scenery on the sometimes foaming torrent. (On this journey it is possible to see storks, ringed plovers and hoopoes.)

Beside the Tatra Mountains, where excessive numbers of tourists are partly limited by National Park regulations, Slovakian areas of the Little Fatras and Lower Tatras are famous for their popular ski resorts. It is true that the Štrbské Pleso in the High Tatra is noted as a modern ski resort, but the Jasna region of the Lower Tatra, culminating in Mt Chopok (2204m) above the Demänovská valley, and the Vrátna valley in the Little Fatras, are becoming more popular among today's skiers. On the Polish side, beside Zakopane, the same could be said of Szczyrk in the Silesian Beskidys, Korbielów at the foot of Mt Pilsko (1557m) in the Zywiec Beskidys, and also the region of Krynica-spa. In the Southern Carpathians, ski centres are in Sinaia and Poiana Brasov, not far from Brasov, the main town of Transylvania. All cableways and lifts go in the direction of the Bucegi Mountains but Sinaia is also known as an important tourist village and former residence of the Romanian monarchy.

Krynica in Poland, as well as Piešt'any at the foot of the Považský Inovec massif in Slovakia, and Băile Herculane in the western part of the Southern Carpathians of Romania, are the more distinguished spas among many smaller resorts like Trenčinské Teplice, Smokovec, Bardejov, Yaremcha and others.

Most of these mountains have been developed for walkers. In Czechoslovakia and Poland there are many kilometres of waymarked footpaths leading to peaks, passes and places of interest. (In all of Poland's mountains, not simply among the Carpathians, there are almost 8400 kilometres of marked tourist trails.) Footpath signs are composed of three stripes: two outer stripes of white and the middle one of either red, blue, green, yellow or black. In Hungary trails have recently been marked in a similar fashion, but in Romania the gamut of signs is much wider, with stripes, crosses, circles or triangles in different colours. In the USSR walking trips are organised along fixed trails from main villages to the ridge of the Gorgany and Chernogora Mountains in the Eastern Beskidys.

Folk customs are kept alive among the Carpathian highlanders and many regional groups may be distinguished by their costumes, music and art. Architectural styles in the mountain villages and farmsteads are distinctive and any visit to Bucharest should at least contain a trip to the Museum of the Romanian Village. (While staying in Zakopane it is also worthwhile visiting the old wooden village of Chocholów.) The growing number of Skansen museums, for example in Zubrzyca, Sanok and Lvov, help to retain a knowledge of time-honoured customs and crafts. Mountain peasants living at the foot of the Tatras, as well as in some parts of the Western Beskidys, in the Pieniny Mountains in Poland and Slovakia, continue to wear traditional costumes, especially on Sundays. In the Eastern Carpathians groups of 'Guruls' live in the shadow of the Chernogora range, near the peak of Goverla (2061m), highest of the Eastern Beskidys on the USSR/Romanian border. The colourful costumes of the mountain people are as well-known as the painted wooden Orthodox churches in the Suceava valley of Romania and the rich variety of artistic activity is likely to arouse the admiration of visitors. Traditional music and dancing are popularised every autumn during the 'International Festival of the Mountain Lands' in Zakopane.

Of course the majority of walkers and climbers visiting the Carpathians are interested mainly in the highest and most rugged parts of the mountains. In the first place then, mention should be made of the Tatras, for theirs are the highest summits between the Alps and the Caucasus. On the Czechoslovak side their highest peak is Gerlachovský (or Gerlach, 2655m); on the Polish side, Rysy (2499m). Other important mountains are the Făgăras in the Southern Carpathians, with the highest peaks being Mt Moldoveanu (2543m) and Mt Negoiu (2536m).

The Tatras, however, are neither high nor extensive by comparison with other mountains. From east to west they stretch only 53 kilometres, while in breadth they measure no more than about 18 kilometres. Between the Hutianské Pass (905m) in the west, and the Zdiarske Pass (1081m) in the east, they cover an area of about 750 square kilometres, and only a fifth of this belongs to Poland.

Situated at the foot of the Tatras are a good many important villages and tourist centres that cater for increasing numbers of visitors, giving these mountains an air of supremacy out of all proportion to their size. Access to them is easy from Zakopane, Kościeliska or Bukowina in Poland, and in Tatranská Lomnica, Smokovec or Štrbské

on the southern side. These are villages and towns with a long tradition as centres of tourism, as spas or as ski resorts. However, their face has been steadily changing in recent years. Zakopane, for example, was simply a small highland village in the nineteenth century but it has now grown into a town of more than 30,000 inhabitants. Some streets, like Kościeliska Street, still preserve the character of the old village and are dominated by the low, wooden houses of the farming communities.

On the Slovakian side a ribbon of villages and hamlets, roads and railway runs parallel to the mountains. The main travellers' centre here is Poprad, but the settlements of Smokovec, and particularly Tatranská Lomnica, are popular with climbers and general tourists alike.

Shepherds' huts in the Chocholowska Pasture—Polish Tatras. (Photo: Jerzy Gajewski.)

142

Mountains huts of the Polish Tatra Association (PTTK) on the north side, and mountain hotels and hostels (some with the character of huts) in valleys on the south, grant easy access to walks and climbs.

The Tatra Mountains belong to the inner Carpathian chain and rise like an island over the valleys of the Dunajec, Poprad, Orohava and Váh rivers which spring from them. The range is divided into three parts: the Zapadné Tatry (the Western Tatras), with the highest point being Mt Bystra (2250m) in Czechoslovakia; the Vysoké Tatry (High Tatras) in the east; and Belanské Tatry on the north-eastern side, culminating in Mt Havran (2154m). These three separate regions are broken by the passes of Liliowe and Kopské.

Huge limestone peaks dominate the Belanské Tatry, particularly in the west, with the so-called 'Red Peaks' (Mt Bobrowiec and Mt Kominiarski) and Mt Giewont whose outline is very much the symbol of Zakopane in the same way that the Matterhorn dominates Zermatt (although Mt Giewont is only 1909 metres high). In the east, Mt Muráň and Zdiarska Vidla are the dominating features. Major valleys like Kościeliska and Chocholowska in Poland, and Tichá, Roháčška, Jalovecká, Jamnicka and Račkova in Czechoslovakia, entice footpaths onto the main ridge of the Western Tatras.

Of more interest to mountaineers are the climbers' trails of the granitic High Tatras. Here, the highest peaks of all are situated on the Slovakian side; rugged, dramatic and offering a jagged crestline: Mt Gerlachovský, Mt Lomnický (2634m), Mt L'adový (2630m), Mt Pyšný and Mt Vysoká. Curiously, Mt Kriváň, the national peak of the Slovakian people, is not among the highest, reaching only 2496 metres. The peaks of L'adový and Vysoká draw the attention of visitors by their fascinating shapes and among the outstanding viewpoints mention must be made of the Rusinowa or Kopieniec pastures on the Polish side, reached even by ordinary tourists after a walk of $1\frac{1}{2}$–2 hours.

Marked trails prepared by the National Park authorities lead to wonderful viewpoints and peaks: to Swinica, Kozi Wierch, Szpiglasowy Wierch, Rysy (with its magnificent view of Mt Gerlachovský and the 300-metre-high crag of the Ganek Gallery), Slavkovský, Kriváň and the passes of Zawrat, Kozia, Chalubiński's Gate, Prielom and Sedielko and many more. Other routes are accessible only to *bona fide* mountaineers who are members of climbing clubs, to those with a permit, or to those in the company of an authorised guide.

On the Polish flanks of the High Tatra, hikers as well as climbers are especially attracted to three major valleys: Sucha Woda (Dry Water), which is headed by the Gasienicowa pastures; Pieciu Stawów Polskich (Valley of the Five Polish Lakes) with the Siklawa Waterfalls being the highest waterfalls in the Tatras; and Rybi Potok (the Fish's Stream) headed by the Morskie Oko lake and its lovely cirque. Some of the most challenging of all the Tatras' rock routes are concentrated around this cirque, and the PTTK hut by the lake (the oldest hut in the Polish Carpathians) serves as a meeting place for climbers and is the starting point for the more serious of Poland's climbing ventures.

The peaks which separate Gasienicowa and the Five Polish Lakes valleys, are threaded on the 'Eagle's Trail', an airy, sheer footpath designed and created in 1903-06. Among the peaks is the inconspicuous top of Zamarla Turnia, whose first ascent of the South Wall in 1910 opened a new era of climbing in the Tatras. There followed successes on difficult routes among the harsh walls of such peaks as Mt Siroká veža, Malý Kežmarský, Rumanov, Ganek Galery, Kozi Wierch (the main peak on the 'Eagle's Trail'), Mnich, Kazalnica and others. The last of these is situated on the pillar of Mt Mieguszowiecki (2438m), and its tremendous crest closes the cirque of the Black and Morskie Oko Lakes. (The traverse of Mieguszowiecki is a noted grade IV route under summer conditions.)

The Slovakian High Tatras open to the south with some great valleys, such as Furkotská and Mlynická (noted for the Skok Waterfall); the Mengusovská valley where the long and easy path to Mt Rysy begins (the *Tatranská magistrala*, a marked trail which runs parallel with the main range, also passes through here), and where the Popradské Lake is as well-loved as Lake Morskie Oko on the Polish side. The Velicka valley (with the 'Sliezsky dom' hotel) is another splendid glen through which an important trail runs from the south to the northern side of the mountains by way of the Pol´sky hreben Pass, and is also the starting point for trips to Mt Gerlachovský. A route also goes to the Batizovská valley, a wild cirque surrounded by great rocky walls, where a classic descent from Mt Gerlachovský finishes. There are the Vel´ka and Malá Studena valleys, easily accessible from the station at Hrebienok (a funicular goes from Stary Smokovec), which are interesting for newcomers to high mountain landscapes. Among the highest tops are Mt Javorovy (a rescue attempt on its North Face in 1910 and the death of Klimek Bachleda are still remembered today), Prostredný hrot, Mt L'adovy, Pyšny and Lomnický. On the other hand, the long northern valleys of Javorová and Bielovodská (the Valley of White Water) create a jagged wall of mountains whose details vanish in the shadow of dark, gloomy rocks.

Until the middle of the nineteenth century Mt Lomnický (Lomnica) was thought to be the highest mountain in the Tatras. In the latter half of the eighteenth century it was a goal for treasure seekers and later for scientists, with the British naturalist Robert Townshead making the first ascent in 1793. In 1805 the summit was reached by Stanislaw Staszic, a Polish scientist, in the company of local guides and huntsmen. Today there is a *téléférique* to the top of Mt Lomnický from the Slovakian side, while on the northern flanks Kasprowy Wierch is reckoned to be Poland's finest skiing kingdom. Its West Face is quite magnificent.

The first recorded ascent of Mt Gerlachovský took place in 1834 by a schoolteacher, J Still, his brother-in-law, Gelhof, a miller by the name of M U Spitzkopf, and two un-named huntsmen. However, it is thought possible that the ubiquitous chamois hunter might have been there before them. John Ball, first President of the Alpine Club, climbed Mt L'adový (Ladowy), third of the Tatra peaks, in 1843, but again it is thought probable that it had been climbed earlier. The trail 'Over the Horse' is the easiest way to the summit.

Above: Hoch Wilde in the Otztal Alps – The Austrian Alps. (Photo: Cecil Davies.)

Below: The view from Erzherzog-Johann Hut on the Adlersruhe – The Austrian Alps. (Photo: Cecil Davies.)

Above: Hay meadow above the Zillertal – The Austrian Alps. (Photo: Kev Reynolds.)

Below: Westfalenhaus and the Längentaler Glacier – The Austrian Alps. (Photo: Cecil Davies.)

Above: Cima Una, formerly known as the Einser Kofel – The Dolomites. (Photo: C Douglas Milner.)

Below: The Catinaccio Hut in the Vajolet district – The Dolomites. (Photo: C Douglas Milner.)

Above: Forcella Giralbo – The Dolomites. (Photo: C Douglas Milner.)

Below: Probably the best-known of all Dolomite summits, the Tre Cima di Lavaredo. (Photo: C Douglas Milner.)

Triglav (2863m) – The Julian Alps. (Photo: Dudley Stevens.)

The lake of Morskie Oko in the Polish Tatras, with the Mnich rising from it – The Carpathians. (Photo: Jerzy Gajewski.)

Above: The canyon of the Dunajec River in the Pieniny Mountains – The Carpathians. The river forms the Czechoslovakia/Poland border. (Photo: Jerzy Gajewski.)

Below: In the Buzau Mountains of Romania – The Carpathians. (Photo: Jerzy Gajewski.)

Above: Shkhelda (4320m) from Ushba – The Caucasus. (Photo: Mick Fowler.)

Below: Dykh Tau; Mummery route on the left spur, Band/Harris route on right – The Caucasus. (Photo: George Band.)

Above: North Face of the Vignemale – The Pyrénées. (Photo: Kev Reynolds.)

Below: Balaitous, most westerly of the 3000 metre peaks, seen here from the summit of Pic de Cambales above the Marcadau valley – The Pyrénées. (Photo: Kev Reynolds.)

Above: Pic du Midi d'Ossau, seen from the west where the Petit Pic appears higher than the Grand Pic – The Pyrénées. (Photo: Kev Reynolds.)

Below: Estany de Mar and Montarto on the western edge of the Encantados region – The Pyrénées. (Photo: Kev Reynolds.)

Peña Vieja – The Picos de Europa. (Photo: Hamish Brown.)

The Picos above Potes – The Picos de Europa. (Photo: Hamish Brown.)

Above: Looking south from the village of Gardhiki on Mt Kakardhitsa – Greece. (Photo: Tim Salmon.)

Below: The western end of the Vikos gorge – Greece. (Photo: Tim Salmon.)

Above: Kali Komi, a typical Pindos village house – Greece. (Photo: Tim Salmon.)

Below: Vlachs shearing their sheep in preparation for the spring transhumance – Greece. (Photo: Tim Salmon.)

The head of the Restonica valley, one of the approaches to Monte Rotondo – Corsica. (Photo: Kev Reynolds.)

The Agnone valley below Monte d'Oro – Corsica. (Photo: Kev Reynolds.)

Exploration of the Tatras was initially a slow affair, but serious rock climbing began with the ascent by Pawlikowski and Sieczka of Mnich (the Monk) in 1879. This little peak has some very hard lines on it today.

Between the wars many difficult face routes were established, among them the North Face of Maly Kiezmarski. But since the Second World War, with an increase in the development of aid climbing, the standard of routes achieved in the Tatras has been impressive, to say the least, while many local climbers (particularly from Poland) who have learned their craft on these small, yet challenging peaks, have gone on to make a name for themselves on some of the world's biggest mountains.

A V SAUNDERS
The Caucasus

Clinton Dent, then President of the Alpine Club, said in 1887 that the Caucasus were without doubt 'the grandest chain of ice mountains that Europe can claim.' This statement has two points of interest. In the first place it is true—and the facts support it. The main peaks are almost 1000 metres taller than their Alpine counterparts, their faces often half as big again as their western equivalent, so in scale the Caucasus are between the Alpine and the Himalayan. Secondly, the words speak from the past, in fact a hundred years ago, for the great bulk of Caucasian climbing literature is from the

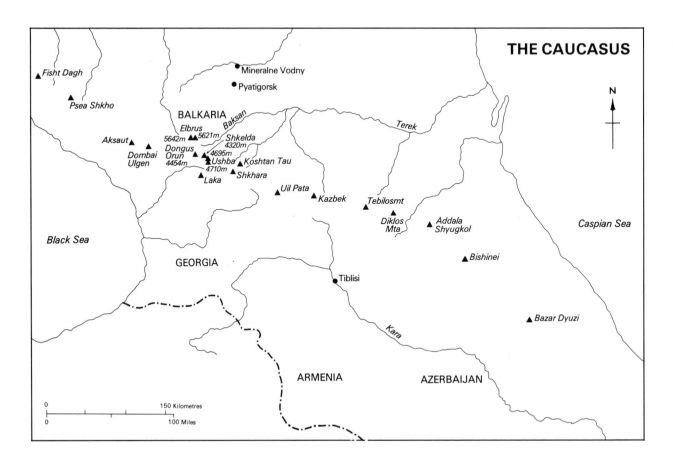

THE CAUCASUS

Fisht Dagh

Psea Shkho

Mineralne Vodny

Pyatigorsk

BALKARIA

Baksan

Terek

Elbrus
Aksaut 5642m 5621m *Shkelda*
Dombai *Dongus* 4320m
Ulgen *Orun* 4695m
4454m *Ushba* *Koshtan Tau*
4710m
Laka *Shkhara*

Uil Pata

Kazbek

Tebilosmt

Diklos Mta *Addala Shyugkol*

Black Sea

GEORGIA

Bishinei

Caspian Sea

Tiblisi

Kara

Bazar Dyuzi

ARMENIA **AZERBAIJAN**

N

0   150 Kilometres
0   100 Miles

nineteenth century. For those who appreciate such things, these mountains exude an almost tangible sensation of history.

The Caucasus form a wall from the Black Sea to the Caspian Sea, a wall that divides Europe from Asia and lies entirely within the political bounds of the Soviet Union. Like so many things within that entity the Caucasus present an ethnological paradox, for the range is peopled by the Balkarians (Central Asian Moslems) in the (European) north, while the (Asian) south is occupied by Georgia, Christendom's second oldest state.

The Tsar subjugated Georgia and her Moslem neighbours in the mid-nineteenth century. Russian unification subsequently brought political stability at a time when, by coincidence, the Golden Age of Mountaineering was coming to a close. The great peaks of the Alps had all been conquered and alpinists looking for virgin summits began to turn their eyes towards the east.

It is fairly well known that Alpine Club members were involved in the early exploration of the Caucasus, but what is perhaps not appreciated is the extent to which the Club dominated that pioneering. Of the ten highest peaks, no fewer than nine were first ascended by members of the A.C. The role call is familiar to students of mountaineering history; the names include, in no particular order: Horace Walker, A W Moore, Clinton Dent, Tom Longstaff, A F Mummery and honorary member, Vittorio Sella. As a rule these gentlemen were accompanied by their guides: Peter Knubel, François Devouassoud, Alexander Burgener and Heinrich Zurfluh—all famous in their own right.

Freshfield's 1868 expedition to Elbrus marked the start of the so-called 'Silver Age' of mountaineering, the first venturings into the Greater Ranges. Freshfield's team not only climbed the lower summit of Elbrus but also made the first ascent of the eastern outlier, Kazbek (5047m), as well as inspecting the enormous range between these two great peaks. A period of intense British activity in the range followed.

During the decade 1886 to 1896 almost all the major peaks were conquered. None survived beyond 1903. There were tragedies, however, as well as successes, and the loss in 1888 of Donkin and Fox was as much a reverse for photography as mountaineering. The Russians accused locals of murdering the mountaineers and the following year a search party led by Freshfield located their last bivouac on Koshtan Tau, then went on to make the first ascent of the mountain. Convinced that Donkin and Fox had been lost in a climbing accident, the search party interceded on behalf of the locals, who had been threatened with Draconian punishment. In 1968 Christopher Brasher was able to write of a local 'his face lit up when Eugene told him we were English. He said his father remembered the first English climbers coming here in the last century . . . [and he] had helped Douglas Freshfield when he came to search for Donkin and Fox.'

By the turn of the century the bulk of exploration in the central Caucasus was complete and mountaineers now turned their attention to the more difficult routes. The twin summits of Ushba (4710m and 4695m), Schkelda (4320m) and similarly technical mountains, as well as the first big traverses, began to feature in the list of ascents. But the British were displaced by strong German and Austrian teams, Harold Raeburn's expedition of 1914 being the last from the British Isles before the Revolution brought this period of Caucasian history to a close.

It was not until the secessionist ambitions of the Caucasians had been suppressed again (the Balkarians had been supported by the West), that the Soviet style of mountaineering established its character during the inter-war years. It officially began in 1923, we are informed by Beletsky (*Alpine Journal* vol 61, 1957), with the mass ascent of Kazbek by 25 Georgian students. Long traverses at consistently high altitudes became fashionable. In 1938, for example, Beletsky himself led an eighteen-day traverse in the Bezingi massif from Shkhara to Lyalver. Later, in 1956, Ivan Galustov's team completed a traverse of 15 summits, spending 31 days above 4000 metres. (It is probable that these two expeditions had the benefit of supply caches *en route*.) A third characteristic of the Soviet style was the ascent of major routes by local farmers and workers, whereas before, the Tsarist tradition had seemed to involve only Muscovites. So the new leading activists included such provincials as Misha Khirgiani from Georgia, and the Abalakov brothers, Eugene and Vitali, from Siberia.

Vitali Abalakov and Misha Khirgiani dominated the scene after the Second World War to such an extent that if you take any great Caucasian face and there is an elegant rock line, that will be the Abalakov route. If the main difficulties are ice, you are probably looking at the Khirgiani route. These were hard men. One Abalakov route, the 'Islands Route' on Nakra Tau, was put up after an enforced 13 year absence from climbing due to frostbite amputations. Khirgiani died in 1962 in the Dolomites, killed by a rockfall. Eugene Abalakov, the younger brother, died of gas poisoning from a malfunctioning stove in the 1940s, but Vitali survived to become the grand old man of Soviet mountaineering. He eventually died in 1986.

After the Revolution, German, Austrian and Italian teams completed first ascents and repeats of several difficult routes. Typical of these classic lines being, perhaps, Muller and Tomaschek's ascent of the 2000 metre north rib of Shkhara in 1930. The route was repeated by the Soviets in 1948 and again by Band, Harris, Bull and Kustovski in 1958. The climbing appears to have been about D+/TD in grade, but the descent was by a route not much easier.

Non-military British involvement during the inter-war years was of little significance, with one notable exception. (A minor contribution was made by the great Scottish mountaineer, J H B Bell, who made the first ascent of the south-west arête of Bashil Tau (4257m) in 1930. He returned in 1932 but had no further successes.) The exception was the 1937 OUMC expedition, comprising Hodgkin, Jenkins, Beaumont and Taylor. The team climbed important new routes on four major peaks; Jailik, Adyr Su Bashi, Tetnuld and Ushba South—all over 4300 metres. The route on Ushba, the direct ascent of the South Peak via the massive 'red wall', was a particularly fine achievement and was not repeated for at least twenty years.

After 1947 the prevailing 'Cold War' brought the problems of access which were only rarely solved. Again this may have something to do with an antipathy between the Russians and the local Balkarian tribes, for during the war the German army had occupied large areas of the Caucasus and there had been bitter fighting around Elbrus. Some of the Balkarians preferred the Germans and were said to have presented Hitler with a white horse. Stalin deported the lot. In 1957 Khrushchev kept his promise to bring the Balkarians back and in the same year, perhaps by coincidence, Joyce Dunsheath was invited to accompany Soviet climbers up Elbrus.

In 1958 a party of nine British climbers visited the Bezingi and Cheget regions. They were stranded on the Ushba Plateau at 4000 metres in appalling weather and forced to retreat empty handed. Better luck was to be had in the Bezingi. There they climbed several routes, the best being the route climbed by George Band and Mike Harris on the South Face of Dykh Tau (5198m), Europe's third summit.

In 1962 and 1970 Hamish MacInnes led strong parties to the Cheget area where they repeated the arduous traverse of Schkelda over twelve days, and one of the hard lines on the North Face of Pik Shchurovski. Meanwhile the main actors on the Caucasian stage were climbers from the eastern bloc. Routes of the most extreme Alpine difficulty were established, on precipices such as Ushba's 'Mirror Wall' and the imposing North Face of Chatyn Tau.

The Soviets inaugurated International Mountaineering Camps in 1974, since when access to these beautiful mountains has become straightforward, if a little long-winded. The system holds many advantages for the visiting westerner—other than the fact that it is unavoidable. There are usually four 'Camps' a year; one in each of the seasons. The summer camp is in two sessions of about four weeks each, which run consecutively and could be linked together to give a longer period in the mountains. This is an option frequently adopted by eastern bloc teams, though less often by westerners. The spring and winter camps offer a certain amount of skiing, in addition to the dubious pleasures of winter mountaineering.

By the standards of a western climber budgeting for say, Chamonix, the cost of visiting the Caucasus is high, but the value is good. For the payment of a lump sum all costs from Moscow to the climbing destination and back are covered. In 1988 this sum was $1000, plus the price of a return journey to Moscow.

Accommodation in the mountains is, almost unbelievably, a four-storey hotel. Food is taken extremely seriously. Breakfast, for example, is a feast of cheeses, cold meats, hamburgers, peas, eggs, rolls, yoghurts and so on. All the food necessary for climbing and walking is freely available from the hotel stores, although a supply of instant coffee and dried milk might be useful for those unable, or unwilling, to make do with Russian black tea and their delicious ground coffee. Fuel for mountain stoves is syphoned from the Camp bus, whose petrol is guaranteed to clog any jet, so a self-pricking petrol stove is essential for those considering the longer or more serious routes. We took an MSR and lost our pricker among the boulders of a bivouac. Using the wires from a head torch we were able to fashion a substitute (useful tip, that), but we still had to dismantle the stove to clear the jet each time we used it.

There are no mountain huts of the kind found in the Alps. Some of the valleys have 'sporting camps' which bear an uncanny resemblance to our holiday camps but these are always far below the snow line. The only apparent exception to this rule is 'Priut', the staging post *en route* to Elbrus. There are no *téléfériques,* except to Priut and to Cheget, neither of which are of significant value to the mountaineer.

This lack of facilities colours the climbing here. Our experience on Ushba is probably fairly typical. We spent Day One walking up to the German bivouac on the North Shkhelda Glacier, carrying a bivouac tent up to this point in order to have a place of retreat in bad weather. Day Two was spent climbing the horrible Ushba icefall to a bivouac on the edge of the Ushba Plateau. Day Three, we sat out a short storm. Day Four, we descended to the start of our route and climbed this to the summit of the mountain. Day Five consisted of a long descent to the German bivouac, and on Day Six we finally returned to our base at Azau. No lifts, no huts. Such 'old-fashioned' mountaineering is only for real amateurs.

The Soviets are very keen on safety. These mountains are large, access to them can be lengthy and rescues are difficult to organise. There used to be a helicopter but that crashed decades ago and the remains can be bivouacked in beneath Nakra Tau. The Soviet answer to the problem is radio. Each party carries a walkie-talkie and has to communicate their position and situation three times a day. The idea is that a party in difficulties can often be helped by another party in the neighbourhood. There used to be strict 'time controls' but the use of radio has made that system redundant. In addition to the radio, the Soviets will require climbers to undertake a training climb before embarking on ambitious projects. The training climb serves for acclimatisation and gives some idea of that party's level of competence.

The International Camp is based in the Upper Baksan valley. Mountains available are those accessed from the tributary valleys: Elbrus, those of the Cheget valley, the Adyl Su and Adyr Su. The Bezingi valley, reached from the lower Baksan, is not currently available to western visitors, but is noted here both because of its intrinsic importance to the region, and in the expectation that it will one day be open again to western climbers.

Elbrus is the highest mountain in Europe (West Peak, 5642m; East Peak, 5621m), and lies north of the main Caucasian massif. While the main range consists largely of plutonic, granite-type rocks, Elbrus has volcanic origins. As a direct result of these origins, its slopes are relatively gentle, and on a good day the mountain looks deceptively harmless. But the lack of features combine with the mountain's height (it is the highest mountain at this end of the Caucasian chain by almost 1000 metres) to allow ferocious winds to sweep over the peak.

The 3500 metre ascent of Elbrus has lost some of the pioneering spirit enjoyed the first time it was climbed. There are now two cable cars and a chair lift; Mir Station at the edge of the Elbrus snowfields, and at 4200 metres, an enormous futuristic hut, Priut. (Priut itself almost beggars description. Imagine a three-storey silver sausage perched on a mound of lava and frozen in mid flow.) This still leaves over 1400 metres of ascent which, although more physically than technically demanding, still offers a challenge to experienced mountaineers.

The western wing of the central Caucasian massif terminates in the vast mass of Donguz Orun and its outlier, Nakra Tau. Climbs are reached from Cheget, the head of the Baksan valley.

The two principal peaks have north faces that typify something special about Caucasian climbing. The North Face of Donguz Orun is a 1500 metre wall of séracs and ice runnels. In common with most of the big ice faces of the Caucasus, the main line was first climbed by the great Svenatian ice climber Khirgiani. Nakra Tau's 1200 metre North Face, by contrast, has two prominent rock lines and the inevitable Abalakov routes.

The classic 'Islands Route' (4B) on Nakra Tau (4277m) takes the three prominent rock islands and the connecting ice ridges, finishing just left of the enormous summit cornices. This is Abalakov country, for he climbed the line after his thirteen-year absence from mountaineering. The route gives enjoyable, if straightforward, climbing; comparable to Chamonix's Frendo Spur but much more serious. There are routes on the right side of the face and a long but technically easy ridge descending to the west.

There is an enjoyable traverse of Donguz Orun (4454m) and Nakra by way of the North-East Ridge, grade 3. Further round on the North Face, a classic Khirgiani, the 'Sevens' route, so-called because the hanging glaciers and ice ramps in the face form a distinct, continental 7. In common with Nakra Tau the descent can pose something of a problem in poor weather. It is essential therefore to take a description from the Russians at the camp before setting out, as the available guidebooks and maps are of very little help.

The Adyl Su is a complex valley system. It is the shape of a hand with a thumb pointing south to Shkelda and the fingers spread out eastwards towards Bhzeduk, Ullu Kara Tau, Bashkara and Jantugan. At the eastern extremity, perhaps where the little finger might point, is a pass, the Via Tau, leading to the Adyr Su. The crossing of this pass is a popular walk involving fine views and no technical difficulties.

A motorable road follows the valley for a few kilometres, but stops short of the Green Bivouac. This is an excellent base for training climbs, as well as some of the classic grade 5 routes. The Bivouac is a magnificent meadow amphitheatre reached by a two-hour walk from the roadhead, along a river bank strewn with flowers, cattle and Russian hikers in long cheerful crocodiles.

From the Green Bivouac the best choices of peak are: Jantugan (3901m), an elegant pyramid boasting both rock and ice routes in the lower grades; Bashkara (4241m), giving fine routes in the harder grades but not without some objective dangers; and Ullu Kara Tau (4302m) which, like the confusingly named Ullu Tau Chana in the Adyr Su, sports an exciting North Face with a fine grade 5 route following the distinctive rocky rib in the centre of the face.

The following peaks, though accessible from the Green Bivouac, are best approached via the Kashkatash Glacier, about two hours below the Bivouac: Pik

Germagenov (3900m) and Cheget Kara Bashi both offer medium grade climbs on mixed terrain; Free Spain Peak (4000m) has popular rock climbs in the higher grades and appears to be something of a test piece for visiting eastern bloc climbers; while Bzeduk (4272m) has classic ridge climbs graded 3 and 4, and can be combined with a traverse of Pik Kavkas for a sporting outing.

The road to the Green Bivouac passes *en route* the mountaineering camp of Spartak. Being the principal climbers' camp (other camps cater for walking and scrambling), Spartak is the operations centre of the rescue services, and boasts the only climbing wall in the Caucasus. This is a timber affair like a serious gymnast's adventure playground—quite terrifying. The camp also contains the area's new-route book. A small library is dedicated to the collection of route descriptions, complete with photographs, diagrams and topos. After all the difficulty we had with guidebooks it was a real eye-opener to find such a wealth of information, all beautifully organised, indexed and catalogued.

From Spartak Camp a delightful path through coniferous forest, carpeted with wild strawberries, leads past the treeline to the Shkhelda Glacier. Crossing onto the glacier under the imposing North Face of Shkhelda, three hours of struggling with the trackless surface debris eventually leads to the German Bivouac. This bivouac is a collection of tent platforms on the edge of the moraine. Clearings in the weather permit awesome views of the North Face of Pik Shchurovsky, which overshadows the bivouac and guards the right bank of the Ushba icefall.

The German Bivouac is base for some of the most technical and demanding climbing in the region and is named after the pioneers who first camped here. There is no greenery, but drinking water is easily accessible and perched on a rock a hundred metres above the glacier is a ramshackle wooden structure which might give a dryish bivouac for two. This is an isolated spot and when no other climbers are in evidence there is a remote flavour, a sensation of seriousness akin to that of the Himalaya. From this bivouac some of the finest climbs in the Caucasus are on offer.

Ushba South (4710m) and North (4695m) make a double-headed granite Matterhorn and it is hard not to be too superlative about this mountain, which is one of the most beautiful in the world. The pick of the routes must surely be the traverse of Ushba, grade 5. The Ushba Plateau (4000m) can be reached from the German Bivouac via the easy, but extremely terrifying, Ushba icefall. From here the North and South summits can be reached at a reasonable grade 4 (ice climbing), or a descent, via the unpleasant Uzbenski icefall, to the West Face where a variety of grade 5 mixed routes up to 1600 metres long reach the same place. There are desperate climbs on the North-East Face, the so-called 'Mirror Wall', and further difficult climbs on the South-East Face, though the latter are best accessed from Svanetia.

Chatyn (4363m) is not visible from the German Bivouac, but it has a steep and rocky North Face popular for its technical difficulty combined with a relatively benign descent.

Pik Shchurovsky (4259m) has a most impressive North Face with grade 5 ice routes

Ushba, from Shkelda.
(Photo: Hamish MacInnes.)

on the left flank and steep rock on the right.

Shkhelda (4320m) is more of a sawtooth ridge than a peak. The North Face dominates the walk up to the bivouac and is seamed with grade 5 rock and mixed lines, all of a high quality. The classic line is the complete traverse, which in the 1960s was the scene of Hamish MacInnes's twelve day epic.

From the village of Old Baksan (which is reminiscent of a solitary tower block in Hackney) the Adyr Su runs almost due south-east for 15 kilometres to the Ullu Tau ice walls. It contains an unsurfaced, but motorable, road with a few *koshes* (Caucasian shepherds' huts), and the sporting camps of Jailik and Ullu Tau. In section it is a typical glacial valley, the steep sides hiding the lateral peaks but displaying the head walls of Ullu Tau to great effect. The sporting camps are connected to Baksan by the road but the Adyr Su is a hanging valley with a short, steep cliff giving access to the long, level valley floor. This cliff is surmounted by a rickety steel stairway and a most peculiar car elevator. To the left a narrow and roaring gorge betrays the hidden Adyr Su waterfall, where a fine mist promotes ferns and mosses. We were told that the car elevator was the choice of local farmers in preference to a more conventional road link, the idea being to restrict tourist access. The immediate consequence for the climber is that unless steps are taken to guarantee motorised transport up the valley, there is an inevitable and blistering 12 kilometre road walk.

From the roadhead at the very organised Ullu Tau camp, a two-hour walk leads to excellent bivouac sites under the magnificent Ullu Tau Chana Wall. For routes on this massif it is worth taking a tent. As these sites are on a descent route the tent can be left at the base of the wall. In 1986 we paid the price for not taking this precaution, for it rained heavily during our bivouac and by dawn we were soaked, cold and feeling aged. Fortunately we were revived by great quantities of tea, cheese and raw garlic gently forced on us by Soviet climbers, but we were unable to raise the enthusiasm for further exploration and chose to return to the dry clothes and warmth of base. The ever-friendly Russians were sympathetic, but could not understand why we were bivouacking without tent or stove. For our part, we were surprised by the selection of raw garlic for breakfast.

The choice of peak from the Adyr Su roadhead is wide. Perhaps the most attractive are: the North Face of Ullu Tau Chana (4363m) which forms the most eye-catching face in the valley and sports several category 5 routes, of which the Abalakov Route to the central summit (5B) looks best. Some relatively minor couloirs below the west summit still await ascents but these look dangerous and difficult. There are easier routes to either side of the North Face which would provide descent routes, as well as enjoyable climbs in their own right.

Jailik (4533m) is the highest peak in the area. This mountain sports several high standard rock climbs and the obvious couloir splitting the South Face is the line of the 1937 British route.

Adyr Su Bashi (4370m) and Cheget Tau Chana (4109m) are attractive peaks flanking Ullu Tau Chana, reached from the same roadhead. These peaks are climbed by classic medium grade routes with reputedly fine views. With the exception of Ullu Tau Chana all the above-mentioned Adyr Su peaks seem infrequently visited.

Visitors to this valley should bear in mind that it lacks the remote feel that the other climbing valleys exude. It is possible to drive deep in to the mountains, up a good road which terminates at the two camps, best described as noisy, thriving holiday centres.

The Bezingi Glacier is the longest in the Caucasus and contains no fewer than eleven of the fourteen 5000 metre peaks in the range. The glacier head is dominated by the Bezingi Wall, 2000 metres of rock and ice. The eastern end of the wall is bounded by the Dykhni-aush and Sella Passes leading to Mirshigi Tau. Enclosing the eastern corner of the Bezingi Glacier is the South-West Face of Dykh Tau and its twin buttresses. The west buttress was used in part by Mummery and Zurfluh during the first ascent of the mountain in July 1888. This buttress was climbed in its entirety by a Polish party in 1959 and its twin was climbed in 1958 by Band and Harris. Due south of Dykh Tau, the Bezingi Wall proper forms the north-south watershed. At the eastern end is Shkhara, with the classic Tomaschek Buttress, mentioned above. The west end is terminated by Lyalver. In between these two lie Gestola, Katyn Tau and Jangi Tau. A number of classic lines culminate in these summits. Perhaps the 1935 Schwarzgruber Rib on Jangi Tau can be taken as typical. This was repeated in 1958 as far as the summit slopes by a British team, which turned back when Lord Hunt (then Sir John) fell down a crevasse. The route appears to equate to about AD/D in difficulty.

KEV REYNOLDS
The Pyrénées

After the Alps the Pyrénées form Europe's second great range of mountains west of the Caucasus. Created during the same period and by similar causes as the Alps, their highest summits reach to more than 3000 metres and although their glaciers are shrinking rapidly and their permanent snowfields are little more than summer napkins, the central portion of the range has a distinctly Alpine appearance about it. Yet with their countless small lakes, their deep shadowed gorges, their great limestone cirques and comparative solitude and isolation, the Pyrénées have a unique atmosphere all their own.

Seen from the low plains of Gascony the Pyrénéan wall rises abruptly with a bold outline of ragged peaks and ridges, thus creating an effective barrier between France and Spain. As a natural frontier the range could scarcely be bettered, separating as it does not only nations and cultures, but also climate and vegetation. To the north stretches the mosaic that is Western Europe, while south of the mountains lies the great Iberian Peninsula, an anachronism whose plains and sierras and remote hilltop villages seem to be dusted by the hot dry breath of Africa.

It's a narrow but unequal divide. The French slopes, well-watered by damp Atlantic mists, are comparatively short and fall steeply to the foothills, while those of

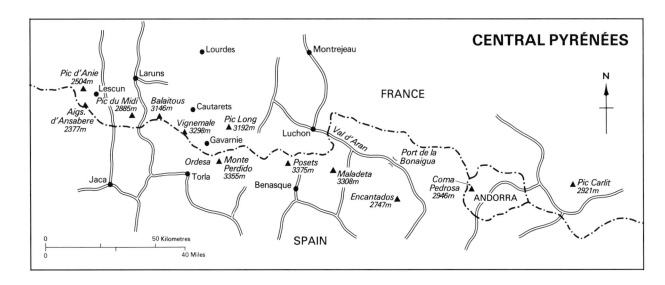

Spain roll away in a succession of baked sierras to the badlands of the Ebro basin. Between Atlantic and Mediterranean the range measures something like 430 kilometres. It is not, however, a single chain, but two lines of more or less equal length that overlap roughly in the centre. Where this overlap occurs the River Garonne flows through the Vall d'Aran, a valley that is politically Spanish but geographically French, and the twin axes are joined at the grassy saddle of the Port de la Bonaigua (2072m). With only one or two notable exceptions the high crest is traced by both watershed and international frontier, and the major peaks are either gathered along this crest, or separated from it by a single valley. The three highest massifs—Maladeta, Posets and Perdido—are all located south of the watershed, while the more dramatic peaks are mostly French.

These are not mountains on which reputations are made, for although the Pyrénées abound in rock climbs of every degree of difficulty, their individual peaks remain little known to all but a comparatively small band of enthusiasts who go there regularly. This is one of the range's attractions. All but a handful of summits are accessible by fairly modest routes; there are few troublesome glaciers and the difference in altitude between valley bed and summit crest is such that bivouacs are rarely necessary and Alpine-like pre-dawn starts a rarity. This is not to say that they should be treated lightly, however, for in the very solitude of some of the most attractive massifs far from villages or even manned refuges, climbing takes on an additional degree of seriousness.

There are few possibilities for ice climbing other than during the winter months, but then there will be much activity, especially on the great walls of the Cirque de Gavarnie. The ice cliffs that adorn the North-East Face of nearby Monte Perdido (Mont Perdu to the French) present a worthwhile challenge, while the Couloir de Gaube on the Vignemale's North Face is a classic mixed route first climbed in 1889 by Henri Brulle's party. A second ascent was not made for 44 years! Winter snowfall attracts a growing ski industry and on both sides of the international frontier resorts are being slowly developed to exploit the potential for downhill skiing. Those who love these mountains most hope that this development is kept in close check. There is, of course, great scope for ski touring, particularly in the Néouvielle and Carlit massifs, and ski ascents are frequently made of a number of summits in various regions.

Perhaps most of all, though, the Pyrénées offer to the mountain walker a series of uncluttered, seemingly remote landscapes of infinite charm and unlimited scope, coloured by the richest flora in all of Europe.

In the west gentle hills rise from the Atlantic – green, rolling, bracken-covered hills, wooded to their summits in many instances and with dense forests of oak and pine in their valleys. 'A very bumpy country,' wrote one traveller to the region in the seventeenth century. Moist Atlantic winds water this lush vegetation and as a consequence, fast-flowing streams dash down the hillsides and through the valleys. The Basques who live here in the seven provinces proudly and defiantly refuse to acknowledge the international frontier, proclaiming themselves to be a separate race owing allegiance neither to France nor to Spain. They have their own language, their own culture, their own distinctive architecture which is as easily recognised in villages to the south of the watershed as it is to the north.

Though of only modest height, La Rhune (900m) is the first of the Basque mountains and the keystone of their country. Most westerly of the peaks, it has a rack-railway leading from Col de St-Ignace to the summit from which extensive views overlook the Atlantic coast, the great Landes Forest to the north and all the confusion of Basque hills on both sides of the watershed. A number of road passes traverse the region across the grain of the country, and also from north to south. For centuries many of the frontier passes were crossed not only by traders and religious pilgrims making for Santiago de Compostela, but especially by armies, the most famous being that of Charlemagne in 778 on his legendary journey to rid Spain of the Saracens.

Heading eastwards the hills grow in stature, but south of the little town of St Jean-Pied-de-Port the dominant feature is not so much mountain height but the vast Forest of Iraty which spills over both sides of the frontier and is managed by a syndicate of local communities. The greenery of this huge tract of beech forest, with green pools hidden within and green pastures above, contrasts dramatically with the nearby region of bare limestone formations and deep gorges—of which that of Kakouetta is the finest—and enormous *gouffres*—the Gouffre de la Pierre St Martin, below Pic d'Arlas, is one of the deepest caves in the world. Neighbouring Pic d'Arlas to the south-east stands the easy Pic d'Anie, at 2504 metres the first of the so-called High Pyrénées.

It is in the High Pyrénées between Pic d'Anie and the Carlit massif to the east of Andorra that the finest scenery, the best climbs and the most challenging walks are to be found. This is an Alpine landscape with sharp jagged peaks, crusty ridges, rock walls and buttresses, small glaciers and snowfields, meadows rich with flowers, tarns and streams and delicate ribbon cascades, great canyons and glacial cirques. Within it there are three National Parks; two in Spain, one in France.

The French National Park (*Parc National des Pyrénées Occidentales*) was created in 1967 and is the most extensive. It follows the Franco-Spanish frontier along a narrow strip eastwards from the Cirque de Lescun for about 110 kilometres, and is nowhere more than 15 kilometres wide. In this Park rise some of the more dramatic peaks: Pic du Midi d'Ossau, Pic Palas, Balaïtous, Vignemale, and the cirques of Gavarnie, Estaubé, Troumouse and Barroude. Among them will be found ample opportunities for climbing at every degree of difficulty. There are more than 400 kilometres of waymarked trails and an abundant wildlife. Isard, the Pyrénéan chamois, will be found in most regions, as will marmots. The European brown bear is said still to inhabit the woods of the Ossau valley, but despite protection by law there are probably no more than about fifty left. In streams the rare desman, with its trumpet-like snout and webbed feet, is found here and in the Caucasus. Vultures are by no means uncommon and will often be seen circling around the crags or feeding in remote country on the carcass of a dead sheep or isard.

Immediately to the south of the Cirque de Gavarnie lies the Ordesa National Park. One of Europe's first, it is also the smallest of the Pyrénéan Parks, comprising the fabulous deep trench of the Ordesa Canyon and adjacent areas, now including the Anisclo Canyon. At its head rises Monte Perdido, third highest of the range's mountains. But Ordesa's northern wall is the most notable feature with the huge multi-coloured cliffs of Mondarruego, Tozal del Mallo and Punta Gallinero soaring out of the mixed forests. On these cliffs some of the more challenging rock climbs have been made in recent years, while along the canyon's southern wall has been created a high, airy pathway known as the *Faja de Pelay*, a scenic walk giving spectacular views across the valley and steeply below to the series of waterfalls that crash through the forest-lined gorge.

Farther east, in Catalonia, lies the third of the National Parks, that of Aigües Tortes-San Mauricio in the Sierra de los Encantados – *The Enchanted Mountains*. This is a wild patch of country wedged between the valleys of Noguera de Tort, Noguera Pallaresa and Vall d'Aran, with the village of Espot conveniently situated on its outskirts. This National Park is a tangled, bewildering region of savage granite peaks and little tarns. Popular with Spanish holidaymakers, one or two of the more accessible regions have been somewhat devalued by the construction of roads, although the heartland remains as remote and challenging as ever. Best-known of the Park's summits are the twin peaks of Els Encantats, but there are numerous possibilities here for some energetic rock climbing on many of the neighbouring walls, and some magnificent walking tours in deserted valleys.

Returning to the west and the first of the High Pyrénées, the limestone Pic d'Anie is approached either from Arette-Pierre-St-Martin by way of a spectacular karst landscape, or from the lovely pastoral village of Lescun in about 5 hours. Lescun itself occupies a sunny meadowland belvedere of great charm. From it a soft green sweep of hillside leads the eye to a backcloth of grey limestone peaks rising from the dark shadow of forest: the Cirque de Lescun. To the west stand sentry-like the twin Pics Billare, while to the south-west one can just make out the summit spike of one of the Aiguilles d'Ansabère; peaks to set a climber's fingers itching.

A country lane which turns into a forest track and then becomes a narrow winding footpath, leads from Lescun to the scree-cluttered ankles of the Petite Aiguille (2350m) and Grande Aiguille d'Ansabère (2377m), peaks that appear to have been transported here from the Dolomites. On them a number of extreme aid routes have been made over many years of activity since the early Twenties. They are indeed challenging peaks, yet the neighbouring Pic d'Ansabère offers an easy scramble by way of the Col de Pétragème, and the classic Pyrénéan high level traverse for mountain walkers passes in their shadow.

South of the frontier here lies a big, empty, largely untravelled countryside with whale-back mountains and trackless valleys. Then, eastwards, the Aspe valley is closed at its head by a handsome cirque that belies its modest altitude. The ancient road pass of the Col du Somport (1632m) writhes over the saddle to one side of this and then, beyond a few more ridges that steadily increase in height, we come to Pic du Midi d'Ossau (2885m), the very symbol of the Pyrénées.

With its distinctive outline, Pic du Midi—or Jean-Pierre as it is affectionately known—appears from the west to resemble Mount Kenya. A lovely, solitary mountain, there are probably more routes on its faces, buttresses and couloirs than on any other mountain throughout the range. These vary from the easy, yet stonefall-troubled, *voie normale* to the exposed lines pioneered by the Ravier twins on the Embarradère Pillar; from the numerous meandering routes on the South Face overlooking the popular Refuge de Pombie, to multi-day winter epics that traverse the four main summits (Pointe Jean Santé, Pointe d'Aragon, Grand Pic and Petit Pic).

Surprising though it may seem, Pic du Midi was first attempted as long ago as 1552 when François de Foix, the Count de Candale, organised an expedition to determine its height. With the assistance of ladders, grapnels and 'climbing irons' the Count and his party managed to climb high enough to see clouds beneath their feet. It is not possible to ascertain exactly how close they got to the summit, but it is certain that the mountain was climbed for the first time in 1787 by an unnamed shepherd from the Aspe valley who set up a cairn on the summit on behalf of the geographers, Reboul and Vidal.

This great rust-coloured peak stands alone amid a tranquil pastureland. To the south and west lie strings of little tarns to throw the mountain on its head, and over the cols that link its surrounding valleys there runs one of the finest of all Pyrénéan walks; the Tour of Pic du Midi, a true classic.

Immediately to the east lies a deep valley threaded by a road which crosses the summer-only Col du Pourtalet, but out of that rises the big granite massif of Balaïtous containing the first of the 3000 metre peaks and the first of the glaciers. By direct contrast with the pasturelands that surround Pic du Midi, the Balaïtous massif is a savage region of bold peaks and long high ridges bristling with gendarmes that rise from boulder slopes and tarns that for much of the year are trapped in ice.

The cone of Pic Palas (2974m) dominates the western sector. When the military surveyors, Peytier and Hossard, were exploring the region in 1825, they climbed Palas under the impression that they were making the first ascent of the Balaïtous and it was only when they actually reached the summit and found the neighbouring peak to be somewhat higher that they realised their mistake. From the summit a ridge plunges off to the south-east, here marking the Franco-Spanish border, and links with the north-west ridge of Balaïtous (3144m).

'This threatening and proud peak', as Henry Russell described it, is noted for its ridges which give long and interesting routes; the traverse of the three main arêtes being a Pyrénéan classic. The Costerillou, or eastern arête, is marked by an individual gendarme, known as the Tour de Costerillou. This rises for about 250 metres out of the steep little Glacier de las Néous and has a fine exposed route on its North Face.

Two manned CAF huts serve the region; Refuge d'Arremoulit below Pic Palas to the west, and Refuge de Larribet to the north. Both give access to entertaining *voies normales*, while an unmanned hut, Refuge Ledormeur, is situated to the north-east below the Crête Fachon.

The pastures of the Marcadau valley make a welcome oasis between the raw massifs of Balaïtous and Vignemale, with superb walking routes around the numerous tarn-sparkling side valleys and easy, yet very pleasant, scrambling to be had on surrounding peaks.

Vignemale, being the highest frontier summit at 3298 metres, is a justifiably popular mountain. On its eastern slopes, by which the normal ascent route is made, sweeps the largest Pyrénéan icefield, the Ossoue Glacier. But it is the great North Face which really impresses. Rising for around 800 metres from the glacial plain of Oulettes de Gaube, this wall offers some of the most serious routes in the whole range, as well as mixed climbing in the shadowed Couloir de Gaube which makes a seam between the triangular wedge of Piton Carré and the main peak. Another fine outing here is to follow the Vignemale's north-west ridge, the Arête de Gaube, from Col des Oulettes to the summit. It is a long, but reasonably safe route, with spectacular views all the way as it overhangs a section of the North Face.

Writing of the Vignemale it is necessary to mention the eccentric pioneer, Count Henry Russell (1834–1909) who, a century ago, created a total of seven grottoes on the mountain in which he spent weeks at a time—even holding dinner parties there and celebrating Mass on the glacier that flowed past his door!

The Cirque de Gavarnie is without doubt the best-known feature of the Pyrénées. A splendid amphitheatre whose 1500 metre walls are terraced with bands of snow and ice and laced with waterfalls. On them are to be found dozens of modern rock climbs of all grades of difficulty, and in winter they receive the attention of ice specialists who have achieved some remarkable successes. Along the rim of the cirque runs the Spanish frontier and in it the fabled Brèche de Roland leads through to the Goriz Hut, from which the standard route on Monte Perdido is tackled, as well as giving access into Ordesa and the neighbouring Anisclo Canyon.

Eastwards from Gavarnie there are more glacial cirques; those of Estaubé, Troumouse and Barroude. Hard climbs are found on the walls of the Cirque de Troumouse and also on the Barroude Wall which backs it. Barroude is a delightful region with long approach marches necessary to locate it. To the north lies the Néouvielle massif; a large area of high granite peaks and scattered lakes—a complex terrain with opportunities for multi-day walking expeditions and hard climbing on remote peaks. Pic Long (3192m) is the highest Pyrénéan summit entirely in France and on its North Face, partly sheathed with glacier, there are some extreme routes. The face was developed in the Thirties by Robert Ollivier and Roger Mailly, founder members of the GPHM (*Groupe Pyrénéiste de Haute Montagne*).

The French side of the watershed becomes sliced now by gentle, wooded, pastoral valleys until a little west of Luchon where the Lac d'Oô makes a pretty site. Above the lake, and accessible from the well-situated Refuge d'Espingo, there's a grand collection of rocky peaks clustered near the frontier ridge; Pics des Spijoles, Gourgs Blancs,

161

Walls of the Cirque de Gavarnie, seen from the west. (Photo: Kev Reynolds.)

Clarabide, Arlaud, Perdiguère, Crabioules, Lézat and Quayrat. Serious rock climbing is to be found on several of these peaks, while others have easy routes to them. Mountain walkers who delight in a wild landscape can spend many days journeying in this largely unsung corner.

Immediately to the south stands the 'viceroy' of the Pyrénées, Pico de Posets (3375m), a bulky massif whose glaciers and snowfields are fast fading away leaving behind a rough desert of boulder and scree and crumbling ridges. Most routes on it are of a moderate grade but more challenging rock climbs are to be found among outlying peaks, especially above the hidden Baticielles valley. The main valley moating the Posets, however, is that of the Estós, a delight of crystal streams and fragrant shrubs.

The Estós stream flows into the Esera a little north of the village of Benasque. At the head of the Esera stands the highest of all Pyrénéan mountains, Pico de Aneto (Néthou to the French; 3404m), main summit of the Maladeta massif. It's an extensive mass of mountain with high crusty ridges and several glaciers. First climbed in 1842 by a Russian, Tchihatcheff, with Albert de Francqueville and the guides Argarot,

Redonnet and Ursule, the standard route to Aneto leads in about five hours from the Renclusa Hut by way of the rocky spine of the Portillon and the Aneto Glacier. Immediately before the summit is reached a short stretch of exposed ridge known as the Pont de Mahommet is crossed. As the highest in the range it is, naturally, a very popular ascent. The neighbouring Pico de la Maladeta has a fine western arête but the grandest ridge of the massif is that of the Salenques which, when linked with that of the Tempêtes to gain Aneto's summit, makes a superb but long outing on bold granite, with a maximum difficulty of grade IV to contend with.

Still in Spain, beyond the high Mulleres ridge and the crumbling Forcanada, lies the deep valley of the Noguera Ribagorzana with its road tunnel leading to the Vall d'Aran. Rising from the Ribagorzana is the Besiberri massif. More high ridges; a region of granite peaks and sparkling tarns. Besiberri Nord (3014m) stands at the junction of three ridges, the traverse of which is a minor classic on firm granite with superb views over a bewildering landscape. Nearby rise the Agulles de Trevassani as a spiky collection of rocks above a trekker's paradise.

All the wild country to the east of Besiberri, as far as the Noguera Pallaresa, is in the Encantados. Dozens of small lakes, low-growing shrubs, gnarled pines and sudden jutting peaks. On the Encantats and Agulles de Amitges there is the prospect of attractive sport on rock that is extremely popular with climbers up from Barcelona, and in summer the region teems with activity.

Between the Encantados and the little independent principality of Andorra there are only three peaks that top the 3000 metre mark and these require only modest ascents from lush valleys. But it is a lovely patch of country all the same, with forests, pastures and yet more tarns. The frontier ridge is remote and largely unvisited, yet for those who love wild places there is an undeniable charm about it.

Andorra has sadly been sacrificed to the whims of the developer and its romance of isolation has been swamped by acres of concrete with roads bringing nose-to-tail traffic where not so long ago mules clattered on lonely paths, and ski tows are changing the face of former lonely valleys. Its highest peak, Coma Pedrosa is, however, as yet undefiled and though it offers only a long walk to reach it, the summit views are extensive and welcome. Of interest to scramblers will be the circuit of Andorra along its frontier ridges, an expedition of note with a number of entertaining pitches (mostly scrambling) to contend with.

Eastwards, on the French side of the watershed, another high granite plateau trapping numerous lakes and with small peaks rising from it, is worthy of a visit. The Carlit massif is ideal for a mountain walking holiday and for easy scrambling on attractive, yet modest, mountains. Pic Carlit (2921m) is the main peak here. It rises to the south-east of Lac de Lanoux and overlooks a tarn-dashed landscape to the east. To the north, beyond the Pics Rouge and Peric, flows the Vallée d'Orlu out of which rises the little twin-peaked Dent d'Orlu, a rock-climbing gem. Although the summit is only 2220 metres, the South Face offers routes of 900 metres and more. It was first climbed in 1964, as was the South-East Face. Several other routes have been developed during the past twenty years, all of which are at least graded TD.

The Carlit empties some of its waters south into the broad, flat-bottomed valley of the Cerdagne; an open, smiling, sun-trap of a valley noted for its wild flowers. The southern wall of the Cerdagne, with the Puigmal as its crown, stretches away towards the east and to Pic du Canigou. This was first climbed as long ago as 1276 by Peter III of Aragon who found a dragon in a lake near the summit! There are no dragons left today and the mountain is the most-visited of all in Roussillon. Although the tourist route is dull and easy, there are rock climbs on the East Face, and on the Barbet Crête. Beyond Canigou there is little of interest as the mountains fall away hot and thirsty to the Mediterranean.

To conclude: the Pyrénées offer a taste of wilderness in some of their more isolated regions. There is rock climbing of all grades of difficulty on both granite and limestone. There are modest ascent routes on high peaks to make the range ideal for aspiring alpinists, and hard ice climbs abound in winter. Unlike the Alps, village bases here do not often make convenient climbing centres, but by use of the many huts on both sides of the frontier one may happily concentrate on specific areas away from tourist resorts. It is, however, an ideal range for the mountain walker, with some spectacular outings to be enjoyed in most regions. The GR10 long-distance footpath crosses from the Atlantic to the Mediterranean along the northern slopes, while the classic Pyrénéan High Route does the same but stays as high along the ridges as possible, sometimes straying into Spain. It is, almost everywhere, a backpacker's paradise.

LOUIS BAUME
The Picos de Europa

The Saracen invaders from North Africa, probing northwards in Spain to extend their rule, clashed in AD 718 with the fierce Christian tribes led by Pelayo near the village of Covadonga, in León. The fight was savage, but this time the Moslem forces were defeated and driven back into the mountains. The tide of Islamic invasion that had swept across much of Europe, spilling over the Pyrénées into France and reaching as far as Touraine, was turning. The soldiers of the Caliphat began to withdraw across the high passes and deep gorges of Mons Vindius (as the Picos de Europa were then known) to Bulnes and Espinama and gradually southwards to Andalusia. Arab rule extended from the Atlas Mountains to the Himalaya, from Kano in Nigeria to Cantabria; but at Covadonga its advance was challenged and repulsed, and for the proud people of that land the way became free for the predominance of the Catholic church and for their own independent way of life. The Reconquista had begun.

Downstream from Covadonga lies the small town of Cangas, capital of the Onis region. It is situated at the northern end of the Sella gorge, close to the main east-west road leading from Bilbao and Santander to Oviedo and Gijón. It boasts several *hostals* and *hospedajas* (guest houses), restaurants and numerous shops. Cangas had been for many years the residence of the royal court and in the plaza before the cathedral stands a statue to Pelayo, the first king of Asturias. A narrow humpbacked medieval bridge still spans the Sella river, close to the modern bridge.

Today Covadonga is a centre of national pilgrimage. A holy grotto, la Cueva de la Señora, with its small chapel dedicated to the Virgin Mary, nestles in the high cliff beyond the ruined monastery and, dominating the scene, is the large basilica in which the first kings of Asturias lie buried.

From the village a road climbs south-eastwards and winds its way up to two lakes, the Lagos Enol and de la Ercina (1108m), and to a large motel. The surrounding grassy plateau, where horses and cattle graze, is the main way into the Macizo Occidental whose rocky peaks, with occasional patches of snow on them, form an impressive back-cloth to the lush mountain meadows. This whole area was created one of Spain's first National Parks in 1918 by Don Pedro Pidal, Marqués de Villaviciosa de Asturias; his grave is not far from the Vega Redonda Hut (*vega* means grassy plateau or pasture) further up the valley.

The small, compact massif of the Picos, measuring about 40 kilometres wide and 25 kilometres deep, with its jumble of serrated ridges and jagged summits rising to between 2000 and 3000 metres, is almost entirely limestone in formation; barren karst

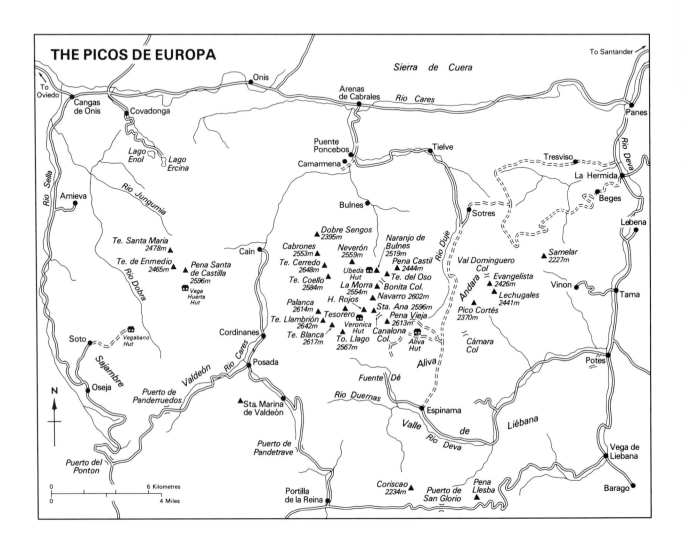

THE PICOS DE EUROPA

To Santander

Sierra de Cuera

To Oviedo

Onis

Cangas de Onis

Covadonga

Arenas de Cabrales

Rio Cares

Panes

Rio Deva

Puente Poncebos

Tielve

Tresviso

La Hermida

Lago Enol

Lago Ercina

Camarmena

Beges

Rio Sella

Rio Jungumia

Amieva

Lebena

Bulnes

Sotres

Te. Santa Maria 2478m

Caín

Dobre Sengos 2395m

Naranjo de Bulnes 2519m

Samelar 2227m

Te. de Enmedio 2465m

Pena Santa de Castilla 2596m

Cabrones 2553m

Neverón 2559m

Pena Castil 2519m

Val Dominguero Col

Rio Duje

Te. Cerredo 2648m

Ubeda Hut

Te. del Oso 2444m

Evangelista 2426m

Vinon

Rio Dobra

Vega Huerta Hut

Te. Coello 2584m

La Morra 2554m

Bonita Col.

Navarro 2602m

Lechugales 2441m

Tama

Palanca 2614m

H. Rojos

Sta. Ana 2596m

Pico Cortés 2370m

Tesorero

Andara

Te. Llambrión 2642m

Veronica Hut

Pena Vieja 2613m

Soto

Vegabano Hut

Cordinanes

Te. Blanca 2617m

To. Llago 2567m

Canalona Col.

Cámara Col

Potes

Sajambre

Aliva Hut

Posada

Aliva

Oseja

Puerto de Panderruedos

Sta Marina de Valdeón

Fuente Dé

Rio Duernas

Espinama

Valle

Rio Deva

de

Liébana

Vega de Liebana

Puerto de Pandetrave

N

Puerto del Ponton

Coriscao 2234m

Pena Llesba 2524m

Barago

Portilla de la Reina

Puerto de San Glorio

0   6 Kilometres
0   4 Miles

country in places but grassy and forested on its lower slopes. It juts out north of the wild Sierra Cantábrica, which stretches east-west from close to the Pyrénées to as far as Galicia and the Atlantic Ocean. To the immediate west of Reinosa, south of Santander, the ground rises quickly to the Alto de Campóo and the Reserva Nacional de Fuentes Carrionas within which are the highest three summits of the Cantabrian range: Espigüete (2450m), Curavacas (2520m) and Peña Prieta (2536m). North of Peña Prieta is an elevated neck of land crossed by the Puerto de San Glorio (1609m); beyond this high pass lies the green and fertile Valle de Liébana on whose far side rise the Picos de Europa themselves.

The Picos are divided into three smaller distinct massifs delimited by four swift-flowing rivers teeming with trout and occasionally with salmon too. The most westerly is the Río Sella; it flows from high in the Sajambre valley (in the south-west corner of the Picos) and, gouging a tortuous way through the mountains, reaches Cangas de Onis from where it winds a more leisurely way to the seaside resort of Ribadesella.

Next, dividing the Macizo Occidental (or de Cornión) from the Macizo Central (or de Urrieles), is the Río Cares, whose source is in the remote southern glens of Valdeón. It runs past the unspoilt village of Posada where the house of Pedro Pidal still stands, then, forcing a narrow way, reaches the hamlet of Caín where there is a memorial to El Cainejo, Pedro Pidal's companion during the historic first ascent of the Naranjo de Bulnes. The Cares continues north-eastward through formidable gorges *(gargantas)* to arrive at Puente Poncebos. This tiny hamlet consists of barely more than a generating station, a bridge *(puente)* across which a road leads up to Sotres, and a modest inn with a restaurant. From Camarmeña, slightly upstream, there is an awe-inspiring view into the narrow ravine (Canal del Tejo) that leads to the small village of Bulnes and, beyond, to the towering Naranjo (2519m).

The third river is the Duje which, rising in the mining area close beneath the eastern flank of Peña Vieja, flows down the wide verdant valley on the north side of the Puertos (a gateway or pass) de Aliva and past the small villages of Sotres and Tielve, thus dividing the Macizo Central from the Macizo Oriental (or de Andara). Then it turns west to Puente Poncebos and joins the Río Cares. Breaking through a narrow gap in the foothills, the Cares reaches Arenas de Cabrales and turns east towards Panes.

There it meets the fourth and longest river of them all, the Deva, which delineates the eastern boundary of the Picos. The Deva rises near Fuente Dé *(fuente* means spring or fountain) and flows past Espinama, one of the ways into the Picos from the south, and down the broad Vallee de Liébana to the small holiday town of Potes. Northwards from Potes to Panes, the river courses through deep defiles (la Garganta de la Hermida), twisting and turning as though seeking to escape from the narrow confines of the towering cliffs and pinnacles that enclose it. From Panes the three rivers Cares, Dujes and Deva together break out to the open sea.

Good metalled roads encircle the Picos and allow reasonably rapid and certainly breath-taking travel from one massif to another. It is this ease of mobility that makes individual transport so much more preferable to local buses or other methods of conveyance, at the cost however of destroying the remoteness and charm of many small villages and hidden valleys. On the west side a road snakes its way down from Puerto del Pontón through the chasms carved by the Sella, crossing and recrossing the torrent until finally it arrives at Cangas. From there a road runs east, through Arenas de Cabrales to Panes. Between this stretch of road and the coast is a low-lying range, the Sierra de Cuera, well-known for its caves, many of which are used by the locals for the storage and maturing of their cheeses. The road branching south off the main Santander-Oviedo highway at Unquera to follow the Deva upstream to Panes continues through the wild Deva gorges to Potes.

Two roads leave Potes: one heads up the wooded Valle de Liébana, following the

Río Deva to Espinama and the Parador (a large hotel complex) at Fuente Dé; the other continues south to La Vega de Liébana and west, tracing a sinuous route up to the Puerto de San Glorio, the link between the Sierra Cantábrica and the Picos. Spectacular panoramas of both can be enjoyed from a viewpoint a little above the Puerto, at the Mirador de Llesba. The road continues via the Portilla de la Reina to Riano from where another road heads north to Puerto del Ponton.

Several roads, some surfaced but others mere jeep tracks, lead into the interior: to villages such as Sotres and Posada de Valdéon, or to mine workings high in the mountains in the Aliva area and in the Andara massif south-east of Sotres. They can be used to advantage but some are quite scaring, particularly the road leading from Cordiñanes to Caín. There are Land Rover hire services at Sotres and Espinama.

Within this framework of rivers lie the three mountain groups. The easternmost one could be of less interest to climbers as its extent, complexity and elevation are more modest. Nevertheless it has 22 summits over 2000 metres, the highest being Tabla de Lechugales (2441m), standing just off the main north-south ridge of the Andara. The traverse of this ridge from the Collado de Cámara north to the Collado Valdominguero over some half-dozen mountain tops, all more than 2000 metres high can provide a very satisfying if long day with difficulties at the start no greater than grade III. These mountains can be approached either from the Aliva side or from the jeep road leading to the zinc mines south-east of Sotres.

The western massif covers the largest area; it has 42 summits over 2000 metres, with the splendid Peña Santa de Castilla (2596m) overtopping her nearest rival, the Torre (or Peña) Santa Maria de Enol (2478m), which rises on the far side of the vast and desolate Jou Santa (*jou* or *hou* in Asturian, *hoyo* in Castilian means an enclosed mountain valley, acting as a funnel or sink-hole for rain water and melted snow). The usual way into this group is from Covadonga to the small Vega Redonda Hut (1560m) in the Jungumia valley, with a stream and fountain on its doorstep. Another way in is from the south, from Oseja de Sajambre in the Sella valley to the Albergue (inn) de Vegabaño (1340m). The Peña Santa de Castilla offers some of the finest rock climbs in the Picos on its south side, which is an immense wall some 550 metres high with routes up to grade VI. There are many other towers, peaks and needles of varying difficulty in this group; most can be approached only by finding a way over broken and confusing terrain for which existing maps offer but limited help.

The central massif is the highest of the three and provides the greatest scope for mountaineers. It contains no less than forty-three summits rising above 2000 metres with Terro Cerredo (2648m) the loftiest of all in the Picos, and Torre del Llambrión (2642m) a close rival. Not far from the latter, across the Garganta del Hoyo Grande, stands the Pico Tesorero (2570m) at whose summit the three provinces of Asturias, Santander and León meet. It is not a difficult mountain to climb; the round trip from the cableway above Fuente Dé can be done in one day, and the keen mountain walker will be rewarded by a most glorious vista from the top. Seen to the east are the two summits of Picos de Santa Ana (2596m) near to which the Agujas (needles) de la

Canalona (2515m) and Bustamente (2380m) rise up, offering exhilarating rock climbs up to grade IV.

The rocky divide between Tesorero and Torre de los Horcados Rojos (2506m) is the hub of this mountain complex and lies roughly half-way on the great north-south divide. To the north an almost indiscernible path drops very steeply over rough ground to Jou de los Boches, leads into the aptly named stony desert of Jou sin Tierre and continues, still between soaring summits, to the Delgado Ubeda Hut (2050m) standing beneath the great west wall of Naranjo de Bulnes. This hut commemorates the first President of the FEM (Spanish Mountaineering Federation); his memorial is at the Mirador del Tombo de Cordiñanes on the road to Caín. From the hut a rough path picks its way down the narrow and tortuous ravines leading to Bulnes and eventually to Puente Poncebos. To the south a path descends, skirting the Hoyos Negros where the small Verónica Hut (2325m) squats, and makes its marked way through the featureless *jous* to meet a track leading down to join the road that descends from the mines and the Aliva Hotel. Close to where the path and track meet, at La Vueltona, there is a spacious shelter-stone and a cave with a spring of clear water. The road continues to the Mirador at the top of the cableway (1843m).

Below the Horcados Rojos (*horcado* means narrow col) another path climbs east from a marked rock to gain the Collado de la Canalona, lying between Santa Ana and the bulky Peña Vieja (2613m), which dominates and divides the areas of Jous sin Tierre and de Lloroza and the upper valley of the Río Duje. The clamber to the collado is not arduous and an obvious path leads up over broken ground, then on to the summit of the Vieja. This is a much-visited mountain with a breathtaking view from its top over most of the Picos and to the far distant mountains of the Cantabrian range. Apart from this easy ascent, there are innumerable climbing routes of a very high standard, particularly on the eastern side whose great cliffs face the Aliva Hotel and the old Chalet Real, the royal hunting lodge.

Easy access to the central massif can be gained from Fuente Dé, the roadhead of the Valle de Liébana where there is a large car park, the state owned Parador, another small hotel, camping areas and other facilities. The cableway at Fuente Dé whisks visitors up the precipitous 800 metre rock wall that forms the southern bastion of the massif. An alternative but very strenuous way down is by the Canal de la Jenduda, a steep narrow cleft in the wall; going up is much worse.

Potes, at the entry to the valley, is a pleasant town and the capital of the region. It is a convenient base, having several modest hotels and eating houses, as well as plenty of shops offering a wide selection of commodities. The local wines are a delight. The town stands astride the Río Deva at an important road intersection; and not far away is the ancient Monasterio de Santo Toribio de Liébana, another excellent viewpoint onto the Macizo Oriental.

The Picos de Europa are impressive and harsh; they are not for the novice or the faint-hearted. The weather, terrain and logistics of movement make an excursion into the region a more serious undertaking than one, for instance, into the Pyrénées. The weather generally is unfavourable, except for a short period from about the last week of August to mid-September. They lie some 20 kilometres inland and the prevailing winds blowing from the Atlantic, sometimes with great force, combine with the warm temperature to produce much rain throughout most of the year with mists or snow on higher ground. This warm humidity accounts for the verdant nature of the coastal region but inland the thick clouds can cause severe problems, not least of route finding in the complicated and often inaccurately mapped confusion of ridges, gullies and scree slopes, and enormous creviced *hoyos* pitted with sump holes. The interior is mostly an arid wilderness of shattered rock and boulders, of bare limestone mountains interspersed with huge *jous,* with occasional névés of frozen snow that necessitate the carrying of ice-axes, if not of crampons.

In the mountains themselves the rock generally is very good, being rough and sound and providing good friction, but occasionally it is broken and fragile and great care is required. The limestone is often of great smooth slabs, elsewhere of well eroded 'organ-pipe' formation *(llambrias),* frequently reaching wall angle. Only a few hardy alpine plants cling to the rocks and the floors of some of the *jous* may be covered with sparse patches of short grass and other small plants; the landscape is devoid of trees and bushes. Despite this there are large numbers of rebecos or local chamois. Golden eagles and other birds of prey circle around the summits, though smaller birds appear to be few. Small lizards are seen, motionless, basking in the warm sun; and large black and yellow salamanders emerge in great numbers from the crannies in the rocks when it is raining and the grass is wet.

Water presents a problem. In higher ground there are no streams, lakes or tarns. All rain water and melting snow runs away and disappears into the crevices of the rocks, reappearing much lower down as *fuentes,* generally marked on maps, though not always correctly. Most of the few mountain huts (nearly all Club-owned and with limited facilities) are sited close to a spring, but if not, the only ready supply is collecting drips from melting snow. The safe but tedious way of having a supply is to carry it with you.

It is not surprising that this wild and wonderful mountain area should have been so little visited. Probably the earliest people to penetrate the interior were hunters and seekers after minerals. Today the forests of beech, oak, lime and chestnut that surround the Picos still provide shelter for fallow deer and wild boar as well as for foxes, badgers and martens. It is said that a few Asturian brown bears still roam the remoter reaches of Valdeón and the mountain fastness around Peña Prieta and in the Saja reserve; wolves too once lived in the forests. But unlike in the Alps, there are no trade routes across the Picos, nor pilgrims crossing to visit the holy cities of Rome and Jerusalem. These mountains remained for long centuries inviolate and unexplored.

It was not until the nineteenth century that surveyors came to make a detailed study of the mountains. Foremost among them was Don Casiano de Prado, a Spanish mining engineer who, accompanied by two French geologists, made short visits in 1847 and 1856; a number of mountains were climbed for the first time, including Torre del

Naranjo de Bulnes, showing typical 'llambrias' striated limestone. (Photo: West Col.)

Llambrión. Their reports in the geological journals, however, went unnoticed. During the following decade Spanish military surveyors mapped the Andara massif; from the summits of the Picos de Jierro and Cortés (also first ascents) they perceived the full extent and complexity of the Picos de Europa.

The first visitor from our islands was an Irish scholar from County Mayo, John Ormsby (1829-1895), an original member of the Alpine Club who had travelled widely in Algiers, Tunis and the Eastern Atlas, as well as in the Sierra Nevada and the Pyrénées. During his explorations of the Cantabrian range and the Picos (about 1870) he achieved the first ascent of possibly Torre Blanca (2617m). No other British travellers seem to have visited the Picos for the next forty years, when brief visits were made by Douglas Freshfield and Haskett Smith.

The person who really opened up the Picos was the Frenchman de Saint-Saud (1856-1936), accompanied by a group of surveyors. He had spent twelve years surveying the Spanish limestone sierras south of the main Pyrénéan divide and in 1890 he handed over his completed working results for drawing up into six maps. A month later de Saint-Saud stood atop the Tabla de Lechugales (its first ascent) believing it to be the highest peak in the Picos. However, 'To the west' he noted, 'the central massif reveals itself, full of surprises, in mysterious grandeur.' De Saint-Saud had visited Covadonga in 1881 when the only maps available would have been the two by Don Francisco Coello (published 1861 and 1870), both inevitably vague and imprecise; as late as 1890 the Picos could be regarded still as *terra incognita*. Subsequently de Saint-Saud made the first ascent of Peña Vieja and recorded from that summit 'the vista of mighty summits, packed close together, a frightening world that . . . discourages the strongest will by the uncertainties it reveals.' Nevertheless he returned the following year with Paul Labrouche to make a detailed exploration of the western massif; the first ascent of Torre Santa Maria de Enol was made, and that of Tiro Llago (2567m) in the Llambrión group. 1892 was to be his outstanding year; he returned accompanied also by the Gavarnie guide, Bernat-Salles. They succeeded in making the first ascent of, among others, Torre Cerredo, the now acknowledged highest summit in the Picos, the second ascent of Torre del Lambrión and, though de Saint-Saud was not one of the party, the first ascent of Peña Santa de Castilla. Only two days later, having crossed a vast tract of still very rough unmapped country, they climbed Espigüete, a trig point in the Alto Carrión.

De Saint-Saud made five more visits between 1893 and 1908 and the results of his labours were published in 1922 in his famous, but now rare, *Monographie des Picos d'Europa (Pyrénées Cantabriques et Asturiennes)*, with a separate folder of maps drawn by Captain L Maury. These maps consist of three sheets scaled 1:50,000 and two smaller maps. Yet there still remained a few small areas unsurveyed and these were indicated in dotted lines.

Others followed, some seeking a way into the central massif from the north to reach the elusive area around Vega de Urriello, dominated by the Naranjo de Bulnes. The first to climb this mountain, after forcing a way from Bulnes, were Pedro Pidal and

Gregorio Pérez, the local hunter known as El Cainejo, in 1904. Two years later Gustav Schulz, an outstanding Munich climber, traversed the mountain solo—an equally astonishing feat. A British attempt was made in 1927 by the Rev. William Elmslie and two friends. They reached the old Camburero Hut from Bulnes and gazed at the Naranjo; Elmslie was astonished by the mountain 'rising sheer a thousand feet or more with smooth repellent sides that at the same time challenge and defy the climber.' Their attempt did not get very far. Nor did Abercrombie and Cope who, in 1933, after climbing Torre Cerredo and Torre del Llambrión, also tried the Naranjo. It was not until seventeen years later that the first British ascent was achieved: in 1950 T Fowle, F Green and F Watson, who were climbing with the Vetusta Mountain Club of Oviedo, managed to reach the top. Since then a number of major routes have been put up on this and other mountains, mainly during the last twenty years, and mostly by Spanish climbers.

At present the Picos de Europa still retain that element of mystery, surprise and awe associated with remote and unknown country: from the savagery of their deeply carved *gargantas,* the silent emptiness of their vast *hoyos* where nothing moves, the intricately carved corrugations of the rock, the jagged crags and *agujas* soaring above the clouds. The Picos are wild and uninhabited, as nature intended. But they are also under threat. Official plans exist for their exploitation by the construction of roads, footpaths, hotels, huts, cableways and hydro-electric schemes. The Picos deserve much better than this. It would be an unmitigated disaster if this unique and precious jewel in the rich treasury of European mountains were destroyed and the Philistine hordes allowed to triumph where more than a thousand years ago the infidel forces of the Caliphat of Ummayad were defeated and driven away.

TIM SALMON
Greece

The special pleasure of the Greek mountains is their almost pristine condition. They have never been developed, least of all as a tamed wilderness playground, as so many of Europe's more dramatic ranges have been. There are few roads, and those mostly dirt tracks built to service the shepherds who still take their flocks to the high pastures in summer.

They are walkers' rather than climbers' mountains, though their remoteness and inaccessibility give them drama and splendour too. They have their crags and precipices, forests and ravines. Numerous peaks are over 2000 metres, and despite their brilliant and balmy summertime climate they behave like mountains anywhere, with unpredictable storms and lightning, mists and snow. In fact for five or six months of the year, from November to April, they are under snow above 1800 metres. Though they are rugged and wild enough to give a real sense of adventure, walking them requires no more skill or expertise than that expected of a fit hill walker and poor navigators can take comfort at least in the good visibility—there is seldom any need to get the compass out!

They are working mountains too, inhabited, scattered with dozens of ancient villages where a handful of mainly old people keep the traditional ways just barely alive, scratching a living with a few sparse crops and a small flock of sheep or goats. Life is basic. Water comes from a spring. Cooking is done on an open hearth or in an outside wood-fired oven. Light in the smaller, more isolated communities is still only an oil lamp. The women weave their own blankets and rugs, and some even the material for their own clothes.

In winter life is at a low ebb. In summer it revives with the return of emigré children from the cities for the summer holiday. The big flocks come up from the lowlands where they were forced to descend to escape the snows. It is a time for village fairs; for dancing and drinking—especially on July 20th, the Prophet Elijah's day, and August 15th, the Assumption of the Virgin Mary.

From the walker's point of view the existence of these villages more than compensates for the absence of any organised amenities, be they hotels, restaurants or rescue services. The people are amazingly hospitable and generous, just as they used to be all over Greece before the days of mass tourism. They will always find you a bed and food—embarrassingly often without charge—and frequently invite you into their homes. Therefore, in addition to the pleasures of walking, you get a real glimpse into a way of life long vanished from other parts of Europe.

GREECE

● Salonica

ALBANIA

▲ *Gramos*
2520m

▲ *Smolikas*
2637m

Konitsa ●

Olympus ▲
2917m

▲ *Gamila*
2497m

● Metsovo

Yanina ●

● Larisa

Pelion ▲
1610m
● Volos

● Arta

AGRAFA

● Karpenisi

Evia

Vardhousia ▲
2495m

Ghiona
▲ *2510m*

▲ *Dhirfi*
1743m

● Amfissa

Helmos
2341m ▲

ATHENS ●

▲
Ohi
1398m

● Kalavrita

Corinth ●

PELOPONNESE

● Sparta

Taÿgetos
▲ *2407m*

N

0   100 Kilometres
0   50 Miles

Aside from the landscape itself, the greatest natural beauty in the mountains is the sight of wild flowers, of which Greece possesses more than 600 endemic species. What you see of course depends on the season, latitude and altitude. But as spring comes late in the mountains, there is plenty of interest until the end of July. Among the richest species are the campanulas, violets, orchids, saxifrages and crocuses, but the variety is legion: irises, butterwort, dogroses, gentians, crimson pools of *geranium subcaulescens* on hot limestone screes, tulips like the Cretan rarity, *bakeri*, fritillaries, narcissus, anemones, lilies—of which the most spectacular are the scarlet *chalcedonicum* and the waxy yellow *albanicum* – while in autumn cyclamen are as common as daisies.

Butterflies are numerous too, with a particularly large variety of fritillaries, and the occasional specimen of Apollo with its distinctive red roundels on black-veined wings. Birds and mammals on the other hand are sadly depleted, largely through indiscriminate hunting. Of the big birds of prey golden eagles are relatively common, as are a variety of hawk. I have seen one lammergeyer and half a dozen vultures, and have occasionally disturbed a covey of rock partridges. Little moves or sings. As to mammals the situation is even sadder. A few bears survive in the north-west; rather more wolves and boar and a few small herds of chamois. I have only ever seen one roe deer and a couple of marten pelts. There are said to be a handful of lynx but I know of no recent sightings. Even the once common hare has become a rarity.

As for the mountains themselves, there are so many areas to walk in that I have organised my description into three or four broad categories simply in order to give it some sort of logic.

First, the doyen of Greek mountains, Olympus. At 2917 metres it is both the highest and the most beautiful. Though not really near any sights you might be visiting, it is not difficult to get to, lying as it does on the main Athens-Salonica road and rail links, about an hour south of Salonica. With its feet literally in the sea every inch of its height counts. And there is no more exciting eve-of-ascent experience than camping at one of the beach-side camp sites and looking up the long wooded cleft of the Mavrólongos ravine into the heart of the mountain as the highest peaks, Mýtikas and Stefáni, darken to a deep indigo against the starlit sky.

The classic ascent begins from the village of Litòhoro at the mouth of the ravine, though most people nowadays take the forest track to Priónia where there is a spring, a stream and Zeus' snack bar! Here the marked path begins, winding steeply up through the hot tangy scent of firs and the contrasting freshness of beech woods. If you are sharp-eyed you might see one of the rarest plants in Europe, endemic to Olympus and the only northern hemisphere relative of the African violet, *Jankaea heldreichii*.

In August at least you will not have the mountain to yourself. That is the price of its fame, but this does also bring compensations, chiefly in the shape of the only two manned refuges in Greece. The first, close to three hours out from Priónia at 2100 metres, is a worthwhile destination in itself. Spectacularly perched on the edge of a rocky bluff among the last of the storm-tormented Balkan pines, it looks east to the sea and up to the stark limestone teeth that ring the summits like a palisade. With hot food and a log fire, it is the best hotel in the land; a little pricey, but then all provisions have to come up by mule.

There are two routes to the top, both about three hours: one by the ridge known as Kaki Skála, the other by the steep Lóuki couloir. Zolotas, keeper of the refuge, recommends the first on the grounds that you are exposed to rockfalls in the couloir if there is a party above you. Both routes involve some mild scrambling. I prefer to go up the ridge and down by the couloir. That way you are nearer to the upper refuge on the Plateau of the Muses at 2600 metres, from where you can descend the beautiful north side of the mountain in about five hours, making a leisurely three-day excursion.

The ridge route is exhilaratingly airy, though not dangerous in good weather, with a 1000 metre drop at your left elbow into a great cirque on whose walls there are a number of climbing routes. The narrow platform of the summit is also splendidly airy for non-climbers, giving you a real sense of achievement, with the secondary summit Stéfani, only 6 metres lower, a short distance to the north—a rather tougher proposition, again with several climbing routes. This latter is the so-called *Throne of Zeus*, where legend has it the gods held court and conducted their tangled amorous intrigues.

Whether it was vestigial fear of the gods or merely the difficult terrain, as far as is known, Mýtikas was climbed for the first time only in 1913, whereas most Greek peaks were trodden at least by the shepherds, as wiry and agile as their sheep. But it is a fickle mountain and you should be prepared for storm and cold even when it is broiling on the beach.

For someone travelling in Greece on a general sight-seeing rather than a specifically mountain holiday, there are a number of good hikes to be made on peaks close to the major sights, especially in the Delphi area. The most obvious is Parnassós, the mountain at whose feet Delphi lies.

The standard route, from the HAC (Hellenic Mountain Club) refuge above the neighbouring village of Aráhova to the 2457 metre Liákoura peak, is rather arid and denuded and best omitted, unless incorporated in a traverse of the entire massif. A prettier and gentler route starts up an old mule trail directly behind the enclosure of the ancient site of Delphi, threads through the forest of Greek fir on the more or less level ledge of ground behind the first steep scarp, to come out on the central plateau by the summer village of Ano Aráhova (about four hours), from where you can easily get a lift off the mountain, or continue for a further two hours up a tougher and more impressive section to the refuge. But the finest route starts on the east side of the mountain at Ano Tithoréa just off the Livadhiá–Amfiklea road, and involves a strenuous six-hour pull up the precipitous Velitsa ravine beneath the eastern faces of the summit ridge, whose crags and crevices hold the snow well into May.

Even so, Parnassós is rather tame by Greek standards, with the country's largest ski resort and a number of Swiss-style chalets beginning to make their appearance. For a more 'real' experience the mountains to the west, Ghióna (2510m) and Vardhóusia (2495m), are better.

Ghióna, which is best reached via the bus station in Amfissa and the hamlet of Viniani, is a long, precipitous spine of rock with several peaks over 2000 metres, fir-clad on its eastern flanks and almost sheer on the west. The classic route is up the Reká ravine, a beetling red-stained trench 300-400 metres deep, which you ascend for about 4¹/₂ hours before clambering out to the north to the HAC refuge where there are a couple of summer sheepfolds. From here you scale the Skasmádha col at 2100 metres, with tremendous views opening out westwards to Vardhóusia and north to the faraway peaks of the southern Pindos. Above, a narrow ridge climbs to Pyramidha, the well-defended summit shaped as its name suggests.

From the cwm below the col you can escape northwards to the villages of Pyrá or Kaloskopi and continue with a two-day traverse of the gentler but green and beautiful Iti (2152m)—whose central plateau must have close to a square kilometre of crocuses in spring—descending the steep north scarp to Lamia, near the ancient pass of Thermopylae, where Leonidas and his Spartans made their heroic stand against the Persian invaders in 480 BC. Alternatively, you can descend the west flank of Ghióna via the knee-trembling course of the Lázos stream, which brings you down to the Mórnos river valley to the village of Sikiá in the shadow of the 1300-metre Pláka wall. (Allow 10-11 hours for the whole traverse. There are climbing routes on the steep western crags.)

From Sikiá it is relatively easy, either on foot or by the dirt road, to reach chestnut-shaded Athanásios Dhiákos, the starting-point for walks and climbs on Vardhóusia. A steep path climbs from the village to the sloping Pitimáliko meadows which fill the jagged ring of peaks that fence the massif. There are two refuges at around 1900 metres and plenty of good camping ground, as long as you watch out for the vicious sheepdogs. This is a favourite spot for HAC summer climbing schools, with numerous routes especially on the western peaks. Most, however, including the summit, Kórakas, are within the grasp of walkers as well. My favourite hike is the eight-hour east-west traverse down to Artotina through some of the best alpine scenery in Greece. Not for nothing is the area known as Little Switzerland.

Another well-placed and beautiful mountain, visible from the peaks of Vardhóusia though across the waters of the Gulf of Corinth, is Helmós (2355m). Close to the Corinth-Patras road, it is most easily accessible via Kalávrita and the delightful rack and pinion railway up the heady Vouraikós gorge. Far the most alluring hike, however, is on the east side, beginning at the remote hamlet of Sólos. Compensation for the difficulty of getting there, for botanists at least, is the presence of the rare white *cyclamen persicum* in the roadside woods. A glorious path climbs through fir and pine woods in five or six hours to the long wavering waterfall of Mavronéri, which the ancients believed was the source of the river Styx separating Hades from the world of the living. Again it is possible to continue right over the mountain via the HAC hut and the Xerókambos plateau down to Kalávrita.

Further south in the Peloponnese the long high range of Taÿgetos forms a magnificent barrier behind the orange groves of the vale of Sparta and the ruined Byzantine hill town of Mistra. If you can get a lift up the dusty 12 kilometres of track from the bus stop at Paliopanayiá, walking time to the highest peak, Profitis Ilias (2407m), is around 4¹/₂ hours via an HAC refuge. On the top is a low troglodytic-looking chapel, dedicated to Elijah (Ilias), where on the prophet's feast day, July 20th, a stout priest and athletic believers gather to celebrate. On a good day—that means early morning—you can see all up the Peloponnese to Helmós and way out to sea towards Crete.

Even in Athens, if you should be overcome by a yearning for the hills, escape is easy. An hour's bus ride from the city centre takes you to the heart of Párnitha, the 1400 metre mountain which forms the city's western border. Amazingly, given the proximity of the great wen, you find yourself surrounded by virgin forest, ravines and crags. There is rock-climbing at Flambóuri and Arma, as well as numerous hiking paths around and across the mountain. There is also a tremendous display of wild flowers from March to May.

Of all the Greek mountain experiences walking the Pindos range is the most telling. Starting in effect on the north shore of the Gulf of Corinth and running all the way to Mt Grámmos on the Albanian border, the range forms the backbone of northern Greece. It takes some thirty days to walk and you cross just two tarmac roads and pass through two small towns of about 4000 people. Although in the past thirty years fine weather tracks have increasingly violated the virginity of the landscape, the greater part of the route can still be travelled on the footpaths and mule trails that since time immemorial have been the only links between the scattered villages. It is this remoteness which makes the area unique. The twentieth century has scarcely touched it. There are no shops, no hotels, no traffic. A week of this and you lose all sense of time and of the workaday western world.

The lack of amenities should not deter you. Every village has a *magazi*, usually a ramshackle establishment that doubles as coffee-shop and general store. This is the place to make for to ask for a meal, shelter, route directions or provisions for the road. These are likely to be cheese, bread, olives and endless tins of sardines or spam.

The route I have worked out is similar to that taken by Lord Hunt's expedition in 1963. It is not waymarked and you will definitely need a guide book. There are stretches which now coincide with the trans-Europe E4 path, recently waymarked by the HAC. However, at the time of writing, there is no available documentation on this.

On the whole the paths are clear, having been worked for so many hundreds of years. However, with depopulation and the advent of Nissan, there is much less mule traffic and the paths have inevitably become overgrown or been washed out in places. But even if you get into difficulty you are not in much danger in summertime, and there is nearly always a shepherd somewhere within earshot. It is surprising how few people it takes to make such a vast landscape seem populated.

The route divides naturally into three sections, each requiring 10-12 days' walking, with plenty of opportunities to escape from it along the way. The first section, in some ways the most arduous because cutting across the grain of the land from valley to valley, begins at Amfissa near Delphi. It goes straight into the traverse of Ghióna and Vardhóusia described above, then angles north-west through unbroken woodland, past half-ruined villages to relatively prosperous Krikelo, where you again strike across country on the old mule trail to Karpenisi.

Although only a small market town on the edge of a bowl ringed by the high peaks, by comparison with where you have come from and what lies ahead, it is a teeming metropolis. It is your last chance of tasting the fleshpots, for the next twelve days, if not the highest, are the wildest of the trip.

It is best to start with a 40-kilometre bus ride west to Kerasohóri, the gateway to the Agrafa mountains, the stuff of folk song and legend, for here many of the half-brigand warriors who fought the Turks out of Greece in the nineteenth century had their lairs, followed in the Second World War by the communist-led guerrillas of the Resistance. From here the route ascends the gorge of the Agrafiótis river closely walled between jagged ridges rising to more than 2000 metres either side. Here and there isolated villages and tiny settlements emerge unsuspected among the woods. Until recently the whole area was innocent of all but hoof and foot. Sadly a carelessly bulldozed track has now buried sections of the old path. It is still beautiful but that magical and total sense of harmony and intimacy with the wild has gone.

There are alternative routes along both eastern and western ridges where the only settlements are summer sheepfolds. The shepherds are mostly Sarakatsani who, until this generation, were almost wholly nomadic, following their sheep winter and summer from lowlands to uplands in search of grazing. Unlike the Vlachs, of whom more later, they are Greek-speaking and on the evidence of their dialect and customs are believed to be perhaps the only true descendants of the ancient Greeks, their integrity preserved by endogamous marriage and their wandering habits.

Beyond the Agrafiótis watershed the way lies west past the Byronically romantic monastery of Spiliá to Petrotó and the serpentine gorges of the Ahelöos, one of the two main rivers draining the southern Pindos. From here there are two options: to keep due north to Mesohóra and up the river to its headwaters at Haliki, or follow its westward loop to Pahtóuri and haul yourself over the fiercely scarped massifs of Kakardhitsa (2429m) and Peristéri (2295m), rejoining the first route at Haliki for the final pull over the watershed to Métsovo.

Both routes have their charms. The western variant, tougher and denuded in the uplands, goes through some fine villages: Matsóuki, Kallarites and Siráko. The valley route is thickly forested, concealing four or five lovely if neglected monasteries and churches on its flanks, while the river itself, a raging torrent in spring, is in summer a delightful chain of turquoise bathing pools.

This is Vlach country, from the upper Ahelöos to the Albanian border in the north. Like the Sarakatsani the Vlachs are a pastoral people, largely nomadic, but with the difference that from around 1600 AD they have had proper summer villages in the mountains. And there is one other major difference: though nearly all bilingual today, the Vlachs have their own mother-tongue which is still recognisably Latin. They grew rich from their sheep and wool products in the sixteenth and seventeenth centuries, diversified into mule haulage and set up trading houses in the capital cities of eastern Europe. Métsovo, commanding the main east-west pass over the Pindos, was their commercial capital. And thanks to the fortune of one of those emigré sons, it remains

The monastery of Ayios Yioryios at Mirófilo on Mt Hadzi, threatened with submersion by a hydro-electric scheme. (Photo: Tim Salmon.)

almost the only unspoilt provincial town in Greece today—a little twee as a result and attracting too much tourism for its own good.

North from here, the last stage of the journey, the country is high, wide, thick with Black pine and beech and largely serpentine in composition, which makes for gentler contours than the wicked limestone to the south, and for a different flora. It is bear country—not that you are likely to see one, for they are few and shy. The nearest I have come to one is fresh prints—enough to give me a *frisson* not entirely of pleasure.

Climbing out of Métsovo, on a tarmac road for the first and only time, you turn into the meadows where rises the river Aöos, which finally reaches the sea on the Albanian coast. (Stop Press: these meadows have recently been churned to pieces by a massive hydro-electric scheme. Even if you were to endure a dusty day's march on the works track, it is by no means certain that you could pick up the old path to Pénde Alónia where the dam has been sited. There are two possibilities. One is to continue along the dirt road from Pénde Alónia to the village of Flambourári described in the guide book, *The Mountains of Greece*—details below. The other is to take a bus from

Métsovo to Háni Baldóuma and then hitch or bus to Flambourári.) Then you head north-west for two or three days through the forest to the imposing stone villages of the Zagóri, strung along the bare southern flanks of Mt Gamíla (2497m). There are several good hikes to be done in the region including the 10 kilometre canyon of the Vikos gorge, while the walls and buttresses of the mountain's north face are a regular challenge to climbers.

Continuing from Skamnéli or Tsepélovo the route scales Gamíla by the col below the 2466 metre Tsóuka Róssa peak, before descending through the only passable gap in the northern cliffs to Vrissohóri in the green depths of the Aöos ravine. Shut between the alpine walls of Gamíla to the south and the wooded slopes of Smólikas, Greece's second highest mountain (2637m) to the north, this is arguably the single finest mountain landscape in the country—now threatened like many of Greece's loveliest areas with dams and tunnels for hydro-electric schemes.

East across Smólikas and down to the famous and still thriving Vlach sheep village of Samarina, the route turns north-west again for the last bee-line bolt for the Albanian border. May is the most entrancing time to be in the area. The peaks are still white above 1800-2000 metres. The north-hanging beech woods are coming into leaf and every inch of open ground is thick with orchids, primulas, crocuses and violets.

Two to three days will take you to the frontier, through Fóurka, Dhrossopiyi, Likórahi and Aetomilitsa, the latter like Samarina inhabited only in summer. The whole area suffered terribly during the 1946–9 Civil War when the Greek Communist partisans made their last stand here against the U.S.-backed government army. There is many a battle-scarred veteran in the villages who spent half a lifetime of exile in Tashkent or Prague before being amnestied and allowed to return. And when you climb above Aetomilitsa to the bare heights of Grámmos, whose 2520 metre summit overhangs the frontier, you will find the ground still littered with rusting steel and pitted with caved-in gun-pits. The Albanians patrol their side of the ridge below the summit, so it is wise not to be too curious.

And that far from exhausts Greek walking possibilities. In the islands Crete's stark and arid White Mountains rise from the sea to a dramatic 2452 metres, cut on the south side by the long rent of the Samariá gorge, itself a day's work to descend. Evia's Dhírfi, Xerovóuni and Ohi, though relatively low, all make good one to two day trips reasonably accessible from Athens. Samos too has potential, though I have not visited since the devastation caused by the forest fire in 1987. Back on the mainland, Pelion just south of Olympus combines beautiful villages, unusually luxuriant vegetation and some fine but rather rapidly disintegrating old footpaths.

Finally, there is Mt Athos whose 2033 metre peak thrusts heavenward like a rocket from the sea at the tip of a long narrow peninsula south-east of Salonica. It offers what is probably the strangest walking experience in Europe, closed unfortunately to women, for no female creature has been allowed to set foot here since the Virgin Mary declared it her private garden. For this is the Monastic Republic of Athos, a curious Byzantine time-warp in which some 1500 monks continue to lead their contemplative and less-so lives in a couple of dozen monasteries up to a thousand years old. The flowers, the woods, the inter-monastery paths—to say nothing of the buildings themselves, in which you can stay—are extraordinary and have scarcely been affected by the hand of man. I say that, yet even here the Forestry has been at work burying millennial footpaths and scarring the mountainside with the rubble from its logging tracks.

The peak is easily walked from the south. From the top you can see Olympus in the west, and in the east they say, even as far as Istanbul on a clear night. The north face is a matter for climbers. A few routes have been put up by Greek climbers, but what the monks would say to such secular assault on the Holy Mountain by non-Orthodox heathen is hard to predict. It would be a brave man who'd drive a piton with a Byzantine anathema upon his head!

KEV REYNOLDS
Corsica

Rising steeply from the Mediterranean, Corsica is very much 'the scented isle', an island of lush flowers and shrubs, of a brilliant luminescence, of clear streams, hidden tarns, deep ravines, open moorlands and some delightful Alpine-style mountains that offer rock routes and challenging walks of considerable charm.

It is not a large island, measuring only about 180 kilometres by 80, but its granite spine is punctuated by a number of peaks well in excess of 2000 metres. There are no glaciers and snow only remains throughout the summer in the most sheltered of couloirs and north-facing slopes, but for the early visitor a coating of late-winter snow adds to the status of the mountains, increasing the impression of overall height.

Politically Corsica belongs to France, even though the Italian coast is only some 80 kilometres away and mainland France more than double that distance. Linguistically and geographically it owes more to Italy than it does to France, and peace is frequently disrupted by nationalist factions demanding independence. Pascale Paoli and Napoleon Bonaparte are honoured for different reasons, while the bandit Antoine Bellacoscia ('King of the Maquis') is recalled as something of a folk hero. But for the climber little of this is evident or, indeed, important, since the mountain experience in Corsica is concentrated away from habitation, and island culture is barely touched upon.

Whilst much of the coast has been developed for tourism, inland there is a natural ruggedness, an untamed, almost primitive splendour that the visiting climber or walker cannot fail to recognise or appreciate. The mountains themselves form the very backbone of Corsica; a spine of granite running north-west to south-east, with minor chains branching south-west and north-east from it. A separate group, composed of crystalline schists and of little interest to climbers, stands apart to the east.

It is the main granite chain which draws the attention of mountaineers and mountain walkers, the latter especially attracted by the *Grande Randonnée* long-distance footpath (GR20) which follows the spine of mountains for 177 kilometres, from Calenzana in the north-west, to Conca, near Porto Vecchio in the south-east. The entire route traverses the Corsican National Park (*Parc Naturel Régional de la Corse*), is considered the most challenging of all GR routes of France, and is an immensely rewarding expedition for fit and experienced hill walkers.

Most of the major peaks were first climbed during the eighteenth century by either surveyors or hunters, but several members of the newly-formed Alpine Club made tentative forays to the island during the latter half of the nineteenth century, among them that much-travelled mountaineer, D W Freshfield, who announced to the AC in

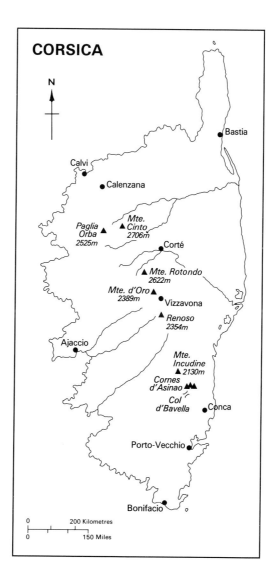

1880 that: 'Corsican mountains clearly come within the scope of our society and call for more attention than we have yet given them.' Yet it was the Germans under the leadership of Dr Félix von Cube who claimed many fine rock peaks in a series of three expeditions undertaken there between 1899 and 1904, while a team of Swiss and Austrians, with the guide Conrad Kain, concentrated on exploration of a cluster of peaks in the north-west of the island around the same time. The brothers G I and M Finch visited Corsica in 1909 with the Norwegian, Alf Bryn, and made—among others—the first traverse of both Tafonato and Cinque Frati, and established a now-classic route on the east face of Paglia Orba (2525m), a mountain considered by many to be among the very finest on the island, and one that is affectionately known as the 'Matterhorn of Corsica'.

But the exploration and development of Corsica's mountains have really been dominated by German and Austrian climbers throughout the twentieth century. Ridges, faces, sturdy buttresses and remote walls have all come under the scrutiny of Germanic ropes, while sporadic noteworthy ascents have been made by visiting French, Italian, Swiss and a few British parties here and there.

Of major interest to mountaineers is the Cinto massif which contains the island's highest peak. This rises in the north-west of the island, with access to it being easiest from the Haut Asco valley where many short technical climbs are possible, as well as major routes on the northern flanks of Cinto itself. The summit of Monte Cinto (2706m) projects from a long ridge rising from Punta Minuta and extending north-eastwards as a major watershed. Impressive cliffs of 400 metres or so slab beneath the summit on the northern side, yet it is from this side, from Haut Asco opposite the Cirque de Trimbolacciu, that the long and somewhat tedious traditional route leads in 6–7 hours. There is some good rock here, and variations of the *voie normale* give an opportunity to sample a little of it and thereby reduce the time required for the ascent.

Between Cinto and Punta Minuta the eye is led through the Trimbolacciu cirque to a glaze of smooth granite walls and the imposing peak of Capo Larghia (2503m). Von Cube's party attacked this during their first raid in 1899, and there are a number of fine routes to enjoy on it today, not only from the north, but also on the south face when approached from the Grotte des Anges, a large cave and a traditional base for climbs in the region.

Punta Minuta sports a cluster of pinnacles—as many as thirty gendarmes perforate its splendid north ridge alone. In 1932 the Swiss team of Amstutz and Risch made the first traverse of this remarkable ridge, which is reckoned among the best of its kind in Corsica, and it remains a serious expedition today with individual pitches of III and IV- and requiring somewhere in the region of fifteen hours of effort to complete in its entirety. Below Minuta's west face is the well-known Cirque de la Solitude, the descent of which is seen as the crux of the whole GR20, fearfully exposed for those unused to such places, albeit aided by a series of fixed ropes, cables and sections of ladder. At the head of the cirque lies Col Perdu which gives access to the West Face Diagonal, now the shortest route to the summit, about grade III.

At the far north-eastern end of the Cinto massif the Popolasca aiguilles contain a true bounty of rock climbing possibilities. The district was not properly explored until the 1960s and an energetic party could happily spend time here continuing that exploration. The villages of Castiglione and Popolasca huddle beneath this barrier of stone to the east.

To the south-west of Monte Cinto the splendid piece of purple sculptured rock that is Paglia Orba (2525m) impresses all who gaze upon it. Again it was von Cube's party who made the first ascent in 1899. It's a gem of a climber's mountain, with numerous routes of all grades on mostly first-rate rock, the most frequented ascent being by way of the western gully and ridge. The walls that adorn the north and north-west faces are separated by the 500 metres of the north pillar which gives climbing of grade V and VI, depending on the line taken, while on the south face there's another grade V pioneered by Moroni, and the Amstutz/Risch route on the south-east ridge with pitches of IV. But perhaps the best-known rock route, not just on Paglia Orba but in all Corsica, is the exposed Finch Route on the east face, still a challenge today at grade IV- and a classic piece of work when it was first climbed in 1909.

Paglia Orba overlooks the Viro valley to the east, while to the south-west stands the great flake of Capo Tafonato (2335m), hugely attractive to rock climbers and with a notable hole below the south summit, some 30 by 10 metres. Again, it was von Cube who first explored here.

The GR20 winds its way below Tafonato, and descends to Col de Verghio where one of the few roads to traverse the island is crossed. The village of Calacuccia lies downhill to the north-east in the Golo valley but GR20 continues away from habitation and comes to Lac de Nino, perched high in the mountains to the west of Punta Artica at the head of the moorland-like sweep of the Tavignano valley. (This valley, incidentally, narrows lower down to a tremendous wooded gorge which is well worth exploring along a mule-track that works its way through from the outskirts of the old capital of the island, Corté.)

Monte Rotondo (2622m) rises to the south-east of Lac de Nino. As the second highest peak in Corsica it gives surprisingly little impression of height or grandeur from a distance. But a closer acquaintance reveals a mountain of some character. (It was one of the few Corsican peaks to be climbed by Freshfield.) When climbed from Refuge de Pétra Piana a series of easy rock bands and slopes of scree lead into a high corrie containing a lake and one or two small pools. Broken crags and little jutting pinnacles embrace this lake and the standard ascent route takes you from it by way of screes, terraces and a gully onto the ridge south-east of the summit. A superb panoramic view is granted from the top (there's a small bivouac hut almost on the summit), with much of the island being displayed. Monte d'Oro appears especially grand to the south.

If the route from Pétra Piana is easy and relatively short, taking only about three hours from the hut, the northern approach from the Restonica valley makes a much more demanding day. Perhaps the worst part is the steady climb through the *maquis*, rising at last with some relief to slabs and gullies, often with snow and ice well into mid-summer (an ice-axe can be useful here even in late July). This route will occupy between five and six hours, with a further three needed for the descent.

The Restonica valley is a magical place. Wonderful forests of Corsican pine clothe the slopes, above which an amazing array of wild flowers and shrubs carpet the hillsides. Cyclamen colour the woods with a dash of scarlet. Fragrance hangs in the air like a great natural perfumery. Semi-wild pigs scavenge through the woods and in islands of rough pasture. And the river that boils through its rocky bed gives out here and there to deep pools that entice the hot and weary climber or trekker with their promise of refreshment.

Standing almost in the very centre of Corsica, and accessible from Vizzavona, Monte d'Oro is clearly seen from the summit of Rotondo. It is a fine, sturdy peak, 2389 metres in height, making for some interesting if not too difficult ascent routes. All approaches are long, while a party prepared to bivouac might well spend several worthwhile days exploring rock climbing possibilities on its north face.

The standard approach route comes from near the Vizzavona col and follows GR20 right onto the west ridge. From here to the summit there is an entertaining scramble of an hour and a half, making a route of more than six hours from Vizzavona. Trekkers with the inclination and sufficient spare energy could enjoy a diversion from the GR20 stage (Refuge de l'Onda to Vizzavona) to make this ascent before tackling the splendours of the Agnone valley, noted for the rather lovely Cascade des Anglais.

South of the Vizzavona-Ajaccio road the mountains of Corsica lose some of their drama but not their appeal. There may not be so much in the way of climbing possibilities here but ascents of modest peaks and days spent following long ridge systems have a charm all their own. On many of these ridges one enjoys a profound sense of space, especially where the main spine teases towards the east and you gaze down nearly 2000 metres onto the island's small flat agricultural plain. And on so many occasions you look westward over a tangled knot of granite to the curving bays of the Mediterranean, then turn eastward and see across a continuing maze of granite to yet more curving bays and the dazzle of sun on sea. This is but one of the pleasures of mountain activity on an island, of course.

GR20 climbs out of the Col de Vizzavona to work its way round the lengthy northern ridge of the Renoso massif, then swings south through woods on its eastern flanks. There is, however, an alternative sporting route to be made onto Monte Renoso (2352m) itself. It first wanders along a spur of hillside, then climbs among *maquis* to a wall of slabs, turrets and spires on a scramble (occasional cairns) onto the ridge south of Punta dell Oriente. Monte Renoso rises along this ridge to the south, with a true surprise on nearing it to find the crest has been flattened and wind-scoured, a great broad stony plateau with the summit obscured among shattered boulders.

Seen from the north-east, this popular peak has a much more elegant face with the lovely Lacs de Bastan lying below in a rocky bowl. Refuge de Capannelle, recently improved and one of the few huts in Corsica to offer meals, is ideally situated for an ascent of Renoso from the north-east.

Between Monte Renoso and the Cappella-Formicola-Incudine ridge system runs the heavily forested Taravo valley. Col de Verde marks the northern-most limits of this valley, and there are several small villages nestling deeply within it. The main north-south road of the island runs through the Taravo, branching away at Zicavo to cross Col de Vaccia *en route* to Sartène.

There is little to interest climbers along this section of ridge. Punta della Cappella

Monte Renoso and Lac de Bastan. (Photo: Kev Reynolds.)

(2041m) is a walker's peak, as is Monte Formicola (1981m) further to the south. A trekker's hut lies between Col de Verde and Punta della Cappella, and another is found on the south side of the ridge below Formicola. From here there are good views across an unfathomable mass of greenery to Monte Incudine (2130m), surely one of the easiest summits in Corsica, and visited by D W Freshfield in 1880.

Incudine has a great whaleback ridge that terminates on the summit and then falls steeply to the south-east. A wonderful panorama can be enjoyed from this peak, overlooking much of southern Corsica and with Mediterranean beaches and coves drawing the eye. But of more interest to climbers is the jagged ridge forming a line of granite fencing to the south-east: the Cornes d'Asinao.

Standing over the road pass of Col de Bavella, the Cornes (or Aiguilles) d'Asinao offer a plethora of routes of varying grades and assorted lengths, and together form one of the most appealing sights on the island. The group consists of seven towers, the highest of which is a modest 1855 metres but appearing much higher as it thrusts out of the pines. Superb climbing is to be enjoyed here, with short approach walks from the road pass. A variation of the GR20 works a route along the western flanks of these towers, then, aided by a short section of fixed rope, crosses through a gap to allow a descent to the col. This entertaining scramble offers trekkers some spectacular views, not the least of which is a close-up profile of the great granite needles.

East of Col de Bavella a complimentary ridge spur running slightly north-east to south-west contains another array of fascinating granite spires and broken turrets. More good climbing is to be had here, although the approach to specific faces is much longer than to those of Asinao. Routes of 300–400 metres are to be found on some of the faces and ridges, with grades of IV and V being common, while on the monolith of Samulaghia (1480m) the west face offers a touch of grade VI. Refuge de Paliri, the most southerly hut in Corsica, serves the eastern side of the Tafunata di Paliri towers (routes up to grade VI), and is gained without difficulty by following the route of GR20 all the way from Col de Bavella.

To summarise Corsica as a destination for climbers and mountain walkers, it may be sufficient to say that the island offers superb wild scenery and, out of the main high-summer season, a true impression of wilderness. There are delectable yet complex granite massifs where climbers may revel in a taste of pioneering. There are hard climbs by the hundreds, and teasingly modest routes to be enjoyed by the low-key scrambler. But because of the relative isolation and remoteness of some of the areas, one should be aware at all times of the added degree of seriousness should an accident occur.

High summer temperatures can be uncomfortably hot. Vegetation is tinder dry and the risk of fire acute. Open fires are banned by the National Park authorities, and cooking on gas or liquid fuel stoves in the open should be attended with great caution. The water source close to some of the huts runs dry in exceptional years, and trekkers in particular should pay heed to the necessity of carrying a good quantity of liquid with them each day.

Perhaps the best months for climbing and walking are June and September. After particularly heavy winter snows, however, June can sometimes make for difficult conditions in places. But the wild flowers are then at their best and will add a new dimension to the valleys and hillsides.

A word of explanation ought to be given with regard to the *maquis*, already mentioned several times in this chapter. Most of the valleys and lower hillsides are covered with a dense growth of scrub consisting of alder, juniper, broom, scrub oak, honeysuckle, myrtle, and a tangled bed of highly fragrant Mediterranean plants. This undergrowth, which often grows chest high and forms a belt right up to the base of many worthwhile cliffs, makes an almost impenetrable barrier in certain areas and is cursed by all who, having strayed from the waymarked trail, attempt to fight a way through. It is one of the memorable, if less desirable, features of inland adventuring on the scented isle.

Appendix

The following fact sheets—each compiled by the relevant contributor—offer practical guidance for anyone planning a visit and suggest further reading material for those inspired to learn more about an area.

SCOTLAND

Area: Highlands, Islands and Cairngorms.
Main Peaks: Ben Nevis (1343m), Ben Macdui (1309m), Braeriach (1296m), Cairn Toul (1291m), Cairngorm (1245m), Lochnagar (1155m), An Teallach (1062m), Liathach (1053m), Buachaille Etive Mor (1022m) and Sgurr Alasdair (993m).
Centres: Fort William—for Ben Nevis and the Marmores; Glen Brittle—for Skye; Aviemore—for the western Cairngorms.
Huts: Seven huts are owned by the SMC, JMCS and BMC. Bothies are a feature of 'back-country' accommodation in many areas. Youth Hostels are also conveniently situated for a number of climbs.
Access: Major airports are at Edinburgh, Glasgow and Aberdeen. Rail services feed Fort William and Oban in the west and Inverness in the east. Local bus services are of little value. Roads give limited access to some districts, and large areas of the country require long approach walks.
Maps: The Ordnance Survey covers the country at scales of 1:50,000. West Col provide maps of Ben Nevis at 1:16,000 scale, and the Cuillin of Skye at 1:15,000. Cicerone Press publish a map at 1:20,000 of the Black Cuillin to accompany the *Scrambles in Skye* guidebook (see below).
Guidebooks: More than a dozen guides are published by the Scottish Mountaineering Trust.
The following are published by Cicerone Press:
Scrambles in Lochaber by Noel Williams, *Scrambles in Skye* by J Wilson Parker (with map at 1:20,000), *Rock Climbs: Glen Nevis & The Lochaber Outcrops* by Ed Grindley, *The Island of Rhum* by Hamish Brown, *Cairngorms: Winter Climbs* by Allen Fyffe, *Winter Climbs: Ben Nevis & Glencoe* by Ed Grindley.

THE LAKE DISTRICT

Area: The English Lake District, Cumbria.
Main Peaks: Scafell Pike (978m), Scafell (964m), Helvellyn (950m) and Skiddaw (931m).
Centres: Keswick and Ambleside are the two chief centres, but there are many others. This is one of the world's great tourist honeypots.
Accommodation: Hotels, Youth Hostels, camp sites, huts. Huts are for club members only, or for those with reciprocal rights.
Access: International airports at Manchester and Newcastle (both approx. 2 hours). Local airports at Barrow and Carlisle. Principal rail access at Oxenholme and Penrith.
Maps: O.S. Outdoor Leisure series: *The Lake District* in 4 sheets 1:25,000.
Guidebooks: FRCC Guides (climbing) in 6 volumes: *Langdale; Eastern Crags; Scafell, Dow & Eskdale; Borrowdale; Pillar Rock; Great Gable.*
Walking guides by A Wainwright (Westmorland Gazette) in 8 volumes: *Eastern Fells; Far Eastern Fells; Central Fells; Southern Fells; Northern Fells; North Western Fells; Western Fells; Outlying Fells.*
Scrambles in the Lake District by R B Evans (Cicerone Press). *Winter Climbs in the Lake District* by Bob Bennett & Bill Birkett (Cicerone Press).

NORTH WALES

Area: North Wales.

Main Peaks: Snowdon/Yr Wyddfa (1085m), Carnedd Llewelyn (1064m), Glyder Fawr (999m), Tryfan (917m).

Centres: Betws y Coed, Capel Curig, Bethesda, Llanberis, Beddgelert and Dolgellau.

Accommodation: Several club huts exist in the main northern area (group bookings only, in advance and on exchange basis with other clubs). Bunkhouses and barns in Capel Curig, the Ogwen Valley and Llanberis Pass (enquire locally). Bed & breakfast accommodation, Youth Hostels and official camp sites in or near all major centres.

Access: By road via the A5 (for those approaching from the south and west) or via the A55 (from the north). By rail from Chester along the North Wales coast (branch line to Betws y Coed) to Bangor.

Maps: The main northern area conveniently appears on the 1:50,000 O.S. Sheet 115 (Snowdon Area). The southern groups appear on 1:50,000 O.S. Sheet 124 (Dolgellau Area). Number 17 (Snowdon) in 1:25,000 Leisure Series is worth having for detailed route finding in the main mountain areas.

Guidebooks: *Hill Walking in Snowdonia* by Steve Ashton (Cicerone Press), *The Mountains of Wales* by Terry Marsh (Hodder & Stoughton), *The Ridges of Snowdonia* by Steve Ashton (Cicerone Press); *Scrambles in Snowdonia* by Steve Ashton (Cicerone Press), *Snowdonia Rock Climbs* by Paul Williams (Constable), *100 Classic Climbs in North Wales* by Steve Ashton (Crowood Press), *Winter Climbs in North Wales* by Malcolm Campbell & Andy Newton (Cicerone Press), *Climbers' Club Guides to Wales*—comprehensive and regularly revised guides to rock climbs, in several volumes.

IRELAND

Main Peaks: Carrauntoohil (1038m), Lugnaquillia (926m), Slieve Donard (850m), Mweelrea (819m).

Main Centres: Dublin, Wicklow, Clonmel, Cahir, Killarney, Kenmare, Dingle, Clifden, Westport, Sligo, Donegal, Letterkenny, Plumbridge, Newcastle (Co. Down), Carlingford.

Huts: There are a few huts owned by Clubs of the Federation of Mountaineering Clubs of Ireland in the Mourne and Wicklow Mountains. The most useful hut-type accommodation is in Youth Hostels or independent hostels.

Access: Airports in Dublin, Cork, Galway, Knock and Belfast. Car ferries to Dublin, Rosslare, Cork and Larne.

Maps: Republic of Ireland: O.S. maps cover the country in 25 sheets at a scale of 1:126,720 ($^1/_2$ in. = 1 mile). Whilst reasonably accurate the scale is too small to show relevant mountain detail. Certain mountain areas are covered by special 1:50,000 sheets.

Northern Ireland: NIOS 1:50,000 maps cover the whole of Northern Ireland in 18 sheets. Areas of the Republic near the border are also covered.

Guidebooks: *Irish Peaks* by Joss Lynam (Constable). Irish walking guides published by Gill & Macmillan are as follows: *North West* by P Simms & G Foley, *North East* by R Rogers, *East* by D Herman etc., *South East* by F Martindale.

Mountains of Connemara by Joss Lynam (Folding Landscapes), *Mountains of Killarney* by J C Coleman (Dundalgan Press), *Dublin & Wicklow Mountains* (Irish Ramblers Club).

Rock climbing guides published by FMCI: *Donegal; Mournes; Fair Head; The Burren; Wicklow; Dalkey* etc.

NORWAY

Main Peaks: Galdhøpiggen (2469m)—Jotunheimen, Glittertind (2452m)—Jotunheimen, Store Skagastølstind (2405m)—Jotunheimen, Trolltindene (1795m)—Romsdalen, Romsdalshorn (1550m)—Romsdalen, Innerdalstårnet (1450m)—Innerdalen, Stetinden (1381m)—Tysfjord.

Centres: Spiterstulen in the Visdalen Valley is best for Galdhøpiggen and Glittertind; Turtagrø for the Hurrungane massif. For Romsdal, the small town of Åndalsnes is ideally situated and has excellent facilities.

Huts: Numerous huts are to be found but mostly in the southern ranges. These are owned by the DNT (Norwegian Touring Association). Some are unmanned and offer limited facilities. Walkers and climbers planning to use the hut network are advised to take out membership of DNT as the cost is more than compensated by reduced hut fees.

Access: There are international airports at Oslo and Bergen. Internally, rail links from Oslo to Åndalsnes, Trondheim, and Bodø. The Arctic Highway goes via Trondheim to North Cape.

Maps: The Norwegian Survey covers the country with a series of maps suitable for walkers at a scale of 1:50,000. Statens Kartverk also produce a series of maps (Turkart) of selected areas at mostly 1:50,000.

Guidebooks: *Mountain Touring Holidays in Norway* by Per Prag (Norway Travel Association, Oslo), *Mountain Touring Holidays in Norway* by Erling Welle Strand (Nortrabooks—Norway Travel Association, Oslo), *Walks and Climbs in Romsdal* by Tony Howard (Cicerone Press). *Scandinavian Mountains* by Peter Lennon (West Col).

Other Reading: *Norway, the Northern Playground* by W C Slingsby (Blackwell 1941, 2nd ed.), *Camps and Climbs in Arctic Norway* by Tom Weir (Cassell 1953).

DAUPHINÉ

Area: Dauphiné—France, South-West Alps, comprising Vercors, Chartreuse, Belledonne, Maurienne, Cerces, Queyras and the Massif des Ecrins.

Main Peaks: Barre des Ecrins (4102m), La Meije (3982m), Ailefroide (3954m), Mont Pelvoux (3946m).

Centres: Massif des Ecrins: La Grave, Briançon, Vallouise-Ailefroide, La Chapelle, Vagaudemar, La Désert, Valjouffrey, La Bérarde.

Huts: Numerous huts, liberally scattered throughout the region, many run by the CAF, others privately owned.

Access: Airports at Lyon and (in Italy) Torino. By rail to Grenoble and Briançon. Bus connections throughout the whole region. There are also buses from the UK (London) to Lyon and Grenoble.

Maps: IGN coverage in 1:50,000 scale. *Massif & Parc National des Ecrins* at 1:50,000 is published by Didier & Richard.

Guidebooks: *Ecrins Massif* by John Brailsford (Alpine Club, 1987). *Escalades du Briançonais* by J-J Rolland and Suzy Péguy. *Massif des Ecrins* by Devies, Laloue and Labonde (in 3 volumes). *Tour of the Oisans: GR54* by Andrew Harper (Cicerone Press). *Tour de l'Oisans: GR54 & GR541* by Roger Cannac (Parc National des Ecrins).

MONT BLANC

Area: Mainly in France and Italy, with a small area in Switzerland.

Main Peaks: Mont Blanc (4807m), Mont Maudit (4465m), Dôme du Goûter (4304m), Mont Blanc du Tacul (4248m), Grandes Jorasses (4208m), Aiguille Verte (4122m), Aiguille de Bionnassay (4052m).

Centres: Chamonix, Argentière and Les Contamines-Montjoie in France, Courmayeur in Italy. Champex-Lac and Orsières in Switzerland.

Huts: Many on all sides, mainly owned by the French, Swiss or Italian Alpine Clubs. Some privately owned, or by Guides Associations. In the valleys on the Tour of Mont Blanc are many refuges or *gîtes d'étape*.

Camp Sites: Many, especially in the Chamonix area. *Camping sauvage* above the tree line in France and Italy but forbidden in Switzerland.

Access: By air from Manchester or London to Geneva, then by train or coach to Chamonix. By rail to Paris and night train to Le Fayet (St-Gervais) and by train or coach to Chamonix.

Maps: *Mont Blanc et Beaufortain* 1:50,000 This map is produced by IGN and overprinted by Didier & Richard with ski routes, hotels and huts in red and walking routes in blue. Whilst there are several other maps available, some in larger scales, this map is the most generally useful.

Guidebooks: *Selected Climbs in the Mont Blanc Range* (Alpine Club)—in three volumes.
A Topo Guide to Rock Climbs of the Mont Blanc Area—the first edition in English (1986) is obtainable from Cordée, Leicester. This remarkable book, with detailed diagrams of no less than 167 rock routes, will appeal to skilled and dedicated rock climbers to whom the sport is more important than reaching a summit. It is especially useful for severe routes at low levels, when conditions are bad at higher altitudes.
La Chaine du Mont Blanc—the Vallots guide in three volumes are the most authoritative works on the region, with details of huts and climbs.
The Tour of Mont Blanc by Andrew Harper (Cicerone Press)—an excellent walking guide, latest edition published 1988.

The Mont Blanc Massif—100 Finest Routes by Gaston Rébuffet (Kaye & Ward 1974)—a lavishly illustrated large-format book by the late well-known guide and mountain writer.
Alpes du Nord—a Michelin Green Guide, very useful as a general introduction to the area.

Other Books: *Mont Blanc & The Seven Valleys* by R Frison-Roche with illustrations by Pierre Tairraz and others (English edition 1961). This book by a French guide is well translated into English, preserving the eloquence of the original. The author is especially knowledgeable on the history of the area, and the splendid photographs, some from the air, complement the text.
Mont Blanc and The Aiguilles by C Douglas Milner (Robert Hale 1955). Illustrated with 70 monochrome photographs, this book deals very largely with the history of mountaineering up to the first of the modern mechanised routes devised in the last 30 years. In the lists of suggested expeditions little has changed, except for the better in enlarged huts. However, the Lognan has been taken over by the military and the Refuge Elena has gone. The Mont Blanc tunnel has greatly helped the appeal of the Courmayeur area.
Savage Snows—The Story of Mont Blanc by Walt Unsworth (Hodder & Stoughton 1986). Substantially another book on the mountaineering history, especially by Englishmen. The last two chapters bring the story of modern hard routes up to date.
La Grande Ronde Autour du Mont Blanc by Samivel, with 97 illustrations in colour by S Norande (1981). Under the pseudonym Samivel, Paul Gayet-Tancrède has become the most renowned satirist, author and artist of mountain matters in France. He was also, in his younger days, an active climber with several first ascents to his credit. This book fully describes the Tour, and is especially worthy of notice for the fine colour illustrations. The text is, of course, in French and one of the many reasons why a sound knowledge of the language should be acquired by intending visitors.

THE PENNINE ALPS

Area: Valais, Switzerland, Piemont and Val d'Aosta, Italy.

Main Peaks: Monte Rosa (Dufourspitze) (4634m) Dom (4545m) Weisshorn (4505m), Matterhorn (4477m), Dent Blanche (4357m), Grand Combin (4314m).

Centres: There are many centres on both sides of the frontier from which climbing, walking or skiing holidays may be based. The major ones are: Zermatt, Saas Fee, Zinal and Arolla in Switzerland; Breuil (Cervinia) and Macugnaga in Italy.

Huts: Around fifty or so huts and emergency bivouac shelters are provided in the district. The majority of these are run by the Swiss and Italian Alpine Clubs but some have been built by local communes or by private enterprise.

Access: Major Swiss airports are Geneva, Zurich and Basle, Geneva being the most convenient for approach to the Pennines. In Italy there is an international airport in Milan. By rail a good service links Geneva with all the main Rhône Valley towns for connections with the major mountain centres. The Trans-European Express runs from Bern-Brig-Domodossola-Milan via the Simplon tunnel. There is a main line in Italy serving Turin-Chivasso-Aosta.

There is no public road connection with Zermatt. Cars should be left in Täsch, from where the railway leads to Zermatt.

Maps: Maps of the official Swiss survey *(Landeskarte der Schweiz)* cover the Pennine Alps in scales of 1:25,000, 1:50,000 and 1:100,000. They are superb and readily available from major map suppliers in Britain and Switzerland, or from Swiss National Tourist Offices.

Guidebooks: *Pennine Alps* (in three volumes—East, Central and West) are the standard English-language climbing guides and are published by the Alpine Club. (Available from West Col.)

High Level Route by Eric Roberts (West Col) covers the classic ski tour from Chamonix.

The Valais by Kev Reynolds (Cicerone Press)—a guidebook for walkers in the Swiss Pennine districts.

A 4-volume series of climbing guides (in French) is published by the Swiss Alpine Club under the general title *Alpes Valaisannes*. Bookshops in major centres listed above will stock these.

Other Books: *Scrambles Amongst the Alps* by Edward Whymper (John Murray) is essential reading for anyone interested in this district of the Alps. *Men and the Matterhorn* by Gaston Rébuffat (Kaye & Ward) is a well-illustrated volume dedicated to the most famous mountain in Europe. *Walking in the Alps* by J Hubert Walker (Oliver & Boyd, 1951) gives many suggestions for walking and climbing tours in the district.

THE BERNESE ALPS

Area: North of the Rhône Valley, between the Grimsel Pass and Lake of Geneva in Switzerland.

Main Peaks: Finsteraarhorn (4274m), Aletschhorn (4195m), Jungfrau (4158m), Schreckhorn (4078m), Eiger (3970m), Bietschhorn (3934m), Wetterhorn (3704m), Blümlisalphorn (3664m).

Centres: There are many centres from which to walk and climb in the district, the best perhaps are: Grindelwald, Lauterbrunnen, Kandersteg on the north side. In the Lötschental there are smaller and less pretentious villages, such as Kippel, Wiler and Blatten.

Huts: In excess of thirty huts and bivouacs, mostly owned by the Swiss Alpine Club.

Access: By air to Geneva, Zurich or Basle; Geneva being the most convenient.

A good rail service connects all the most important parts of the region with major towns such as Geneva, Bern, Basle and Zurich. The Lötschberg Tunnel provides access via Kandersteg with the Rhône Valley and southern parts of Switzerland.

Maps: Official Swiss survey maps (*Landeskarte der Schweiz*) cover the Bernese Alps in scales of 1:25,000, 1:50,000 and 1:100,000. Superbly executed they are readily available from major map suppliers in Britain and Switzerland, or from Swiss National Tourist Offices.

Guidebooks: *Bernese Alps East* and *Bernese Alps Central* are the standard English-language climbing guides. Published by the Alpine Club and produced by West Col.

The Bernese Oberland by Kev Reynolds (Cicerone Press) covers walking routes on the northern side of the watershed. For walks on the southern side, see *The Valais* also by Kev Reynolds and published by Cicerone Press.

A series of German-language climbing guides to the region is published by the Swiss Alpine Club.

BERNINA/BREGAGLIA

Area: Rhaetian Alps—south-east Switzerland and part Italy.

Main Peaks: Piz Bernina (4049m), Piz Zupo (3996m), Piz Scerscen (3971m), Piz Roseg (3937m), Piz Palü (3905m), Monte della Disgrazia (3678m), Piz Cengalo (3370m), Piz Badile (3308m).

Centres: St Moritz and Pontresina for Bernina. Maloja, Promontogno, Bondo, Vicosoprano for Bregaglia. Chiesa or San Martino for the Italian valleys.

Huts: Several huts exist on both sides of the frontier, mostly owned by the Swiss or Italian Alpine Clubs but one or two are privately run.

Access: Zurich is the most convenient Swiss airport. A first class rail link is then made via Chur to Samedan, St Moritz and Poschiavo. Trains also run through the Engadine to Scuol. From St Moritz a Postbus serves the whole Engadine and Val Bregaglia.

Maps: Official Swiss survey maps (*Landeskarte der Schweiz*) cover the region in a variety of scales: 1:25,000, 1:50,000 and 1:100,000. Superbly executed and readily available from major map suppliers in Britain and Switzerland, or from Swiss National Tourist Offices.

West Col Productions stock a specially-drawn map prepared by Alpina Technica to cover the Bregaglia region at 1:35,000 scale. Ideal for climbers.

Guidebooks: English-language guidebooks for climbers are published by West Col. Coverage for the Bernina/Bregaglia is as follows: *Bregaglia East* and *Bregaglia West, Bernina Alps*.

A walker's guidebook covering all Swiss terrain in the region is *Walks in the Engadine* by Kev Reynolds (Cicerone Press).

THE AUSTRIAN ALPS

Area: Western Austria, Vorarlberg, Tirol, Ost Tirol, Salzburg, Styria, Southern Bavaria.

Main Peaks: Grossglockner (3798m), Grossvenediger (3674m), Hochfeiler (3510m), Zuckerhutl (3507m), Wildspitze (3772m), Zugspitze (2962m)

Centres: There are numerous villages, small towns and resorts that make convenient bases for climbing or walking holidays. The following are some of the principal centres: Bludenz, St Anton, Imst, Sölden, Innsbruck, Mayrhofen, Matrei-in-Osttirol, Heiligenblut, Kufstein, Berchtesgaden, Salzburg, Schladming.

Huts: Over 500 Alpenverein huts and more than 500 run by other associations or privately owned. (See the AV Hut Book).

Access: Principal international airports: Munich, Zürich. Regular summer services to Innsbruck and Salzburg. Rail travel via Bregenz or Salzburg. Good services on main west to east routes. Otherwise use the excellent Postbus service.

By road via Bregenz, Innsbruck or Salzburg. International road communications are excellent.

Maps: For mountaineering: *Alpenvereinskarten* (Alpine Club Maps) at a scale usually 1:25,000.
For walking: *Kompass Wanderkarten* (Kompass Walking Maps) 1:50,000.
Freytag-Berndt also publish *Wanderkarten* 1:50,000.

Guidebooks: *Mountain Walking in Austria* by Cecil Davies (Cicerone Press). *Walking Austria's Alps Hut to Hut* by Jonathan Hurdle (Cordée). *Hut Hopping in the Austrian Alps* by William Reifsnyder (Sierra Club). *100 Best Walks in the Alps* by Walter Pause (Harrap). *Felix Austria* by Philip Tallantire (Eden Press) in 4 volumes. (Now out of print and difficult to obtain.)

For climbing, the Alpenverein Guide Books published by Rudolf Rother (Munich) cover all aspects, including climbs. They are all written in German.

In English, West Col publish a series of mountaineering guides as follows: *Ortler Alps, Otztal Alps, Stubai Alps, Zillertal Alps, Glockner Region.*

THE DOLOMITES

Area: North-east Italy.

Main Peaks: Marmolada (3343m), Anteleo (3263m), Monte Cristallo (3221m), Cimon della Pala (3186m), Cima Tosa (3173m), Croda dei Toni (3094m).

There is also great interest in pinnacles: Campanile Basso (Guglia di Brenta) (2883m), Tre Cime di Lavaredo (2999m), Cima della Madonna (2751m).

Centres: Bolzano, Cortina d'Ampezzo, Madonna di Campiglio, San Martino di Castrozza.

Huts: Hundreds in the area, mainly owned by the Italian Alpine Club. Usually well appointed with good food and wine.

Access: By rail from Calais or Boulogne to Milan or Verona, thence to Bolzano. In particular the motor-rail as far as Milan. By air to Venice, then by motor coach to San Martino or Cortina. By road from Switzerland via the Stelvio Pass, or from Austria over the Brenner.

Maps: Touring Club Italiano—6 maps scale 1:50,000. Tabacco Wanderkarte series, also 1:50,000. Kompass Carta Turistica for Brenta, at 1:30,000.

Guidebooks: *Guide di Monte d'Italia* in 6 volumes published by the Touring Club Italiano and the Italian Alpine Club. *Da Rifugio a Rifugio* (Italian Touring Club). *Alta Via—High Level Walks in the Dolomites* by Martin Collins (Cicerone Press 1986). *Via Ferrata—Scrambles in the Dolomites* translated from the German by Cecil Davies (Cicerone Press 1982). *Classic Climbs in the Dolomites* translated by Al Churcher (Cicerone Press 1986). *Selected Climbs in the Dolomites* by Ron James (Alpine Club 1988).

General Books: *The Dolomites* by C Douglas Milner (Robert Hale 1951) with 150 illustrations in monochrome. *The Dolomites* (Manfrini, Rovereto 1966) translated from the Italian. *The Brenta Dolomites* (Manfrini, Rovereto 1966) translated from the Italian. In both the last two books there are superb illustrations in colour.

Historic Books: *The Dolomite Mountains* by Gilbert & Churchill (1864). *Untrodden Peaks & Unfrequented Valleys* by Amelia B Edwards (1873). *Tirol & The Dolomites* (Baedeker 1927). This is especially interesting as it is the first of the Baedeker Guidebooks issued after the Great War and includes details of the fighting in the area.

THE JULIAN ALPS

Area: Yugoslavia/Italy.

Main Peaks: Yugoslavia (Eastern Julians): Triglav (2863m), Škrlatica (2738m), Jalovec (2643m), Razor (2601m), Prisojnik (2541m).

Italy (Western Julians): Poliški Špik (Iof di Montasio) (2754m), Viš (2666m).

Centres: Mojstrana, Kranjska Gora, Lake Bohinj, Bled in Yugoslavia. Tarvisio in Italy.

Huts: About 40 huts dispersed throughout the region, mostly owned by the Slovenian Alpine Association and the Italian Alpine Club.

Access: International flights to Ljubljana. Bus/coach from here to Kranj and Lake Bohinj, or to Jesenice. By rail from Paris to Jesenice or Bohinj via Swarzach St Veit (Austria). Bus services to most towns within the Julians.

Maps: Of the official Slovene maps the latest and best are: *Julian Alps—Triglav—Planinska Karta* (Blue cover), *Julian Alps—Bohinj* (Green cover) both at 1:20,000.

Three further Slovenian sheets at a scale of 1:50,000 may be found. *Julian Alps, East; Julian Alps, West;* and one sheet covering both these, *Julian Alps.*

Austrian maps published by Freytag-Berndt: *Julische Alpen* and *Ostkarawanken & Steiner Alpen* at 1:100,000.

Guidebooks: *Julian Alps* by Robin Collomb (West Col).

Other Reading: *Son of the Mountains* and *Alpine Pilgrimage* by Julius Kugy, both long out of print but occasionally obtainable from specialist book dealers, or on loan from some libraries.

The Irresistible Challenge by Dudley Stevens— translated into Slovenian by Marijan Lipovšek (as *Neubranljivi Izziv*) (Državna založba Slovenije, Ljubljana).

Alpine Clubs: Every small town has its climbing club, organised now into the Slovenian Alpine Association which has done much good work. Among other things, the condition of routes is checked, waymarks kept clear and huts maintained.

Address: Planinsko Društvo Slovenija
Miklošiceva 38
61000 Ljubljana,
Jugoslavija

Language: The Slovenian language is one of the Slav languages, a group to which Russian also belongs, but mercifully it is written in the Roman alphabet like ours, not in Cyrillic script. In vocabulary it is somewhat different to the Serbo-Croat spoken in most seaside towns and usually offered in phrase-books. But it is possible to buy a Slovenian/English dictionary or phrase-book in Ljubljana, or enquire at Kompas, the travel agency in any sizeable place such as Jesenice. Pronunciation of some letters seems to us very 'soft': thus *v* is almost *u* (enabling *Vrh* to be pronounced) and *j* is like our *y*. However, *c* between vowels is *ts*.

Older Slovenians speak fluent German because they were previously under the rule of the Austro-Hungarian Empire. Most younger Slovenians have now learnt English at school.

The Country: Yugoslavia today is a troubled country, economically and politically. It is a federation of republics as diverse as Montenegro in the south—Turkish in influence, and hope-shatteringly poor—and alpine Slovenia, progressive and hard-working, where people from Western Europe find it so easy to make friends.

Their inflation, of course, is our gain, and travel in Yugoslavia is relatively inexpensive for Britons.

THE CARPATHIANS

Area: Czechoslovakia, Poland, USSR, Romania and Hungary.

Main Peaks: Gerlachovský (Gerlach) (2655m)—High Tatra. Moldoveanu (2543m)—Fǎgǎras Mountains. Paringul Mare (2518m)—Paring Mountains. Peleaga (2509m)—Retezat Mountains. Omul (2507m)—Bucegi Mountains. Bystra (2248m)—Western Tatra. Goverla (2061m)—Eastern Beskidys. Dumbier (2043m)—Lower Tatras.

Centres: Strbské Pleso, Smokovec, Tatranska Lomnica and Zakopane on both sides of the Tatra (Poland/Czechoslovakia).

Liptovský Mikuláš for the Western and Lower Tatras.

Martin for the Malá and Vel'ka Fatras.

Zywiec, Zawoja, Rabka and Krynica for the Western Beskidys.

Szczawnica for the Polish Pieninys.

Yablonitsa, Yaremcha and Cosov for the Gorganys and Chernogora range.

Borsa, Cimpulung Moldovenesc and Vatra Dornei for the Romanian Eastern Carpathians.

Sinaia and Brasov for the Bucegi and Buzǎu Mountains.

Curtea de Arges and Fǎgǎras for the Fǎgǎras Mountains.

Sibiu and Petrosani for western massifs of the Southern Carpathians.

Huts: Numerous mountain huts are situated in the mountain areas of Poland and Romania, mostly owned by touring associations such as the PTTK. There are many mountain hotels, inns and hostels in Czechoslovakia in all the major valleys (usually under the 'Inter-hotel' administration), some of which have the character of mountain huts or bungalow villages. In the USSR tourist bases ('Turbase') hostels are provided for organised groups by regional councils for tourism.

Access: To Czechoslovakia—international flights to Bratislava and Tatry-Poprad airports; domestic flights to Ostrava, Košice and several other towns.

To Poland—international flights to Cracow (Warsaw is too far from the mountains to be of use other than to change for domestic flights). Domestic flights to Katowice and Rzeszów.

To the USSR—Lvov airport.

To Romania—via Bucharest airport.

To Hungary—flights to Budapest.

Maps: Official Czechoslovakian maps in the scale 1:50,000 published by Slovenská kartografia. There are 29 sheets (some still in preparation).

In Poland, maps of all mountain regions, mostly published to a scale of 1:75,000, but those of the Tatra and Pieniny National Parks are at 1:30,000.

For the USSR, a general map of the Carpathians is available, or better than this is a tourist atlas *Ukrainskiye Carpati,* published in 1987 by the Principal Geodesic and Ordnance Survey of the USSR Ministries Council.

Romanian maps are published (varying scales) by Editura Sport-Turism in the collection: *Harti turistica montane Carpati.* More general maps are edited by regional tourist offices.

In Hungary, 8 sheets of the 26 tourist maps edited by Cartographia—a Hungarian survey and mapping company. The scales vary from 1:60,000 to 1:40,000.

Guidebooks: In Czechoslovakia there are many volumes covering each of the mountain areas, published by 'Sport Publishers' in the collection: *Touristicky sprievodca CSSR.* Some of these, covering popular regions like the Tatras, appear in English, German and Russian translations. (F Kroutil and A Puskas are noted authors of climbing guides to the High Tatra.)

In Poland guidebooks for walkers are published by 'Sport i Turystyka' and 'Kraj'. An English-language guide to selected climbs in the Tatra is published by Fregata Travel—official Polish travel agency in London. *Tatry Wysokie,* by W H Paryski is a 25-volume series covering climbs throughout the High Tatra.

Romania has a guidebook collection of about 30 volumes entitled *Muntii nostri* (in German, *Unsere Berg*) published by 'Editura Sport-Turism'. The guidebook for the Fagaras Mountains, by V Bǎlǎceanu, M Cicotti & E Cristea was published in 1975.

THE CAUCASUS

Area: Caucasus, USSR.

Main Peaks: Elbrus (5642m and 5621m), Ushba (4710m and 4695m), Shkhelda (4320m), Dongus Orun (4454m).

Centres: Azau Sporting Camp, Baksan Valley. (The 'Camp' is a 4-storey hotel.)

Huts: Other than Priut beneath the summit slopes of Elbrus, there are no mountain huts. It will be necessary to bivouac below, or on, almost all climbs.

Access: Travel to the Camp is arranged from Moscow. All arrangements are made through:

Directorate of International Mountaineering Camps
Luzhnezkaja Quay 8
Moscow 119270
USSR

Maps: There are no high-quality contour maps for the Caucasus obtainable in the west. An orthographical map, published in the Alpine Journal vol 86 (1981), author John Town, is about the best available. The Soviets have produced a tourist map which is of some use for gaining an impression of the general layout of the valleys but is not very specific about the peaks. This map is available in the Caucasus.

Guidebooks: There are no English language guides to climbing and walking in the Caucasus. The Russian 3-volume guide to the region: *Baksanskaya Dolina* by A F Naumov (Physkultur i Sport, Moscow 1972), a reference copy of which can be seen in the library of the Alpine Club, is neither up to date, nor helpful about descent routes. More useful, but extremely elusive, is a German guide, published in Dresden: *Deutscher Verband Fur Wandern, Bergstein, Orienterungslave* by Frederick Bender and Rudor Schneider. This contains clear diagrams and reasonable route descriptions.

Other Reading: *Travels in the Central Caucasus and Bashan* by D W Freshfield (Longmans, 1869). *The Exploration of the Caucasus* by D W Freshfield (Edward Arnold, 1896). *My Climbs in the Alps and Caucasus* by A F Mummery (Fisher Unwin, 1895). *Guest of the Soviets* by Joyce Dunsheath (Constable, 1959). *The Red Snows* by John Hunt and Christopher Brasher (Hutchinson, 1960).

Grading: A numerical grading system is in use throughout the region, and corresponds to Alpine grades as follows:

Russian	Alpine (French)
1A	F
1B	F+
2A	PD
2B	PD+
3A	AD
3B	AD+
4A	D
4B	D+
5A	TD
5B	TD+
6A	ED

THE PYRÉNÉES

Area: France, Spain, Andorra.
Main Peaks: Pico de Aneto (3404m), Pico de Posets (3375m), Monte Perdido (3355m), Vignemale (3298m), Pic du Midi d'Ossau (2885m).
Centres: Laruns, Gavarnie, Cauterets and Luchon in France. Torla, Bielsa, Benasque and Espot in Spain. Andorra la Vella in Andorra.
Huts: A number of huts are situated on both sides of the watershed and serve the more popular areas. Mostly owned by the CAF (French Alpine Club) or Catalan Alpine Club but others provided by the French National Parks authority.
Access: Nearest airports in France are Tarbes-Lourdes and Toulouse. In Spain, these are Zaragoza and Barcelona. By rail there are good connections via Paris to Pau, Lourdes, Luchon and Ax-les-Thermes, and L'Hospitalet for Andorra. Road access is easy on both sides, if somewhat devious in Spain.
Maps: The IGN survey for the French side is good and accurate. For the Spanish side Editorial Alpina maps are more widely available than the official IGC, but are not of the strictest accuracy.
Guidebooks: *Walks and Climbs in the Pyrénées* by Kev Reynolds (Cicerone Press). *Classic Walks in the Pyrénées* by Kev Reynolds (Oxford Illustrated Press).
Coverage by Gastons/West Col is in three volumes: *Pyrénées West*, *Pyrénées Central* and *Pyrénées East* by Arthur Battagel.
A series of climbing guides in French is published by Robert Ollivier (Pau). These are widely available in the French mountain towns.

THE PICOS DE EUROPA

Area: North-western Spain.
Main Peaks: Torre Cerredo (2648m), Peña Santa de Castilla (2596m), Naranjo de Bulnes (2519m), Tabla de Lechugales (2441m).
Centres: Potes, Fuente Dé, Cangas.
Huts: Aliva—a hotel rather than a hut, run by the State Tourist Board. A few huts (none in the eastern massif) mostly belonging to the FEM. These are mainly small with only very basic facilities; not all have adjacent running water; usually but not invariably kept unlocked during late summer.
Access: Car ferry from Plymouth to Santander. Onward journeys by public transport complicated; enquire before leaving the U.K. Fly/drive via Bilbao. New motorway out of town and along the north coast is being planned. Sondica airport (Bilbao) is due for removal at some time to Vitoria.
Maps: FEM 1:25,000 are the best; one for each massif, if available.
Editorial Alpina 1:25,000 with short 28-page guide in Spanish: I. Macizo Occidental. II. Macizo Central y Oriental.
FEM 1:50,000 covers the entire Picos with a panorama and information on the reverse.
FAM (Oviedo) 1:50,000 covers the entire Picos. Kammkarte, coloured.
(Note, however, none of the mapping is of a high standard and there are many inaccuracies.)
Guidebooks: *Picos de Europa* by R G Collomb (West Col), covers touring, mountain walking, principal ascents. Illustrated. (In English.)
Los Picos de Europa by J R Lueje (Everest S.A., León). A general guide, in Spanish. Illustrated, text maps.
Los Picos de Europa by M A Adrados & J Lopez (Privately published in Oviedo). A climbing guide, in Spanish.
Guia del Macizo del Alto Carrión (FPM—Palencia). Climbing guide in Spanish. Illustrated, maps.

GREECE

Area: The northern Greek mainland and Peloponnese.

Main Peaks: Northern Greece—Olympus (2917m), Smólikas (2637m), Ghióna (2510m), Vardhóusia (2495m). The Peloponnese—Taÿgetos (2407m), Ziria (2376m), Helmós (2355m).

Centres: Northern Greece—Amfissa, Karpenisi, Kónitsa, Métsovo.

The Peloponnese—Kalávrita and Sparta.

Huts: Huts are few and far between. Only the two on Mount Olympus are manned. The usefulness of the others in summertime at least is generally outweighed by the difficulty of obtaining and returning the keys. A list of huts is available from the National Tourist Office of Greece, 195-197 Regent Street, London W1R 8DL, and the Hellenic Alpine Club, Karageorgis Servias 7, Athens, Greece.

Access: Athens is the most accessible base for the mountains of the Peloponnese and Central Greece. For the north, there are direct flights from London to Salonica. Alternatively, domestic flights connect Athens with Yánina in the centre of the Pindos. In the main you have to rely on the extensive local bus network.

Maps: Though the situation is better than it was, maps remain a bit of a problem. The most readily available are those produced by the National Statistical Service of Greece (Likourgou 14, Omonia, Athens). They are stocked by Stanford, and Robertson McCarta in London. The scale is only 1:200,000 with contours at 200 metre intervals. More detailed, but covering only a limited area, are the maps of individual peaks reproduced in the outdoor magazine, *Korfés*, back numbers of which are obtainable from Mr Epaminondas Nikas, HAC Aharnes, Kentriki Platia 16, Aharnes 13671, Greece. Best of all are the army's 1:50,000 series, now released with some reluctance to the public and even posted abroad—though it is hard for a foreigner to get hold of more than two sheets at a time. The address to write to is: Hellenic Army Cartography Service, Pedhion Areos, Athens.

Guidebooks: *The Mountains of Greece: A Walker's Guide* by Tim Salmon (Cicerone Press). *Greece on Foot: Mountain Treks, Island Trails* by Marc Dubin (Cordée).

CORSICA

Main Peaks: Monte Cinto (2706m), Monte Rotondo (2622m), Punta Minuta (2556m), Paglia Orba (2525m), Monte d'Oro (2389m), Monte Renoso (2354m).

Centres: There are few villages of real value as true mountain bases, since most are too far from the climbing areas. The following, however, may be considered as much for restocking with supplies as centres in themselves. Albertacce (above Calacuccia); Calacuccia; Asco (for the Cinto massif); Bastelica; Corté; Vizzavona.

Huts: About a dozen huts are found along the main spine of mountains, mostly run by the National Park authorities. Not all have guardians and meals and food supplies are rarely available, even where guardians are in occupation. Facilities are minimal as a general rule, although cooking equipment, ie: gas stoves, are provided. Camping is generally allowed in the vicinity of huts, often within a fenced compound to keep the semi-wild pigs out. A fee is charged for camping by a hut.

Access: Frequent flights operate from the UK to Corsica. Airports are at Ajaccio and Bastia. Flights from France are usually to Calvi.

By boat a variety of services ply from French ports eg: Marseilles-Ajaccio; Toulon-Propriano; Nice-Calvi etc.

Travel in Corsica is by rail (one line, Ajaccio-Bastia and branch-line to Calvi via Ponte Leccia). This is useful for reaching the start of GR20, or for access to the Monte d'Oro/Renoso districts via the station at Vizzavona.

Bus routes serve principal towns; taxis are generally expensive. Car hire is worth considering for those who wish to sample a mixture of mountain and beach.

Maps: IGN publish a series of sheets covering the mountain areas to scales of 1:50,000 and 1:25,000. Didier & Richard publish two sheets at 1:50,000 (*Corse Nord* and *Corse Sud*) of use to GR20 walkers. The route and huts are clearly marked in blue.

Guidebooks: *Corsica Mountains* by Robin Collomb (West Col) offers a good general introduction to the mountains, with a selection of climbing routes.
Guide des Montagnes Corses by Michel Fabrikant —2 volumes of climbs, in French.
The Corsican High Level Route by Alan Castle (Cicerone Press) gives a description of the GR20.

Notes on Contributors

Steve Ashton began mountaineering in 1969 and has since climbed throughout Britain and in several Alpine regions. He has lived in Snowdonia since 1973 and has written a number of books on mountain subjects, including four guidebooks to walks and climbs in North Wales. He is a regular columnist for *High* magazine.

Louis Baume is of Swiss origin, from the Franches Montagnes. Horologist; fellow and past Chairman of the British Horological Institute; book collector, dealer and publisher. He is author of *Sivalaya—the Himalayan 8000ers* and of technical, mountaineering and travel articles, and is a member of CAS (1946) and AC (1952). He first visited the Alps in 1937 and has climbed in many European and more distant ranges, including two exploratory visits to the Picos de Europa with ascents of several peaks, including the Naranjo. He was in the Antarctic with the South Georgia Survey Expedition 1955–6; Mount Baume was subsequently named after him.

John Brailsford is an international mountain guide and former President of the Association of British Mountain Guides; Honorary Member of the Ailefroide-Vallouise Syndicate in l'Oisans and former Secretary of the Alpine Climbing Group. He is author of two Alpine Club guidebooks to the Dauphiné (1967 & 1987) and two volumes to the Dolomites (1970). He has had thirty-five Alpine seasons, twenty-eight of them in Dauphiné during which he made many early and first British ascents of most of the classic hard routes of the region. He was formerly Head of Outdoor Education at the Normal College, Bangor, North Wales.

Cecil Davies became interested in climbing in the 1950s when his work in Manchester University took him annually to a Summer School at Bangor. Attending a conference near Salzburg in 1964 he discovered the Austrian Alps and since then has been there practically every summer—and several times in winter. An experienced mountain photographer, he has written and illustrated *Mountain Walking in Austria,* and translated from German *Via Ferrata: Scrambles in the Dolomites.* He is a member of the Austrian Alpine Club (1964), the Mynydd Climbing Club (1959) and the Wayfarers' Club. A former actor, schoolmaster and university teacher, his academic interests lie in the fields of English and German Literature and Drama.

Dave Durkan is 40 and was brought up in Holyhead, North Wales. From walking he progressed to 'mother's clothes-line' climbing on Holyhead Mountain and was soon ticking off the crags of Britain. On joining the RAF he served overseas, ending up in Norway, where he remained to become a guide and climbing instructor, and later the manager of a large sports shop. Today he combines equipment design and market consultancy with journalism. He has travelled and climbed virtually the world over, with thirteen visits to Nepal to date, organising trekking and small expeditions. In Norway he has walked, skied and climbed extensively in both summer and winter.

Jerzy Gajewski was born in 1946 in Cracow, Poland. He graduated in architecture and journalism, and for many years has worked in the fields of tourism. A member of the Mountain Tourism Committee of the Polish Tourist Association, he has contributed many articles about mountains, both in his native Poland and, recently, in the *Alpine Journal*, and is the author of three books on mountain walking. He has wandered among the mountains of Eastern Europe, throughout the Carpathians, in Bulgaria and also in the Alps and North Wales. He is married and lives still in Cracow.

Joss Lynam has been walking and climbing in Ireland and many other parts of the world for nearly 50 years. He has edited nearly a dozen rock climbing and hill walking guides to Ireland, including very recently *The Mountains of Connemara*. He is President of AFAS, the co-ordinating body for Adventure Sports in Ireland, Chairman of the National Sports Council's Committee for Long-Distance Walks, Chairman of the Irish Mountain Training Board, and edits *Irish Mountain Log* for the FMCI. He has climbed in the Himalaya (7 expeditions), the Andes and Greenland. In between these activities he earns a living as a Civil Engineer.

Cameron NcNeish is a full-time journalist and broadcaster specialising in outdoor environmental topics. He is editor of *Climber and Hillwalker*, Britain's oldest outdoors magazine, presents regular programmes on BBC Radio Scotland and is author of a number of books on the outdoors, including *Classic Walks in Scotland* (Oxford Illustrated Press, 1988). He is a keen climber, hill walker and backpacker with interests in folk music and photography. Cameron is also very involved with his local Christian fellowship group and speaks regularly at Christian meetings throughout the country.

C Douglas Milner has considerable Alpine climbing experience and first visited the Mont Blanc range in 1938. Formerly a bank manager in his professional life, he is a past Vice-President of the Alpine Club, author of numerous articles on mountaineering subjects and a noted mountain photographer. His books include *Mont Blanc and the Aiguilles, The Dolomites, Rock for Climbing* and *Mountain Photography*.

Kev Reynolds began climbing at the age of sixteen and has since spent thirty years under the spell of mountains. A member of the Alpine Club, he has climbed and walked in many regions including the Alps, Atlas, Corsica and the Pyrénées. For nearly twenty years he worked as a Youth Hostel Warden in Switzerland and in England, but since 1986 has concentrated on full-time writing and lecturing, with the emphasis on mountains and the countryside. Author of more than a dozen books, including guidebooks to the Swiss Alps and the Pyrénées, one of his most recent works is *Classic Walks in the Pyrénées* (Oxford Illustrated Press, 1989). He is married and has two daughters.

Tim Salmon is a teacher-turned-writer, and author of—among other things—*The Rough Guide to France* and *The Rough Guide to Paris*. He is a classicist by training, which is what first took him to Greece some thirty years ago. Since then he has spent a large part of his life there, pursuing his obsession with mountains and sheep. His book *The Mountains of Greece: A Walker's Guide* (Cicerone Press) is required reading for all who plan to explore the mountains of that country. Tim Salmon is married to a Greek journalist who is Athens correspondent for *The Guardian*.

Victor Saunders, an architect by profession, took up mountaineering in 1978 at the age of 28. Since that time he has been trying to make amends for a well-spent youth. In 1986 he climbed in the Caucasus with a small team from north London. They climbed throughout the Upper Baksan valley area, following a number of classic lines and adding a new route on Ushba. He has since achieved a number of fine ascents in the Himalaya, including (1988) a new route on Jitchu Drake in Bhutan with Doug Scott. He regularly contributes articles to the *Alpine Journal*.

Dudley Stevens was a pioneer of mountain education and the first person in England to offer mountain courses open to the general public. He ran Outdoor Pursuits courses and lectures for most of the major P.E. Training Colleges until they were able to establish their own specialist departments. He targeted Yugoslavia as a possible area for his students to gain experience on larger mountains and from 1960 took two expeditions there almost every year. In 1968 he was invited to give the Mountaineering Association's annual January lecture but was struck down by illness. He died in March 1988. The Julians expedition booked for 1968 was led by his wife, H Stevens, who also completed the preparation of the Julian Alps chapter for this present book. Dudley Stevens' own book *The Irresistible Challenge* was published in a Slovenian translation in 1987.

Walt Unsworth was born in the shadow of the Pennine Hills and has spent a lifetime looking beyond the last blue mountain, walking and climbing in many parts of the world. *Classic Walks of the World* and *Savage Snows* are two of his recent books: one reflecting his interest in topography and the other in mountain history. He has written several books on the Lake District, as well as a highly acclaimed 'biography' of Everest. One of Britain's leading mountain writers, he is also Editorial Director of Cicerone Press, the well-known guidebook company.